The Richness of my Yesterdays

D1160617

The Richness of My Yesterdays

A Memoir continued

by

Marguerite Chien Eng Church

All rights reserved. No part of this book shall be reproduced or transmitted in any form or by any means, electronic, mechanical, magnetic, photographic including photocopying, recording or by any information storage and retrieval system, without prior written permission of the publisher. No patent liability is assumed with respect to the use of the information contained herein. Although every precaution has been taken in the preparation of this book, the publisher and author assume no responsibility for errors or omissions. Neither is any liability assumed for damages resulting from the use of the information contained herein.

Copyright © 2015 by Marguerite Chien Eng Church

ISBN 978-1-4958-0709-1
Library of Congress Control Number: 2015909638

Published June 2015

INFINITY PUBLISHING
1094 New DeHaven Street, Suite 100
West Conshohocken, PA 19428-2713
Toll-free (877) BUY BOOK
Local Phone (610) 941-9999
Fax (610) 941-9959
Info@buybooksontheweb.com
www.buybooksontheweb.com

For my children,
Eric, Kathy, and Bean
And their children,
Stepher, Mason, Jae, Emmy, and Peter

With the hope that this book will spare them the
regret I have often felt at knowing so little about
my parents' and grandparents' lives before me

Acknowledgments

I am deeply indebted to Marcia Boyles and Betsy Renner, without whose help this book would not have been begun or finished. Marcia's invitation to join her class in creative writing gave me the impetus to start writing, and their joint encouragement spurred me on to its completion. During our monthly meetings over the past three years, their critiques have without doubt improved the quality of my writing as well as the content of this memoir. Thank you Marcia, and thank you Betsy for your help, your time, and your friendship.

I am more grateful than I can say to Carol Subick for the many hours she spent in cropping, sizing, and inserting the many pictures in this book, and also for formatting my manuscript for submission to my publisher. I want to thank also Mary Jane Dryden for sharing her recollections of Subic Bay in the Philippines where we were both stationed many years ago, and Megan Donovan for providing pictures of my first home in America. My thanks also to my old friend Marion Ciaccio, who edited my first memoir, *Adopted, the Chinese Way*, and once again was good enough to do the final editing of this book. And as in the past, I am ever grateful to my daughter-in-law Carolyn Eng for being available for technical help whenever needed. Finally, my thanks to my two good friends Mike Shoesmith and Mary Dean for reading every word of this memoir as it was in progress, and for encouraging me along the way.

Contents

Chapter 1
The Immigrant

I've never thought of myself as an immigrant, but I suppose I am one. I did come from a foreign country and I did settle in America, later to become an American citizen. But when I think "immigrant," what I see is a straggling line of Mexicans crossing the deserts of Arizona. Or in the case of Chinese immigrants, my mind conjures up age-old images of bodies huddled in the steerage of some great ocean liner. That is definitely not the way I arrived in America. No, I sailed under that Golden Gate together with a crew of four or five hundred clean-shaven young American men in dungarees and white sailor caps who manned the U.S. Navy ship that brought me to America.

USS *Lavaca* (APA-180)

I should not have been on that ship at all. I was Chinese, and this ship, a US Navy Attack Transport, was for Americans. During World War II, these ships had been used for transporting troops to battle areas, but now, the war over, many of them, in a massive sea lift dubbed Operation Magic Carpet, were diverted to transporting American personnel from the Pacific war zone back to the West Coast. In October 1945, two months after VJ Day, our ship, the USS Lavaca, was part of that program and was to ferry back to the U. S. those American civilians who had been stranded in the Pacific during the war. My mother and the other Americans in Peking had been notified by the Red Cross that in twenty-four hours the ship would be leaving from the Tientsin port of Ta-ku, just three hours away from Peking by train. My American mother jumped at the chance.

As for me, being Chinese, and not even half American, I was not entitled to a place on the ship. I was an adopted child, but without even formal adoption papers to prove that I was my mother's child. My adoptive parents had met when my father was a student at Harvard. He and his American bride were married in 1912. The Boston papers had carried an article on the inter-racial marriage, captioned, "Local Girl Marries Pagan Prince." Together, they had returned to China, to his home in Peking. When they found that they could not have children of their own, they had adopted children from within my father's family. I was, by birth, his niece, the daughter of his younger brother, merely transferred from one branch of the family to another in the traditional Chinese manner termed *kuo chi*. So, from the age of one month, my uncle and aunt became my parents. (For readers who are interested in this Chinese custom, I refer them to my earlier memoir, *Adopted the Chinese Way*, in which the Chinese *kuo chi* system is explained at length in the book's first chapter.)

When the Sino-Japanese war broke out in the summer of 1937 and the Chinese government was forced to retreat to the interior province of Ssuchuan, my father, a government official, had gone with it. From that day on, my mother was left with the sole care of my older sister Lois—returned home after an unhappy divorce—her infant son, my little sister Jeanne, then only two, and me. When America entered the war, other Americans were taken to concentration camps in various parts of North China, but in a supposed act of compassion on the part of the Japanese, my mother was exempted because she had minor Chinese children. From that day forward she was constantly harassed by the Japanese, woken from her bed at 3:00 A.M. to be hauled to the Japanese gendarmerie, and subjected to countless interrogations. Having endured eight years under Japanese occupation, four of which as an enemy national had brought her untold hardship, she was more than ready to leave.

I was twenty years old at the time. I had already taken my College Board exams in my Junior year at the Peking American School and been accepted at Smith College for the 1942 school year. America's entry into the war had intervened. My mother pleaded with the Red Cross officials administering the program to allow me on board. With the letter of my acceptance from Smith in hand, she was able to convince them that the U.S. immigration authorities surely would admit me as a student. The Red Cross officials relented, but with the admonition that I might still be turned back at San Francisco if a student visa was not granted. My little sister Jeannie, then only six years old, as a minor child of my mother, was permitted to accompany us.

I believe there were about three hundred passengers on board the ship, corralled from all parts of North China. Some joked that it was a shipload of missionaries and prostitutes. The elderly and women with small children were assigned to the officers' quarters, which held about fifty bunks, some stacked three deep and others with just an upper and lower. My mother, being the most senior in age, was appointed as matron. Being part of her family, Jeannie and I also were permitted in the officers' quarters. I let Jeannie take the lower bunk and I slept above her, with no third bunk above me. The rest of the women were relegated to the enlisted quarters where the bunks were stacked five deep. Whereas we in the officers' quarters slept in relative luxury on comfortable mattresses, they had only tarps laced over metal frames.

The excitement of being on a US Navy ship bound for America buoyed my spirits through the first few days of mild seasickness. After that, there was the novelty of exploring the ship and getting adjusted to the ship's routine. I quickly got used to eating off metal trays in the mess hall, but found the reconstituted potatoes and vegetables hard to swallow. The weather in October was mild and many of us spent much of our time on deck. Others entertained themselves with books, cards, and board games in the mess hall; but those things soon became stale, and there was only the prospect of the interminable sea, the sea, and more sea. Boredom set in.

But for me, far from being bored, I was having the time of my life. Never had I had so much attention. These young sailors, who had probably not seen a woman in months, were suddenly confronted with women and girls. And I was not *just* a girl. I was a Chinese girl, something they had never seen before. They were interested, curious. How come I spoke such good English? Where did I learn it? How come I was on the ship? Where was I going? The questions never stopped. They sought me out when off duty, peppering me with questions. And I too had questions; they gave me answers. Paul Lanius, a native American, told me about life on the reservation. Jim Henderson regaled me with stories of life on his family's farm. They showed me pictures, taught me songs. We went through all ninety-nine verses of *Ninety-nine Bottles of Beer on the Wall*, and others. Bob Malezzie taught me, or tried to teach me, to yodel. Two others joined us in the effort. The four of us produced the most amazing cacophony of sounds. I had never laughed so much in my life. When we got to Okinawa, Bob Cotton and Henry something-or-other urged me to join them on the mail pick-up. I was game for anything. But when they were ready to make the run, it was pouring rain and the sea was rough. They were in slickers and had gotten me into one too. They threw out the rope ladder; Henry went over the side. I leaned over the rail and watched him go down. The ladder was flapping against the side of the ship as he descended. The boat in the water was pitching, lurching, and banging against the ship. Bob said, "Now you. Your turn." I was scared to death. What if the boat lurched away while I was jumping off the ladder? Mercifully, just then, one of the ship's officers appeared. I did not recognize him. Quite firmly he said, "I can't allow you to do this, Miss." Then he lit into the boys. They were chagrined and made the run without me. I know they both faced severe reprimands after that incident.

While I was having all this fun with the sailors, my fellow passengers were getting restless. After a week of cards, board games, and reading, there was nothing to keep them occupied. However, missionaries are resourceful, and a group decided to put on a show for the other passengers. Planning sessions and rehearsals followed. A skit lampooning the experiences of various Americans in China; a group dance number orchestrated by a former dancing teacher; a solo number by the teacher herself; a really good story-teller, again with tales of China; and then, me, with an American popular song, *This is a Lovely Way to Spend an Evening.* There had been much applause for each number, but after my song the sailors hollered and whistled, yelling for an encore. I had not prepared one and stood awkwardly waiting for the rest of the cast to come back on stage. The band struck up with *California Here I Come* and everyone, performers and audience together joined in. The following morning the sailors made a big show of swooning at my feet, some wailing "O-o-o-oh Frankie! Others "O-o-o-o-oh Marguerite." I did not learn till later who this Frankie was.

But even with all this attention, for me the greatest thrill was being singled out by the ship's executive officer Commander Guy Jubitz. To the sailors he was the "Exec." Early on, at the first of the twice-weekly movies that were shown on the forward deck, I had been looking for a place to sit when he had taken me aside and said, "You can stop looking for a seat, young lady. Come sit with me and Captain Gabel on the bridge." Thereafter, on movie nights I always sat on the bridge with the two of them while the other passengers vied for the few folding chairs available or sat uncomfortably on the forward hatch. The same with the special dinners at which each ship's officer invited a guest. Even though Captain Gabel invited a different person each time, including my mother on one occasion, I became the Exec's regular date. Looking back, I wondered if others might have suspected a romantic interest, but I never sensed any. I felt as if his attentions were almost protective, as if he wanted to make sure I was taken care of. In any case, I enjoyed an enviable position, being recognized by all aboard as the Exec's favored one. In fact, the month-long voyage was for me the most exciting and wonderful adventure. I was almost sorry when the trip came to an end.

We docked in San Francisco early in the morning, but were not cleared for disembarkation for several hours. Consular officials came aboard, and on the spot I was granted a student visa. Captain Gabel had cabled Smith College on my behalf, and their reply, not only accepting me, but offering a full scholarship, was ample evidence that I would be a legitimate student. While we were still waiting to be processed I was approached also by a crewmember, somewhat older than most of the sailors. I believe he was a Navy Chief. I had not met him before, but he evidently knew who I was and knew that I was to be a college student. He explained that in civilian life he was a performers' agent. "Your voice has an unusual appeal, and you have a certain presence," he said. "I'm pretty sure I could line up singing engagements for you during your summer vacations if you're interested. "These would be at summer resorts where they provide entertainment for the summer season only," he explained. "They wouldn't be high-paying jobs, but might be fun for you and you'd earn some pin money."

I was flattered, thrilled, exhilarated, all of these together. My cup truly was running over. I was so taken aback that I didn't know what to say. "You don't need to commit yourself; just take my card and think about it. If you find you'd like to give it a try, call me." "But give me a couple of months notice," he added. With that, he was gone. I was so excited. Here I had already had such a wonderful time during the trip, I had gotten my student visa, and now, without even setting foot in the country I was being offered a job, or at least the possibility of one. No one could have asked for a better welcome to America.

When we finally descended the gangplank—it was the end of October, 1945—I could see many familiar faces on the dock, but it was Dr. William Pettus, former head of the College of Chinese Studies in Peking, who pushed himself forward to greet my mother. He had a white envelope in his hand. After little more than a handshake and a few words of welcome, he said, "I wanted to be the first to greet you and to turn this over to you. I hope you'll be pleased." With that, he handed my mother the envelope. Somewhat perplexed, she opened it rather tentatively, and found to her great surprise and joy a check for almost six thousand dollars. Dr. Pettus, though not a particularly close friend of my mother's, had taken it upon himself to collect all the monies she had lent to fellow Americans in Peking during the war.

The money had come from the sale of our family home in Peking. At the height of the war, remittances from my father had been coming through only sporadically or not at all. We were desperately in need of money, and the house, already confiscated by the Japanese military, was for all practical purposes, lost to us. When a wealthy Chinese, one of the despicable group who were collaborating with the Japanese at immense profit to themselves, offered to buy the house, my mother saw no alternative but to sell. To the best of my recollection the proceeds were about the equivalent of US $6000, an amount that could have bought no more than a small starter home in the United States. The money was received in cash, in Chinese dollars. With daily currency devaluation, it could have been worthless in weeks. Other Americans, whose remittances were no longer coming from America, were also in financial straits. Mother lent almost the entire amount to friends who, in return, gave her promissory notes for the then equivalent amounts in U.S. dollars. My mother had dreaded the thought of having to contact old Peking friends individually to remind them of the money they owed, but Dr. Pettus had spared her that onerous task. She would be forever grateful for his kindness. With this money in hand my mother was able to start our new life in America.

After a two-day visit with friends at their home in Palo Alto, we started by train on a whirlwind visit to my mother's family. When she married my father in1912, U.S. laws were such that a woman lost her U.S. citizenship when she married a foreign national. My mother had never been comfortable with that loss, and when that law was rescinded in 1935, she had made the trip back to the United States to regain her citizenship, and at the same time to visit her family. Now it had been ten years since she had last seen them.

In short order we visited all of my mother's siblings. First, two weeks with one sister in Detroit; then two weeks with another in Peabody, Massachusetts. Another two weeks with each of her two brothers. Until my arrival there had been a preponderance of boys among their children. Aunt Irene had three boys. Uncle Harvey also had three boys. The family had longed for a girl. Now, at last, they had one; not just a girl, but a very special Chinese one. Uncles, aunts, and cousins all showered me with love and nearly smothered me with attention.

When we arrived in America, with almost no money in hand, my mother had expected to stay with each of her siblings for a given period until we could get settled in a home of our own. During that time she had expected to contact the Peking friends to whom she had lent money during the war. Now, with those sums already recovered for her by Dr. Pettus, her family presented her with yet another gift, the proceeds from the sale of their mother's house. Years before, my parents had bought for my grandmother the small house in which she lived until she died. Upon her death there had been no squabbling over who should get the proceeds. All had agreed that the money should go to my mother. And now, that money was added to her store of funds.

From a home base at Aunt Mildred's in Peabody, my mother made weekly trips to Cambridge to look for a property. She had lived there before her marriage and was familiar with the area. Also, my brother Luther, who had left China before America entered the war, was a student at Harvard. Cambridge seemed the logical place to make our home. Mother found a beautiful old house not far from the Harvard campus and only one block from the bus line. It had three floors, the bottom one a self-contained apartment, already rented to a middle-aged widow. Years ago, she and Aunt Irene had rented rooms to Harvard students. Now, once again she would rent out the rooms on

24 Agassiz Street, Cambridge

the third floor, and she, Jeannie, and I would live on the second floor. My mother and I shopped for furniture in second hand stores. She had a good eye and acquired some lovely pieces, pieces that in those days were considered used furniture, but today would probably command substantial prices as antiques. In no time at all she had made the apartment into an attractive home.

By Christmas, only two months after our arrival in America, we were completely and comfortably settled in. Mother had put ads in the paper. The third floor rooms, two singles and one double, were all rented. One single was taken immediately by a music student at the Peabody Music School. The double and remaining single were snapped up by three Harvard students who were to move in right after Christmas. With the rents from the first floor apartment and the third floor rooms, we could manage if we lived frugally. At the close of the year 1945 we were ready to begin our lives in America.

Chapter 2
The Student

In May 1947 I received my Bachelor of Arts degree in English from Smith College. Though I had attended for only a year and a half, entering in the second half of my junior year, Smith was generous in giving me her degree. At the time, my oldest brother Richard was visiting from London where he had chosen to make his home, and my father, who was still living in China, had come to America to be at my graduation. It was one of the few times when all the members of our Chien family, with the exception of sister Lois, who was still in China, were all together.

Back row: Luther and Richard
Front: Jeannie, my mother, me, my father

Smith was not easy for me. After a euphoric trip across the Pacific, followed by a virtual lovefest with my mother's family, I was coming off a real high. Now, suddenly I was in unfamiliar territory without the support of friends or family. For months I had been made to feel I was someone special, but now, to the houseful of girls at Gillette House, I was just another transfer student arriving in the middle of the school year. I had never felt so alone. The room to which I was assigned was on the fourth floor, occupied by freshmen and sophomores. Consequently it was among them that I found friends and not among my own classmates. The juniors and seniors on the lower floors had already made their friendships; they took no interest in a new arrival. None of my classmates reached out to the new student from China.

Also, I struggled to maintain the good grades expected of a scholarship student. I was unaccustomed to the enormous amounts of reading required. In my one year at Fu Jen University in Peking, where all classes were in Chinese, other than our textbooks, we were assigned no additional reading. The same applied to the year and a half I had spent at St. John's University in Shanghai. Though classes were in English at St. Johns, we were given no additional reading assignments. I was majoring in English, but prior to coming to Smith, had taken only one English course, that, in Shakespeare. Consequently, my senior year at Smith was crammed with the English courses required for an English major. Sometimes I felt I was drowning in reading material. I spent many late hours in the library, often being the last to leave at night.

In addition to the above problems, for the first time in my life I felt poor. I was no stranger to doing without. The war years under Japanese occupation in Peking had been hard, but wartime deprivation and hardship were shared by all. At Smith, I felt as if I was alone in my "poorness" among a crowd of affluent others. I had a full tuition scholarship from Smith, at that time $600 a year, but room and board were another $600, an amount that in itself was a fortune for our family. Luckily, many of the professors did not object to students knitting in class. I took advantage of that and earned my spending money by knitting socks and sweaters on order for friends and for friends of friends. Other than working a few hours a week in the library for a pittance, I literally knit my way through college. I had a steady order of hand-knit argyle socks from Mr. Crane of Crane plumbing.

Apart from the trials and tribulations experienced above, my memories of the time spent at Smith are fragmented.

I remember another scholarship student and I making do with soda crackers and bouillon in our dorm rooms while wishing we could afford to be among the girls who went off to the student hangouts on Green Street for hamburgers and cokes.

I remember how annoyed I was that someone was stealing great chunks from the cakes my mother occasionally sent me. These I always shared with my floormates, storing the remains in a breadbox *inside* my closet. The thief made no effort to hide her thefts. I couldn't fail to notice. The cake was always taken, not in neat slices, but in great gouges. I never found out who the culprit was.

I remember too being surprised at the free use of what I had been brought up thinking of as unmentionable swear words. God damn it! Jesus Christ! Hell! My mother would have been shocked.

I remember the scramble for the use of the vacuum cleaner just before weekly room inspections made by our housemother Mrs. Brown. She ran a tissue over picture surfaces to test for dust.

I remember sitting down daily for both lunch and dinner at tables for six or eight—no cafeteria meals then—with the student at the head of each table doing the serving, much as family meals were served in the past. Breakfast was buffet style.

I remember how the girls vied for places at the two dinner tables hosted by Mrs. Brown our house-mother and by our resident faculty member Mrs. Hill. I remember how the girls from the South said they did not dare to tell their parents that Mrs. Hill was black.

I also remember the smoke that filled the lounge before and after dinner when the girls sat around on the floor playing bridge.

I remember too the stunned silence when I, hitherto a quiet foreign student, spoke up loudly and clearly on whether smoking should be allowed in the dining room during after-dinner coffee. "We non-smokers already have to put up with smoking in the living room before and after dinner. We shouldn't have to endure it in the dining room as well." I won my case, but the smokers eyed me warily after that.

Picture for Yearbook

I remember making the Junior class basketball team and finding the rules at Smith peculiar and regressive, the court divided into three sections. In China, girls had long ago left behind the old half-court game and were playing full-court basketball.

I remember auditioning for the class performance at Smith's annual Rally Day and being given a solo singing part. It made my mother proud.

I remember too the annual house party at Gillette House, at which, apart from my American date—the son of an old family friend—not a single other boy asked me to dance. It was the first time in my life that I had felt like a wallflower, stuck with my partner— invited only at my mother's urging—and he with me, for the whole evening. In those days, inter-racial dating was rare. We dated within our race. Three Chinese fraternities, *Rho Psi, F. F.*, and A.*L.* were active on many of the major college campuses, and it was through these fraternities that Chinese girls met Chinese boys. At the time

I was seeing a *Rho Psi* boy, and many a weekend, he would drive up to Northampton to pick me up for a fraternity dance, picnic, or other activity. It was a welcome respite from the weekday grind of endless studying.

A last memory of the time I spent at Smith remains vivid in my mind, even as I have had to reach back over sixty-five years and dig deep to bring back the others. My professor in Comparative Religion announced in class that he wanted to read aloud a paper submitted by one of his students. It was a paper on racial prejudice and discrimination. As he started reading, I realized that the paper was mine. In it I had told of my personal experience, of my total unawareness of racial prejudices until I reached America. I couldn't help feeling pleased, but also a little embarrassed as all eyes turned toward me. But whatever joy I felt was quickly dispelled by what followed. At the end of the class, as students swarmed out of the classroom and headed down the stairs, one raced past me, turning to shout as she passed, "I thought that was a lot of bull."

I can hardly find the words to express how I felt at the time. Today, after sixty-seven years in America, I am all too aware that Americans are more outspoken than Chinese and that I was possibly overly sensitive to the blunt putdown. Today I could weather a comment like that and possibly even retaliate in kind, but at that time, the words had stung. They had hurt. I didn't know what to make of it. It seemed so mean spirited. Why would anyone want to inflict a hurt on a fellow student whom she hardly knew?

My year and a half at Smith passed quickly. Today I call myself a graduate of Smith College, but a Smith graduate should have a Smith education. That, I did not have. I worked hard, earned creditable grades, but will always be sorry that I never had a music course, nor an art course, nor, as an English major, a course in writing. Through the years I have often felt undeserving of my Smith degree. That degree was received at the culmination of attendance at four different universities: two and a half years at schools in China, at one of which all classes were taught in Chinese. Another summer course at Boston University to make up for missing credits for my English major; and then the final year and a half at Smith. If the secretarial course I took at Katherine Gibbs during the summer between my junior and senior years were added to the others, I would have attended five colleges en route to receiving my B.A.

But, all that said, have I had a good education? Yes, despite not having had an orthodox liberal arts education, I would say I have. I have been educated by my own life experiences; by the two cultures into which I was brought at birth; by the countries in which I've lived; by the books I've read; by the people I've known, and by observing the world around me. I've been educated by seeing my mother's strength in adversity; by watching my children mature and grow; by knowing the joy of their successes and of my own; by recovering with strength from hardship and failures; by caring for ones I've loved; and finally, by coping with loss.

Yes, I believe I have had a good education, and, whether deserved or not, I have a degree from Smith.

Chapter 3
The Working Girl

I sat there with a big silly smile on my face surveying my new domain. I felt as if I must be just about the luckiest girl in the world. Just two weeks ago I had been sitting at home in Cambridge, disconsolate, wondering what I was going to do with my life. I had naively thought that once I had my college degree I would of course find a job, but not so. No longer a student, my student visa had been replaced with an Alien Registration Certificate, which did not permit me to work while in the United States. The only exceptions were working with the United Nations or with a foreign embassy. A month earlier I had filled out a lengthy application form for a job with the U.N., but had had no reply. I was discouraged.

Now, here I was, sitting at a great big desk looking out over the beautiful grounds of Twin Oaks, home of the Chinese Ambassador in Washington, D.C. The job had simply dropped into my lap. A phone call from an old friend from Peking whose summer home in the Western Hills had been just above ours on the hillside. Thelma's husband had recently been posted to Washington and she had learned that the wife of the ambassador was in need of a personal secretary. She thought of me. "Are you interested?" "Of course I am." That, followed by a quick trip to Washington for an interview with Madame Koo. She seemed to like me. The job was mine.

So, I am now the private and social secretary to Madame Wellington Koo. I look around the room where I will be spending

Madame Koo

my working hours for the next six years. It's large. Has an adjoining bathroom and a coat closet. Besides the enormous desk, a couch against one wall and a single easy chair beside it, an oriental rug covering the floor. Altogether an enviably luxurious office for a young girl's first job. Surely this is going to be the cushiest job imaginable. The only drawback is the salary, which even in 1947 is a mere pittance. My salary is a paltry $155 a month.

Earlier in the week I had scoured the "rooms for rent" columns in the newspaper. I had found a wonderful room only a mile from Twin Oaks, a short walk through quiet residential streets. It was also only one block from the bus stop on Connecticut Avenue, a major artery into the city, a perfect location. Again, I couldn't quite believe my good fortune. It was a beautiful old house on a corner lot. I had the corner room on the second floor. It was large, and bright. On the front it had a large bay window looking out onto a tree-lined street, and another window on the side. The other bedroom was occupied by two sisters, both waitresses at the Wardman Park Hotel. In between the two bedrooms was a bathroom that we shared. My monthly rent was $30.00. Combined with the $50 I sent home each month to my mother, that left me with $75 for myself. It didn't seem like much, but I had few expenses. My lunch I had daily with Madame Koo at Twin Oaks. (The Ambassador did not return for lunch.) With one good meal a day taken care of, a sandwich and milkshake at the drugstore on the way home was enough for dinner.

I had been told that Madame Koo could be difficult. Being the daughter of a man reputed to have been the wealthiest man in Indonesia, and often referred to as the world's sugar king, she was independently wealthy in her own right. She had an imperious manner that did not endear her to the Embassy staff. However, I found her very easy to work for. She was often curt and peremptory when issuing orders, but she seldom criticized and always seemed approving of my services. I handled all her correspondence, wrote all her letters: letters of appreciation, of congratulations, of condolence, of thanks. Though she had initially told me what to say, I was soon composing her letters myself. She simply reviewed what I had written and then signed her name. I bought gifts for all kinds of social occasions: weddings, graduations, new-born babies. She seldom found fault with my choices. On occasion, when Thomas the chauffeur was unavailable, I also served as personal driver. (My boyfriend had taught me to drive when I was in college.) She could be extremely generous. When I got married, she gave me four sterling silver place settings. When she received gifts of chocolates she would share them with me, often giving me half the box. Or, when she received flowers after a dinner party, she would frequently tell me to take them home. Best of all were the perishable gifts of fruit from Harry & Davids, which she would tell me to take home to share with my husband. (I was married in 1950.) When his sisters and their husbands came to visit from Hong Kong, she asked, "How are you going to squeeze them into that little car of yours?" When I assured her that we could manage, she said, "Nonsense, you'd better take my car." When she found they would be staying beyond the weekend, she insisted that I take two days off. "You're not so invaluable that I can't live without you for a few extra days." So, I drove my in-laws around for four days in her luxurious Fleetwood Cadillac. When my husband and I bought our first home and she learned that I was shopping for shrubs at Sears, she said, "There's no sense in your spending all that money. I'll have Dixon dig up some plants from here." Dixon was the elderly Scottish gardener who took care of the grounds at Twin Oaks. I remember the trunk of my car being jammed with forsythia, bridal wreath, ivy, and chrysanthemum cuttings and other plants that I can't remember. Dixon spent the better part of a day planting them for me.

I know that Madame Koo was fond of me, and I also know that she really appreciated the jobs I took on that were above and beyond those of a personal secretary. Among these was making curtains. The curtains at Twin Oaks were in shameful condition and badly in need of replacement. Unfortunately, the estimates that came in were astronomical and the costs prohibitive. At the time, the Chinese government was in dire financial straits. The funds for new curtains were simply unavailable. One of my first expenditures after I had saved enough from my meager salary was to buy a sewing machine, a Singer Featherweight. I had been making full use of it, making myself a new wardrobe of Chinese *ch'i p'ao*. Shortly after my arrival in Washington, Thelma, who had gotten me the job at the Embassy, had taught me how to make the simple sheaths, and from that time forward I discarded my western-style clothing and wore Chinese *ch'i p'ao* exclusively. Besides being easy to make—I could put a simple unlined one together in one evening—they fit my limited budget. A dress took only a yard and a half of fabric.

When the subject of curtains for the Embassy came up, I thought, "Curtains are so easy. It's just hems, plus channels for the rods. I can do that." I made the suggestion to Madame Koo. She was somewhat skeptical but willing to let me give it a try. The next week I measured windows and bought the material, but just for one room. Madame Koo was not about to have me do all the rooms until she had seen how good a job I could do. I brought my sewing machine to my office and for the next few days sandwiched the sewing in between my other tasks. Madame Koo was delighted with my sample products. I then bought material for all the other rooms. It was such an easy job, I hardly felt I deserved the thanks that were heaped upon me. It had cost the Embassy nothing more than the cost of the material.

In the years I worked for Madame Koo, she reprimanded me only once and it was a well-deserved reprimand. I had failed to stand when being introduced to Madame Chiang Kai Shek. The incident occurred at the large reception the Embassy was hosting in Madame Chiang's honor. She had come to Washington to address a joint session of congress appealing for U.S. aid for China. I was to pour tea. I had already seated myself at the head of the dining table and was checking out the tea service and the positioning of the cups when the Ambassador brought Madame Chiang in to the dining room to introduce me. Guests had not yet started to arrive. Looking back, I cannot imagine what I was thinking of not to have immediately stood up. But I didn't. Madame Chiang graciously put out her hand. I put out mine. But from a seated position. What a monumental breach of protocol!

Protocol was something I learned a great deal about in the years I worked at the Chinese Embassy. I learned who was *The Honorable*, who was *His Excellency*, and who was a mere *Mister*. I learned about orders of precedence, whether an Ambassador outranked a Senator, whether a military chief of staff outranked a Congressman, or whether a retired four- star general outranked a sitting two-star. Whenever in doubt I could always consult Mrs. Shaw. Carolyn Hagner Shaw was the social arbiter of official Washington. Her felt-covered "green book" was on the desk of every social secretary in the city. If the green book did not have the needed answers, I could always call Mrs. Shaw herself. She was always ready and willing to help. I also learned how incredibly sensitive some people could be if they were seated lower than they felt was their due. I remember how furious Madame Koo had been when one woman, having noted on the seating chart that she was seated lower than her expectations, had actually repositioned her name on the chart and then managed to get into the dining room and move the place cards accordingly.

As Madame Koo's personal secretary, I was of course fully responsible for her personal social engagements and the lunches and teas she gave. However, I had no responsibility for official social functions. That was the job of the Embassy's Second Secretary. My attendance was not required at dinner parties, but I was expected to be present at all receptions and cocktail parties. Other than pouring tea on occasion, I had no particular assigned duties, but was just told to "make yourself useful," and to "take care of the guests." Often Madame Koo would spot guests who were in need of care and she would simply dispatch me to go and talk to them, but one of the guests was a particular charge. Mrs. Hamilton-Wright was an elderly dowager who must have once been of some social prominence. Madame Koo would order, "Go take care of Mrs. Hamilton-Wright. Can't you see, she's sitting all alone. Go introduce her to Admiral so-and-so or Senator so-and-so." I then had to lead Mrs.Hamilton-Wright to the Admiral or Senator and insert myself into whatever group he was engaged with. "Admiral so-and-so, "May I present————." With that, I would make my escape without daring to look back to see how Mrs.Hamilton-Wright was faring.

Apart from being on the guest list for large receptions, Mrs. Hamilton-Wright was also often included in smaller ladies affairs. I remember the time she mistakenly walked off with the beautiful mink coat of Madame Belt, wife of the Cuban Ambassador, leaving her own worn fur in its place. Madame Belt was the last to leave. Though annoyed, she couldn't have been more gracious about the error. But I recall her saying with some indignation, "I don't see how anyone, even Mrs. Hamilton-Wright, could possibly have mistaken my mink for this ratty old thing she left behind." Her coat was of course returned the next day with profuse apologies.

At the many luncheons we shared, Madame Koo would often voice her complaints about the behavior of the wives of the Embassy's junior officers at official functions. "Who do they think they are? They should be assisting with the hostessing. Instead, they cluster together in their own little circle sipping their drinks and nibbling on refreshments as if they were guests." Or sometimes, when guests lingered long after the specified reception hours, or when the Embassy rooms had been constantly filled to overflowing, she would complain, "Don't people know that 6:00 to 8:00 doesn't mean you're supposed to stay the whole time? They're supposed to come for a short while and then leave to make room for other guests."

During the years I worked at the Embassy I met many prominent people, among them President Nixon, then a Senator, and Senator Joe McCarthy. They were both frequent guests at the Embassy receptions. However, I found that merely having shaken hands with them at a big reception meant little if one didn't really know them or they you. My husband and I attended one small informal dinner where Senator McCarthy was among the guests. It was at the home of the Embassy's First Secretary. He was responsible for press relations, and despite the miserably tiny house they lived in, he and his wife entertained frequently. This was a fun evening ending with the ten of us all gathered in the basement, some sitting on the floor, while we sang old favorites. I found Senator McCarthy somewhat bombastic but otherwise good company. At that time I don't believe he had as yet embarked on his Communist witch hunt.

Among the other notables that I met was Bishop Fulton Sheen. Madame Koo was converting to Catholicism, and for a short period, Bishop Sheen, then a Monsignor, came weekly to give her instruction. I was always pleased when he took the time to say a few words to me, but could not help feeling somewhat intimidated. He had these piercing eyes which I felt could look right through me

Among Madame Koo's friends was an Austrian businesswoman, a dynamic no-nonsense kind of woman whom I took to instantly. I know she was fond of me. During the months she was in the United States she was a frequent luncheon guest at Twin Oaks. She had some business meetings scheduled in New York and needed someone to take notes. She asked Madame Koo if she could release me for a few days to accompany her to New York. Madame Koo readily agreed. In New York I met Madame Haberer's husband and was surprised at how meek and ineffectual he appeared. His manner toward Madame Haberer struck me as being almost obsequious. It seemed like an incongruous match, a milktoast of a man and a dominant confident woman. The two occupied a large hotel suite. They had an extra cot set up for me in the living room.

The following day, Mme. Haberer and I attended a series of meetings in downtown offices. She was negotiating the sale of heavy-duty trucks and equipment to China. I took notes and occasionally raised a few questions. Madame Haberer later commended me on what she thought were astute observations. I cannot even remember what they were (something about tires).

Later, back in the hotel suite she and her husband had retired to their bedroom and I was lying on my cot reading a book. At first I heard muffled sounds of an argument coming from the bedroom. The sounds grew louder and more vehement. I could hear some scuffling. I couldn't tell what they were saying but was getting quite alarmed when suddenly Madame Haberer was yelling, "Marguerite, Marguerite, come help! Come! Come!" I hopped out of bed and went rushing into the bedroom. The window was open, the curtains flapping. Mr. Haberer, fully clothed, had one leg over the window sill. He was disheveled and crying. He kept saying, "let me go, let me go." Madame Haberer was yelling, "no, no, it'll be all right." She was yanking on his arm. We must have been at least ten floors up. Madame Haberer was screaming at me, "Help me. Pull him back." Between the two of us we got him away from the window. He collapsed on the bed, engulfed in great gut-wrenching sobs. I was so shaken. I didn't know what to do. But Madame Haberer soon recovered her composure. Very quietly she said, "You can go, Marguerite. Thank you. You were a big help." I slept fitfully that night.

The next morning, Madame Haberer said not a word about what had transpired the night before and never again mentioned the subject to me. On the train back to Washington, I wondered, "should I tell Madame Koo what had happened?" But then I thought, "if I had a husband who had tried to commit suicide, would I want others to know?" I thought not. Besides, I really didn't think that Mr. Haberer had had any intention of jumping. He had let us pull him back from the window all to easily. When Madame Koo asked how the trip had gone, I told her of the business meetings, but said nothing about the night's incident. Later, though, Madame Haberer herself evidently reported on what had happened. Madame Koo said to me later, "You were very wise to have kept it to yourself."

Two things happened after the Haberer incident that I believe were the direct results of that one instance of good judgment on my part. Normally, except for seeing him at social functions and the occasional good mornings as he left for the office, I hardly ever saw the Ambassador. The only chore he had ever asked of me was to place orders for his shoes. He had very small feet, I believe size 7½, and his shoes had to be specially ordered. On this morning, he stopped in my office and asked me to order some flowers to be delivered to Mrs. X in New York. I cannot remember her name, but it was well known that she was his long-time mistress. From that day forward he frequently asked me to order flowers or other gifts for her on special occasions. He did not need to tell me that these requests were to be confidential. I was quite tickled that I had been entrusted with this new assignment.

A more substantial reward was that given to me by Madame Haberer. She had not known me long before she noticed that my ears protruded quite visibly from my head, often even through my hair. As a child I had hated it when my mother stuck my ears down at night with adhesive tape, but of course it had done no good. Now, Madame Haberer was determined to get my ears fixed. She had a friend, an eminent Austrian surgeon, who was temporarily in New York. Dr. Pribram agreed to do the surgery as a personal favor. So off I went again to New York with Madame Haberer. The surgery was done at a New York hospital under local anaesthetic. The surgery took almost three hours, and again and again I would hear the attending doctor say, "Superficial, superficial." Each time I heard these words I found myself wondering if there had been a slip of the scalpel and if Dr. Pribram had ever worked on ears before. The end result was that my ears were flat, but slightly misshapen. I spent one night in the hospital. Looking back, I find it surprising that in those days this type of surgery had required an overnight stay. Madame Haberer took care of all expenses, which even then must have been substantial. I have often wondered how big a part my one act of discretion played in Madame Haberer's decision to take on this expense. But whatever prompted her generosity, I will be forever grateful. My ears no longer protrude.

I worked at the Embassy for six years, from 1947 to 1953, through my marriage, and through the birth of my first child. I did not leave the job until my husband was assigned to an overseas post with the U.S. government. As I had thought at the very beginning, it had been the cushiest job imaginable and I had enjoyed it tremendously. I had also learned a lot, all of which would serve me well in later years, but I was ready to move on, to another world and another chapter in my life.

Chapter 4
The Bride-in-Waiting

General Wedemeyer always thought he was the one who had brought us together: his wartime Chinese-American Aide and the young Chinese girl he had known briefly as a child. In the early thirties, when he was a young Second Lieutenant stationed in the Philippines, he and his family had spent a summer in Peking. They had been among the early guests at my mother's guesthouse. My mother had started the guesthouse when my father's job with the Chinese government had moved him to Nanking and she needed something to occupy her time during his absence. She had always wanted to show foreign visitors the "real" Peking, and the guesthouse had seemed the ideal way of realizing that wish. During the summer that the Wedemeyers had spent at the guesthouse, they had come to know our family well, and the general had become especially fond of the little Chinese girl who had been his sons' constant playmate during those months. Now, at a cocktail party in his home, the General wanted me to meet "someone very special, Captain Horace Eng." He seemed so pleased to be making the introduction that

Horace

neither of us had the heart to tell him we had already met. In fact, through mutual friends at the Chinese Embassy, I had met Horace within the first week of my arrival in Washington. Horace had an illustrious military record. Though he had been inducted into the Army in 1943 as a private, the following year he was commissioned directly as a second lieutenant "as a convenience to the United States Government," and served as Aide-de-camp to General Patrick Hurley during the initial stages of U.S. efforts to bring the Chinese Communist to terms with the Nationalists. When Communist Party Chairman Mao Tze Tung met with Generalissimo Chiang Kai Shek at the Nationalist Party headquarters in Chungking, Horace had been the sole liaison between General Hurley and both Nationalist and Communist leaders. During the final years of the war he was assigned as Aide to General Wedemeyer, then China Theatre Commander, and served as principal liaison between General Wedemeyer and Generalissimo Chiang Kai Shek. Later, he also served as Aide to

**Horace (seated), Mao Tze Tung (standing behind
Horace), and General Marshall at Yenan**

General George Marshall. When Marshall visited Mao Tze Tung in Yenan late in 1945 in an attempt to broker peace between the Chinese Communists and Nationalists, Horace again served as liaison officer and also as the official interpreter. In these positions Horace had become well known to both the American military officers with whom he had served as well as to many of the officers of the Chinese Embassy. He was a popular figure among both groups.

Much was made of his illustrious military service, but also of his eminent eligibility. He was single, had recently lost his wife. Thelma and my other friends at the Embassy could not say enough about how wonderful he was. I found it hard to believe that he could measure up to all these accolades, but when I met him, I found him all of those things. He had a warm, easygoing personality and seemed as comfortable with himself as with others. And he was undoubtedly attractive. I couldn't help liking him immediately and could see why others were so drawn to him. It seemed that all the young Chinese women of Washington were being thrown at him including the daughters of the more prominent members of the Chinese community. When he called me a few days after our first meeting I was thrilled that I had caught his attention. He took me to the Willard Hotel's Jungle Room for dinner. We learned more about each other. He had been born in America when his father was a student at Harvard. He was thirty-two years old. Actually, he lied about his age and was in reality thirty-four at the time, twelve years older than I. He was brought up in Canton and had his early schooling in China. He had graduated from St. Johns University in Shanghai, where I had also been a student for a year and a half during the war. Later he went on to get his law degree from Soochow University's Law School. He then returned to America to continue his legal studies and received his Doctorate in Jurisprudence from Indiana University. And then the war. As I already knew, he was now a Captain.

I told him about myself: raised in Peking by an American mother. No, I was *not* half American. My parents were my adoptive parents, in reality my uncle and aunt. My father too had gone to Harvard. I had attended a Chinese grade school; then an American high school. I had come to America to finish my studies and had just graduated from Smith. We danced. I later learned he had learned to dance in Shanghai's dance halls, from the dance hostesses lined up along the walls to accommodate paying customers. They had done a good job of teaching; Horace was a beautiful dancer. In the ensuing months I met all his friends. I became his regular partner. We partied with his military buddies and with our mutual friends from the Chinese Embassy. To all social gatherings we were invited as a couple. He met my family. My mother loved him; started to dream of wedding bells.

Within the first few months I knew that he was the one I wanted to spend my life with. But our courtship was no whirlwind

Horace and Elsie

affair. Though he professed his love for me countless times and spoke often of marriage, it was three years before he could bring himself to take the step. During that time he never once spoke of his earlier marriage or the loss of his wife. I learned of it through friends. Even after we were married, other than the bare facts, he spoke little of their romance. He and Elsie had been college sweethearts, both attending St. Johns together, and both moving on together to Soochow University to earn their law degrees. They had traveled on the same ship to the U.S. and both earned their JDs at the University of Indiana at the same time. They had been married for five years, though separated for much of the time during the war years. Their romance had been long and deep. It was from Horace's youngest sister Weiping, a gynecologist, then visiting from Hong Kong, that I learned of the circumstances surrounding Elsie's death. She had been hospitalized—I can't recall the reason—and had died from a wrongful dose of sulfa drugs. To compound the tragedy for Horace, Elsie had been pregnant at the time. Weiping said she had urged Horace to bring suit against the hospital, but that Horace could not bring himself to pursue the case. The loss of Elsie and dealing with his grief was as much as he could cope with.

As for me, I waited patiently, but with each passing month I was becoming more and more convinced that he would never put Elsie behind him. Though he didn't speak of her, photographs of her in his apartment were a constant reminder to me of her presence. I could see how beautiful she was, and I knew she must have been a brilliant woman. To earn a law degree in the mid thirties was an achievement for any woman, and for a Chinese woman an even greater accomplishment. I couldn't help feeling that in Horace's eyes I may not have measured up. I was also so much younger, not just in age, but in maturity. I did not drink, did not smoke, and had seen little of the life that he and his friends had experienced. I wondered if the age difference was a concern to him. But then, one day, just before

Christmas, while we were driving up to Cambridge to spend the week with my mother, he said, not so much to me, but almost as if he were thinking out loud, "I think on this visit it would be a good time to get married." I had waited so long to hear these words that I found it hard to accept that he had said them. It had been more than three years that we had been going together; I had been seriously doubting that he really wanted to spend his life with me. I asked, "Horace, are you sure? Are you really sure you want to marry me?" He turned toward me and covered my hand with his own. "Yes, Marguerite, I'm sure. I'm very sure." It was not the most romantic of proposals, but for me it was enough; it was everything.

With that, our whirlwind preparations began. Nothing could be done on Christmas day, but the day after, we started. First, the church.

Both our fathers had been students at Harvard; also, my brother Luther. We were definitely eligible to use the Harvard chapel. Would it even be available during that Christmas week? Yes, we could have it on the 30th, but only in the evening. Great, we'll take it. That gave us five days to put our wedding together. My mother's minister and the Chapel's regular organist were speedily pinned down

The Bride and Groom

by phone. Getting the marriage license was simple, but first there was an unexpected requirement: blood tests. A visit to the doctor took care of that. A phone call to an old friend of Horace's yielded a best man. A close friend and classmate from my Peking days was thrilled to be Maid of Honor. Then, the wedding dress. A quick trip by subway into Boston to the Jordan Marsh department store. It was the quickest shopping I had ever done. The choice was easy. It was the first dress the salesgirl showed me: long-sleeved Chantilly lace over a strapless satin bodice. Simple. Beautiful. Except for shortening its long train, no other alterations were necessary. It fit me perfectly. Then the bouquet. At the florist's, camelias or gardenias? Camelias, definitely. I could picture their velvety white petals overlaid on the dark glossy green leaves. All plans for the wedding ceremony itself completed in record time. The wedding came off without a hitch. Lit entirely by candelabra lining its wide center aisle, the chapel looked beautiful. In the four rows of pews, all facing the aisle in ascending tiers, some thirty-odd friends and family members beamed down upon me as I came down the aisle on the arm of my Uncle Irving. Horace waited for me at the altar. Mother, smiling through tears, gave me away.

Then, on to the reception at my mother's house. The table was laden with food: ham, turkey, scalloped potatoes, salads, aspics, biscuits, and more. Other than the two-tiered wedding cake, everything was prepared by my mother and my aunt. The punch was Horace's responsibility. It was heavily spiked, courtesy of his fraternity brothers. Prim, proper Aunt Mildred declared, her words slightly slurred, "Bess punch ever ad. I'll ave another please." Spirits were high. The party was humming. Horace and I escaped amid a shower of rice. With tin cans and other junk trailing the car, new bride and groom went clattering off into the night.

Chapter 5
The American Dream

With all the frenzy that had gone into the wedding preparations, we had not had time to even think of our wedding night. No plans had been made for a romantic hideaway. Horace was scheduled to be back at work in Washington the day after the New Year holiday so we knew only that we must head south. Surely we would find some roadside cabins where we could spend the night. As chance would have it, the first ones we came to looked unbelievably inviting. Five small cabins nestled in the woods, set far back from the roadside. The cabins' owners gave us a key to one of them. A light snow covered the ground, and as we pulled up in front of our cabin, the scene was like a picture post card. I thought that this was as romantic a setting as anyone could hope for.

One would have thought, that having waited so long for this marriage, I would remember vividly all the details of that wedding night, but today, sixty-five years later, only one memory remains clear in my mind. I cannot help smiling when I think of it. Lodged securely in Horace's navel was a single kernel of rice. We were both amazed that it had found its way through all his layers of clothing into that little crevice. When I found it, we both laughed at the discovery and Horace said, "Some Chinese fortune teller would probably say it's a sign that our marriage will be fruitful." And of course it was, though the fruit did not materialize as quickly as many people surmised. It was a full two years before we had our first child.

On the drive back to Washington, at one of the many rest stops, we ran into a group of Horace's fraternity brothers and their dates. When Horace, told them we had just been married, they heaped congratulations on us both, but I'm sure there was much conjecture as to why the wedding had taken place so suddenly and without any advance notice. The general consensus was, "She has to be pregnant." When the months passed and my figure showed no change whatsoever, there may have been disappointment in some quarters, but my mother surely must have breathed a sigh of relief. I think even she had resigned herself to the possibility that she might soon have to tell her friends that I had given birth "prematurely." That was the acceptable way it was done in those days. For "nice girls" the admission of sex before marriage was unthinkable.

On New Year's day we moved my things into Horace's one-bedroom apartment in Virginia. Miraculously, all photographs of Elsie had disappeared. I told myself, "Elsie is in the past." She was no longer a part of the present or of the future. Those would be totally mine. And so began a marriage that could have been a prototype for the American Dream: a house in the suburbs, a garden, a dog, babies, barbecues in the back yard, chats over the fence, pot luck with the neighbors.

When Horace and I first met in 1947, he had already returned to civilian life and was working at the Pentagon as a military intelligence officer. But just before our marriage at the end of 1950, he had transferred to the Central Intelligence Agency. The CIA was the nation's first civilian intelligence agency, and as such was for those interested in intelligence work, *the* place to be. Though it had been commissioned in 1947, it was still operating out of temporary buildings down near Washington's Tidal Basin. The workload in those early days was heavy. Many an evening I would arrive at 5:30 to pick up Horace, only to be kept waiting for two or three hours in the parking lot. In warm weather the wait was not too onerous. At least I could read a book until darkness descended, but in the winter, reading was impossible and I had a hard time keeping warm. I kept a blanket in the car and wrapped myself in it when I had to give the heater a rest.

Although I kept my job at the Embassy, I was determined to be a wife Horace could be proud of. This was for me a new and challenging experience. I cleaned, I polished, I washed, I ironed. In my early zeal I even ironed his underwear. More important, however, than anything else was learning to cook. In China, where we had always had a cook, I had seldom been in the kitchen. Despite the fact my mother had been known for her cooking expertise, my only experience with cooking had been making brownies for my Girl Scout merit badge. However, cookbooks are wonderful things, and with the help of Fanny Farmer and the Boston Cookbook I soon became a creditable western cook. Chinese food, however, was another thing. The few Chinese cookbooks available were not very good, and the single Chinese cookbook (in Chinese) that a friend sent me from China gave no precise measurements whatsoever. Directions would be the English equivalent of "add seasonings" or "add soy sauce to taste" or "add garlic." No indication of whether "to taste" meant a teaspoon, a tablespoon, or half a cup, or whether "garlic" meant two slices or ten cloves. So, with cooking Chinese food, it was strictly trial and error. I tried many recipes that looked promising, but in the first months of our marriage Horace poured soy sauce liberally on every dish I presented. What was the point of my following the recipes so precisely? However, I was undeterred, and when he eventually dispensed with that extra soy, I knew I was finally on my way to becoming a good cook.

In a period when large housing developments were springing up with not a tree in sight, we were lucky to find a small group of houses in the near-in suburb of Kensington, Maryland, where the builder had actually left the trees standing. We were so excited to have found a community that actually had trees that we were ready to sign the contract on sight. What clinched the deal was the two large apple trees on the lot we were eyeing. The house cost all of $4,400 But it was tiny. The so-called master bedroom was so small that I spent a sleepless night after signing the contract, worried that the room would not hold both a double bed and a dresser and leave space to walk between them. The living/dining room was only slightly larger than

Our first home. 3410 Anderson Road, Kensington, MD

a 9 x 12 rug. I wanted a separate dining room, so we created one by cutting through the living room wall into the adjacent bedroom.

Now we had a house, but unfortunately no furniture—Horace had been living in a furnished apartment, and I in a furnished room. Through the yellow pages we found a discount furniture wholesaler. In one fell swoop we selected living room, dining room, and bedroom furniture, all in solid rock maple—it was popular then for young couples just starting out. Having just incurred a mortgage debt, the additional bill for our selections seemed staggering. We decided to pay for it on the installment plan. In China, mortgages and installment plans were still unheard of. One did not buy things one couldn't pay for. But this was America. Paying by installment was commonplace. But when the first payment was due, neither of us could stand the thought of that additional debt, and we paid off the total amount.

Though small, the house did have a full basement. Horace would finish it himself the "do-it-yourself" American way. Having been raised in China, where the privileged classes did not indulge in manual labor, Horace had no experience whatsoever with carpentry, but nonetheless started valiantly on paneling the basement. He was not good with a hammer and was not naturally handy, but he was determined. Many a finger was banged, and many many times I thought he would throw me out of the house when I would suggest very tentatively that a panel was crooked or that a two-by-four was off by several inches. I discovered then that Horace had a temper. The basement project almost brought an early end to our idyllic marriage, but when the job was done, all was forgiven. Many an evening we settled ourselves in that basement room luxuriating in Horace's accomplishment.

The next step in our new suburban life was to have a dog. We picked up Spooky at the local animal shelter, a year-old mixed breed, but mostly cocker spaniel. We bought a dog house and had a chain link fence installed, but found out all too soon that it could not contain him. When we got home from work, Spooky, totally covered in mud, came bounding toward us. He had dug his way under the fence. We hosed him off and filled the hole, but the next day, he had again dug his way out. This time he did not rush up to greet us, but again covered with mud, was sitting on the front stoop waiting. This time we filled the hole with rocks, only to find the next day that Spooky had simply dug a new hole. And so it went. By the time four holes had been dug and refilled, we gave up. We had no idea where he spent his days, whether inside or outside the fence, but it was a joy to see him each day on our return, sitting on the front stoop wagging his tail furiously in greeting.

After Spooky, came babies. First, Eric, born in January 1953. An easy delivery, a beautiful baby. With the guidance of Dr. Spock's book on babies and childcare, Eric was weaned early from the bottle, was toilet trained at a year and a half. In those days children were put on the toilet seat every two hours with the faucet turned on. If the sound of running water and a parent making "ss—ss—ss" sounds brought success, the child would then be praised, much as we housebreak a puppy today. Eric was a good baby and he was easy. We advertised in the paper for a baby sitter. Again, we were lucky. The first person who answered the ad was a young black girl whom both Horace and I liked on sight. Frannie was a mere slip of a thing, and surprisingly well spoken. She had no references other than a letter from her landlady stating that she was a lovely girl of good character who she was sure would be a conscientious and caring baby sitter. Knowing so little about her, we were hesitant, but took her on anyway. It was one of the best decisions we ever made. Frannie fell in love with Eric instantly. The neighbors saw her in the back yard rocking him, singing to him, playing with him. She dressed him up and pushed him through the neighborhood in his stroller, showing him off as proudly as if he were her own. The neighbors asked, "Where on earth

Horace and me, with Eric and Kathy

did you find her? Do you realize how lucky you are?" Yes, we did realize it. Frannie worked for us for over two years, through the birth of our second child, right up to the time we left for our first overseas assignment in the fall of 1954. When we left, she took Spooky with her, and with Spooky, his doghouse as well.

Our second child, Kathy, was born in May 1954, just sixteen months after Eric. The delivery was easy, but Kathy was *not* a beautiful baby. The back of her head was flat, and her forehead sloped back to form a kind of wedge. In later years, Horace's secretary said she always remembered how each time Horace left the office for a hospital visit, he had said, "I always wait until there is no one else around viewing their babies. I don't want them to know the one with the peculiar head is mine." Of course, as expected, Kathy's head soon rounded out to a normal shape, but she was a difficult baby. Suffering from colic, she cried continually, stopping only when she was held. I was up most of the night cradling her and rocking her, but the minute I put her down, her crying would resume. Since Eric was still occupying the crib, I had made a makeshift bassinet out of a Chinese wicker basket for Kathy. We kept her in our bedroom, and both Horace and I had many sleepless nights during Kathy's infancy.

In those days, we didn't have many of the conveniences of today's world: no air conditioning, no dishwashers, no automatic washers or dryers. In the humid, sweltering heat of Washington summers, sleep was possible only with a rotating electric fan trained fully upon us throughout the night. My weekends were spent in shorts and halter tops. Laundry was done in a wringer-type washing machine. It churned the clothes in soapsuds, but every item had to be put through the wringer for a rinsing in clear water in the double laundry tub. Then through the wringer again into a laundry basket. From there to an outside laundry line. Diapers were a chore. No disposable ones in those days. I remember the unpleasant job of swishing soiled diapers around in the toilet bowl before consigning them to the laundry basket. The day that we decided to splurge on diaper service was a liberating day for me. What luxury it was to have the used diapers picked up and washed by someone else, and having them replaced each week by a tidy packet of clean ones.

It was early in 1954 when Horace was told he would soon be assigned to a post in Japan. CIA requirements for an officer going on an overseas assignment stipulated that the spouse must be an American citizen. Even though I was married to an American, I was still a Chinese national. I was proud of my Chinese heritage and had no desire to change, but now I was to become an American citizen. Getting that citizenship proved to be a simple matter, all arranged and facilitated by the CIA. Following instructions, I simply left the country for Montreal for a few days, applied at the American Consulate there for reentry, and within a few weeks was sworn in as a U.S. citizen. Looking back, I am ashamed to admit how little that citizenship, treasured so much today, meant to me at the time. It was a major event in my life. Yet, I have no recollection of the swearing in ceremony, of raising my hand and swearing allegiance to my new country. It had come too easily.

Autumn was upon us when we started preparing for departure. The house was put up for rent and immediately taken by a young Navy couple with one child. The apple trees were loaded with fruit. Ripened apples were already beginning to litter the ground. We didn't want to leave our new tenants with a yard full of rotting apples, so we shook the trees down even though many were still green. The two trees yielded twenty bushels, all of which we distributed to delighted neighbors. Spooky, and his doghouse, were delivered to Frannie's house. It was hard leaving him behind, but we knew he would be loved and cared for. I could see Frannie walking Spooky on the city sidewalks just as proudly as she had paraded Eric around our suburban neighborhood. The moving vans came and all our furniture and those of our belongings that would be put in storage were packed. The rest, our personal belongings, would be shipped directly to our post in Japan.

As we left the empty house, I couldn't help feeling sad. I was excited about our overseas assignment and looking forward to it, but I hated to leave the home in which we had been so happy. Our lives in those years by most standards would not have been considered remarkable in any way. They were probably not that much different from the lives of countless young couples across America. Yet, for me, raised in a different culture, it *had been* remarkable; it had been different. It had been my first real hands-on experience with *living* the American way, the do-it-yourself way. In China, even in the leanest years, the war years, there had always been servants to do the work. Servants cleaned the house, servants laundered our clothes, servants prepared our meals. Here, in America, coming home to household chores after a full day at work, admittedly I often longed for those servants of my China years. And yet, there was something immensely satisfying about doing things for ourselves. It was knowing that our house was clean because *I* had cleaned it; our meals were good because *I* had cooked them; and our house was a home we were proud of because *we* had worked with our hands to make it so. And oftentimes, when I buried my nose in the clean fresh smell of laundry just off the line, or bit into an apple picked from a tree in our own back yard, or looked down on our two children sleeping peacefully in their beds, I thought that life could not hold much more than this. It felt great just to be alive.

Chapter 6
Japan

At the end of October 1954 we boarded the SS President Wilson and began sixteen years of life overseas along with home leaves every two or three years. Life on board the passenger liner was a far cry from the Navy transport ship that had brought me to America nine years earlier. The ocean liner seemed the height of luxury: spacious quarters—U.S. government employees traveled first class in those days—sumptuous meals, and all kinds of amenities I hadn't known existed. Yet, by today's standards when luxury cruises are practically floating cities, the President Wilson would seem small and insignificant.

On our arrival in Tokyo we were met by our Chief of Station Desmond F. He and his wife Barbara drove us directly to Kamakura to the house they had rented for us. "It's not much of a house," Barbara explained, "but it's near us, and it's only temporary while you look for a permanent place." But when we drew up at the house my only concern was not about the house itself. It had been a long drive and my immediate need was for a bathroom. The houseboy pointed me toward a door, but inside, there was a wash basin and a tub; no sign of a toilet. "No, no. The toilet. I want the toilet," I said desperately. Seeing my anguish, he hastily yanked open another door. Blessedly, a toilet. I rushed in, pulling the door shut behind me, and sat myself down with a sigh of relief. But on looking up, I found I was in a tiny room, no more than a cubicle really. And on the floor before me, on a slightly raised platform, was the most beautiful flower arrangement, two blossoms at the base of a few bare branches, almost sparse in its simplicity. Up until that moment I had been completely keyed up by all the excitement of arrival in Japan, seeing new sights and sounds, and catching up with old friends, but on seeing that simple flower arrangement, all the pent up tension that had built up in me simply fell away. I felt calm, composed. Not even wanting to get up, I lingered for a few minutes on that unlikely throne. As I rejoined the others, I couldn't help thinking what an odd spot it had been to find peace and serenity. I wondered too how a people with such love of beauty could have at the same time the cruelty and ruthlessness they had shown during the war? During the time we spent in Japan, each time I saw a thing of beauty, or noted an act of gentle humility, that same thought came to me again and again. How could one people have two such different sides?

In our search for permanent housing, the agent had four houses for us to look at. The first two were western style, adequate, but unimpressive. And then, a Japanese house. Our search stopped there. One look and Horace and I both knew that that was where we wanted to live. "But I have another to show you," the agent said eagerly. "No, no, we don't need to look further. We like this one." It was lovely. Its

Our house in Kamakura

wide double gate of weathered wood opened onto a beautiful Japanese garden where the grass was laid out, not in an expanse of lawn, but in oval patches of varied sizes. Pathways of bare earth meandered through and around the grassy ovals. It was like an artist's creation, a collage of greens and browns, green grass overlaid on brown earth. The house itself, L-shaped, was at the back of the garden, all glass and mellow wood, raised slightly above the ground on stilts, and crowned with a roof of earthen tiles.

We loved our year in that Japanese house, and I think it was the major reason we enjoyed our stay in Japan so much. I loved its cleanliness and simplicity. I loved the feel of its cool *tatami* floors on bare or stockinged feet. I loved the papered doors and the way they slid smoothly along their polished tracks. I loved the way the entire house could be closed up with glass panels when the weather was cool, yet opened to the fresh air when the panels were slid aside. I loved the way the house could be closed up completely at night with additional wooden panels that slid out on their separate tracks. And I marveled at how all these panels, both glass and wood, could be slid tidily into their own compartments when not in use.

Most of all I loved our Japanese teahouse. It was at the far end of the long passageway onto which all the separate rooms opened. It formed an L with the rest of the house. It was completely open on two sides, but it too could be enclosed with glass panels in cool weather. From it, a small wooden bridge, flanked by a cherry tree, led to the garden. It seemed almost sacrilegious to use the room for anything but a tea ceremony, but nonetheless, we could not resist making the teahouse into our bedroom. At night, when we slid the wood panels in place, we were cocooned in darkness. But waking in the morning, we opened the panels to the morning light and air. Looking across the bridge into that Japanese garden, I felt that if I inhaled deeply enough I could breathe all that beauty into my lungs and that it would become a part of me. It was an almost spiritual way to begin the day.

Though we had chosen to live in a Japanese house, unfortunately, we were incapable of adapting to the simplicity of the Japanese lifestyle. We had to have chairs to sit on and beds to sleep on. But it pained me to see the movers plant the western style furniture, the usual beds, tables, chairs, sofas, all Navy issue, onto the pristine *tatami* floors. Even as the heavy bed was being positioned, I could see the dents being made in the *tatami*, and at mealtimes the scratches made by the dining chairs as we pulled them in and out. I often wondered what our Japanese servants thought of the damage caused by our way of life. I felt as if it must be something of an affront to them, the lifestyle of these foreign barbarians who misused without remorse what was theirs. The one concession we did make to Japanese custom was that we did remove our shoes on entering the house (we required this of all our guests as well). Looking back, I can't help smiling at my memories of men in coats and ties, and women in full cocktail attire balancing their cocktail glasses and hors d'oeuvres, all shoeless in their stockinged feet.

But there were drawbacks to a Japanese house as well. Chief among these was the lack of central heating. The rooms were heated with oil-burning space heaters. These were skinny, box-like affairs that sat in aluminum-lined trays and seemed so unstable that a child at play could have knocked them over. In a country prone to earthquakes, it was a constant concern that one could fall over and set the house on fire. I remember, whenever we felt the slightest tremor, which was frequently, both Horace and I, *and* the maids, would all rush to turn off the heaters. Insufficient closet space was another problem. I hated seeing the simplicity of the Japanese rooms almost defiled by the addition of furniture that we needed for our western clutter. In addition, there were frequent problems with clogged drains and toilets that wouldn't flush. Plumbers came so frequently that I often felt they were a part of our regular staff. I could not understand how a country that had the capability of mounting a massive war on the most developed nations in the world could not handle the mundane functions of daily living such as simple plumbing, or design a stable heating unit. This same thought would occur to me again and again as we saw small Japanese cars frequently disabled along the roadside. How on earth had they managed to wage a devastating war? The fact that Japanese cars kept breaking down was a boon to Americans whose cars were much in demand by the Japanese. When we left Japan, we sold ours for twice what we had paid for it.

Our house was on a short lane just off Kamakura's main street, and only a block from the *Daibutsu* (Big Buddha) Temple. When friends came to visit, it was easy to describe the street where it was located, but finding the house was another matter. Houses were not numbered consecutively on the street, but rather by the date on which they had been built. Thus #7 could be adjacent to #35, #7 being the seventh house built on that street, and #35 the thirty-fifth. When we found that friends were frequently unable to find our house, we had our weathered wooden gates painted a bright red. It was only after the deed was done that we learned red was used only for temples and that we had violated an unwritten rule. I am sure that after our departure, our office must have had to pay dearly for replacing that gate as well as the *tatami* floors.

While in Japan the Navy issued numerous pamphlets on adjusting to life in Japan. Among these were cautionary notices about not eating the local bread (known to contain bacteria), avoiding raw fish, and not allowing the children to go barefoot for fear of contracting worms. The first few weeks we followed these directives faithfully, but soon, thinking almost as one, Horace and I decided that this advice was not for us. We had been raised in a country far less hygienic than Japan and had managed to survive to a healthy adulthood. Thereafter, we ignored most of the Navy's notices. We found the local bread delicious. And how could we live in Japan and be denied the joys of *sashimi*? We enjoyed raw seafood of every type: octopus, squid, and the many varieties of fish (all raw), without any ill effects. *Soba* and *udong* noodles became a staple of our diets. We embraced whatever foods the Japanese had to offer. The only things I never acquired a taste for were *miso* soup and the hyper sweet red bean confections. The children played barefoot on occasion and never had worms.

I was totally ignorant of the circumstances of Horace's work, but every day he was off to the U.S. Naval base in Yokosuka, and I to engage in the normal women's activities. Once again we had servants: two maids and a gardener: Ishi, Masako and Oki. The three of them, like most Japanese, loved children, and showered their attention on our two and spoiled them beyond belief. I can still see Eric on his tricycle happily pedaling around the pathways that divided the garden's grassy ovals. Behind him would be Kathy, just starting to walk, teetering along, with her hand held firmly by Ishi or Masako.

We women had lots of leisure time. We played bridge. Some of us took painting lessons. Almost all of us took flower arranging in one or the other of the many schools and styles. My teacher was of the *Sugetsu* School. She complimented me profusely on my arrangements, telling me I had great talent, but I noticed that even as she offered praise, she always found it necessary to tweak ever so slightly a single stem or branch in every one of my arrangements. We also shopped, both at the Navy Commissary and PX, and in the local stores. Japan was a shopper's heaven. There was so much to shop for, most of it inexpensive by U.S. standards. We acquired whole sets of western style glassware and dishes for a pittance. A set of Blue Danube china for twelve, including serving platters, sugar and cream pitcher and even a soup tureen, all for U.S. $36. I am still using that set today, but adding a single coffee mug a few years ago cost me $22. Silver too was cheap. It didn't compare in quality or weight to American silver, but the designs were lovely and most of us loaded up on candelabra, serving dishes, and picture frames. I loved shopping in the local stores. First of all because of the artistry of the local crafts and the unbelievably low prices, but also because it was such a joy having every purchase, even the most insignificant dime-store type item, wrapped and tied with loving care and presented as if it were some treasured object.

For Horace and me, one of our greatest joys of living in Kamakura was strolling along the streets in the evenings. The *Daibutsu* Temple, being the main attraction of Kamakura, drew many tourists during the day, but after sundown the town was quiet. It was then that Horace and I, both passing easily for Japanese, donned our *yukatas* and wooden clogs and delighted in joining the local populace as they returned home from their evening baths.

When I look back at the time we spent in Japan I can't help thinking of how ambivalent I had been when we first learned of the assignment. On the one hand, I had been excited about the prospect of seeing a new country—I had been eager to learn about Japan itself and its culture. On the other, fully nine years after the war had ended, I still harbored a deep antipathy towards the Japanese. Having lived for four years under Japanese occupation, I had known them as cruel and ruthless oppressors. I could not forget the many nights when Japanese gendarmes had come banging on our gate and the harsh way they had treated my mother as they hauled her off forcibly to the gendarmerie for questioning. Yet, when our tour was cut short at the end of a year, my earlier ambivalence had been totally dispelled. I had seen a different Japanese people from those who had occupied Peking during the war. We had had a small taste of the Japanese culture. We had done the usual things that foreigners do; visited countless temples, sat through hours of *kabuki* performances, participated in tea ceremonies, learned something of various Japanese traditions, and admired the spectacular show of cherry blossoms in full bloom. Unfortunately, we did not make any friends among the Japanese. Being a part of a small minority in a foreign country, we tended to do things together. We made weekly play dates for our children; we shopped together; we partied often. We played games. Charades was the game of choice. It became a competitive sport, men against the women. All these activities with fellow Americans, and friendships were forged that continued through our lifetimes.

Chapter 7
The Philippines

Though our assignment to Japan was intended as a two-year tour of duty, barely a year into our stay we were told that the entire station was being transferred to Subic Bay, the U.S.Navy Base in the Philippines. We would be airlifted by Navy planes in shifts. Women and children were to go first with only a bare minimum of personal belongings. In the dead of night we were bused to the Air Force base in Atsugi where we were loaded onto a small Navy plane. Wicker baskets for the infants were lined up and roped together in the center of the plane. We women buckled ourselves up in bucket seats along the sides. It was not exactly a deluxe form of travel, and there was no possibility of sleep, but the trip was charged with excitement. We made one stop in Okinawa and landed at Subic Bay the next morning exhausted, but none the worse for wear.

An advance team met us at the airport and took us directly to our housing area to the houses to which we had been assigned. They were located on the side of a hill and were quite luxurious compared to the Quonset huts occupied by most of the Navy personnel. The houses were all two and three-bedroom duplexes. Earlier, having been asked by our Chief of Administration Bob W. if we would like to share a duplex with his family, I was quite sure we would be in a choice location. True to expectations, our unit was located at the top of the hill and would surely get more breeze than those which were lower down. The houses were very open—no air conditioning in those days—with lots of windows and a fully screened porch. Floors were

Our duplex house at Subic Bay

asphalt tile. Kitchens were well equipped, with exceptionally large refrigerators and freezing compartments. And a feature I had never heard of or encountered before, "hot closets." These were truly a godsend, for in the high humidity of the Philippines, dampness was a constant scourge. The "hot closets" were equipped with electric coils and each house had two. We used one for salt, sugar, flour, and other dry goods, the other for linens. The only drawback in our housing, as we learned after we were settled in, was the complete lack of privacy. The houses were located a good distance apart, but because of the heat, all the slatted windows were kept open all the time. Day and night, not only could we see into the open windows of our neighbors, but we could also hear everything. We often felt we were living in each other's living rooms. And at night, until lights were out, we could well have been in each other's bedrooms as well.

Our presence on the Base was something of an anomaly. Our privileged accommodations must have been obvious to the Base personnel, as they dubbed our housing area "Nob Hill." I'm not sure how welcome we were, but we were given access to all the Base facilities. Though we were located about ten minutes drive from the Base itself, they ran an hourly shuttle service to and from our housing area. Certainly, all our needs were met.

All in all, we were very well taken care of, but life on a US Navy Base is not exactly a cultural experience and we hardly had any exposure to either the people or the culture of the Philippines. On arrival at Subic we did make a few forays into the nearby town of Olongapo. We explored the open markets and poked into some of the shops looking for local crafts, but the heat was oppressive, and the dust churned up by the jeepneys (jeeps converted into buses) hurtling about the streets discouraged further visits. We also made one trip to Clark Airforce Base, about a two hour drive away, but driving too far afield was frowned upon as we were told there was always the possibility, however remote, of an attack by deserted Communist insurgent Huks hidden in the hills. We did, however, get a brief glimpse of life in the Philippine countryside. Along the road were many small woven huts, all built on stilts, often with a pig or other livestock below. Little children ran about either totally naked or sometimes clad only in a loose shirt but no pants. Occasionally, through the windows we could see lines of women and children. We were told they were de-lousing each others' heads. We saw water buffalo plowing the earth, and countless rice paddies, fields of sugar cane, and many many banana and papaya trees. All interesting, but not enough so that we wanted to brave heat and dust to learn more.

The few trips we took beyond the Base constituted our total association with the outside world. We had seen it, we had rejected it, and we had retreated to the insular and sterile life of the Base. We lived mostly among ourselves without even much contact with our Navy neighbors. Our sole exposure to the local populace was through our own housemaids and the workmen who took care of the grounds. I made a real effort to get to know our maid Esperanza, but she was a dour individual who was unresponsive to all my attempts to draw her out. I praised her often, trying to get a smile out of her, but she was singularly uncommunicative and all I could get from her were monosyllabic responses. "Yes, Mum," "No, Mum," "Thank you, Mum." I said to her once, "Esperanza, I am very happy with the work you do for me, but sometimes I worry that you are not happy here. I never see you smile." Her reply, again expressionless: "Thank you,

Mum. I cannot help it, Mum. That is my habit." The only time she appeared to be enjoying herself was when she was polishing the floors. With one foot placed firmly on half of a coconut husk, or sometimes with both feet on separate husks, she half skated and half shuffled on the tiled floors until they literally gleamed. All the while she would be humming to herself as if she were dancing to the rhythmic beat of her own music. Sometimes her movements were slow and measured. A lullaby perhaps? Or a sad ballad? Other times she moved as if she were dancing to a native drum beat. And sometimes there was a half smile on her face.

Looking back on our stay in the Philippines, I would say it was pleasant, but uneventful. There was, however, one event of major consequence, the birth of our third child. When we first arrived at Subic, our medical needs were taken care of by the Navy doctors, but the addition of our CIA contingent required that we provide our own doctor. He arrived just before my baby was due and I was somewhat concerned when I learned that my delivery would be his first since his internship some twenty years earlier. My concerns, however, were somewhat allayed when I learned that he had requested that the Navy obstetrician also be in attendance. This delivery was a fascinating event for me. My first two deliveries had been under general anaesthetic and I had been unconscious throughout the deliveries. Though "natural childbirth" was being heavily promoted at those times, I was not one to endure pain if modern science had provided a means of avoiding it. However, I did have some curiosity about the process of childbirth and this time elected to have an epidural. I was assured that I would feel no pain but would be awake throughout the procedure. I found it a fascinating experience. Admittedly, though, it was nerve wracking to hear the Navy doctor giving non-ending instructions to our doctor throughout the delivery. "Here comes the head. Looks like it's going to an easy one. Now, put your hand here. No, no, not that way. This way. Can you feel the shoulder?" and so on. Every time an instruction was preceded with the words "no, no," I wondered what our doctor was doing wrong. A healthy baby boy was delivered on June 4, 1956. His birth certificate listed his place of birth as Olongapo, the Philippines. We named him Laurence.

From the time he was brought home from the hospital, that child was fussed over, cradled, and rocked by more people than I can count. He never lacked for attention. Whenever friends were at the house, if he made the slightest murmur, someone would pick him up. If a bridge game was in progress, it would be whoever held the dummy hand. Throughout the game he would then be passed on from dummy to dummy, whether male or female. Our Chief of Station Des F. and Bob W., Admin chief, both took their turns. Friends were constantly dropping by to check on his progress. One neighbor dropped by each afternoon without fail. Her first words were always, "How's the old bean today?" Eric, now three and a half, and Kathy, sixteen months, immediately picked up on those words and started calling him Old Bean. "Mommy, Old Bean"s awake." "Mommy, Old Bean's crying." Before too long "Old Bean" morphed into just plain "Bean." Among friends and family he remains Bean to this day, though there was a brief period when he was in high school that he asked us to call him Laurence. Bean, like Eric before him, was an easy baby, and for me, once again with help to do the housework, life was easy. For the first few weeks after Bean's birth I indulged in a daily steam bath and massage. It was before saunas had become popular, and the steam bath consisted of sitting in a steam box with just my head poking through a hole at the top. The steam heat left one totally drained of energy, and having one's limp body massaged afterwards was the single most wonderfully soothing, relaxing, and almost mesmerizing indulgence that I have ever experienced.

As in Japan, I had no idea what Horace's job involved. He left for work at the Base in the morning, returning late in the afternoon. It appeared to be a routine nine-to-five job. While we were at Subic the friendships forged in Japan were solidified, and we did have some good times. I have pleasant memories of loafing by the pool and lazy afternoon naps with the fragrance of ginger blossoms wafting through the windows. The hula lessons were fun, as were the luaus. The men joined us in casual evenings with gin-and-tonics or ice tea in hand. We continued our bridge games, enjoyed the continual battles between men and women at charades and the occasional scavenger hunts, one of which revealed an embarrassing cache of canned goods, obviously stolen, hidden under the mattress of one of the maids. I had enjoyed all these activities, but, other than bringing a beautiful child into the world, I had learned little, contributed nothing, and through sheer inertia accomplished nothing.

We left Subic in the fall of 1956. I was not sorry to be leaving. In later years, when asked if I had ever been to the Philippines, I always answered, "Yes, we spent a year there." Yes, physically, we had been there, but we had not *lived* in the Philippines. We had merely *lived* in a small part of the United States, a US Naval base.

Chapter 8
Home Again

On our return home, our first stop was at my brother Luther's new home in Pitman, New Jersey. During the two years we had been abroad, my mother had sold her house in Cambridge and was now living with Luther. With the proceeds from the sale, Luther had built a house that included an apartment for my mother and Jeannie. I was glad that she now was relieved of the responsibility of the large Cambridge house. She was seventy-nine years old, well beyond the age she should be cleaning rooms and doing laundry for four roomers.

It was wonderful being with family again after two full years away. My children had a chance to get to know their grandmother and she to know them. Luther's two boys, Ken and David, each a year older than Eric and Kathy, got on well together. We had two fine weeks of togetherness, but the time went quickly, and soon we were off to Washington. Since it would be another week before our household effects would arrive from the Philippines, we moved into a temporary apartment near Horace's office. He was off daily to his office, but the children and I were pretty much confined to the apartment. It was while we were there that I had the most frightening experience of my life, one that still gives me chills when I think of it.

I had called the front desk to report that the bathroom lights were not working, and an electrician had been sent up promptly to make the repairs. Eric, not yet four, and Kathy, two and a half, had both been quite good, but the long days of confinement were beginning to make them restless. The arrival of the repairman was a welcome diversion, and they were at his heels from the moment he entered the apartment. "Leave him alone," I said to the two of them. "Come into the bedroom with me. I'm going to give Bean his bottle." But as I settled down with Bean, they did not follow. I called out, "Eric, Kathy, come on, don't bother the poor man. He has a job to do." But there was no reply. With that, Bean in my arms, I stepped into the living room, but there was no sign of the children. The repairman was still in the bathroom. I looked in the other bedroom. No children. Then I noticed that the apartment door was open. With Bean still in my arms I went to the door. Immediately, I could feel a draft. Looking down the hall I could see an open door and caught just a glimpse of Kathy's dress beyond it. "Oh my God! The fire escape!" Without even thinking I put Bean on the floor, bottle and all, and went racing down the hall. Kathy was standing with her back to me on that narrow platform, oblivious to the danger. I yanked her into the hall. Before seeing him I could hear Eric whimpering, "Mo-o-o-mmy, Mo-o-o-mmy." I was out again for him He was four steps down and was trying to crawl back up the stairs. I stepped down two steps, grabbed his hand, and half pulled, half dragged him up and into the hall. On my knees, I clutched them both to me. I was gasping, and the tears were pouring out of me. I couldn't stop them. I clung to the two children, couldn't let go. But finally, I gathered myself and stood up. Suddenly I remembered Bean, still on the hallway floor. He was starting to cry. His bottle had rolled away. With Eric and Kathy clinging to me, we went back down the hall. I picked Bean up, and as we were reentering the apartment, the electrician was leaving. He saw that I was distraught and asked, "Are you all right, ma'am?" Couldn't he see? Wasn't he even aware of what he had done? I screamed at him, "What were you thinking? What were you thinking? How could you leave the door open?" He looked at me blankly, still unaware; then started to say something, but I didn't want to hear it. "Never mind. Never mind. Just go! Go!" I yelled at him. "Just go!" I herded the children into the room and closed the door.

When Horace came home, I was still shaken and weak in the knees, but at least had stopped crying. But as I recounted the story, again and again the tears would start flowing. We had been five or six flights up and the thought of what could have happened was more than I could bear.

Two days later we moved back into our home in the suburbs. When we had left for Japan the house had been rented to a nice young Navy couple with one small child. But less than a year later the couple had been transferred and the real estate agent without consulting us had re-rented the house to another Navy couple with four boys, ages three through twelve. It was too many for that small house and we had been upset, but there was nothing we could do. Now, we approached the house with some apprehension. Expecting the worst, we were surprised to find the refrigerator spotless, a box of soda on one of the shelves. The burners on the stove were clean, as was the oven. There were some smudges and scratches on the walls, and nail holes where pictures had been hung, but there was no real damage of any kind. I could hardly believe how lucky we had been. Some spackle and a single coat of paint and the house was ready for us.

Though I had enjoyed our tour abroad, I was glad to be back in America. This time, however, life was different for me. This time I did not have Frannie to help me with the children. And now I had three children to care for rather than two. I had become accustomed to the servants we had abroad, and now had to readjust to once again doing the chores myself. Friends offered sympathy. They spoke of my being *saddled with* the children, of being *tied to* the house. They said, "Marguerite, you need to take a day off a week to *get away from* the children." But I neither wanted nor needed sympathy. I didn't feel *tied* to the house, or *saddled with* the children, and I had no wish to get away from them. I was not working, did not have to go to an office every day, and I loved being a stay-at-home mom. I was young and healthy, and though I couldn't exactly say I loved housework, it came easily to me and I was happy and content with my life.

In June that year—it was 1957—Horace was offered an assignment in Hong Kong. It was not a total surprise. When we were in the Philippines, the Chief of the Agency's Far East Division had made a trip to the station at Subic Bay. He had spoken then to Horace about the possibility of a Hong Kong tour. As Horace's father and four sisters were all living in Hong Kong, Horace couldn't have asked for a better posting, but he didn't think for a minute that it would come through. In Hong Kong his job would have to be in the U. S. Consulate, and at the time, State Department policy did not permit the assignment of officers of foreign descent to their countries of origin. Thus, when we were told the tour was firm, Horace couldn't have been more pleased. I, on the other hand, had some misgivings. I did not share these doubts with Horace. The prospect of two years in Hong Kong was exciting—it was a much-coveted post—but I was not sure what it would be like living at such close quarters with his family.

I had already met three of Horace's sisters. His third sister Weiping, a gynecologist, I had met before we were married. She had done her training in China but was doing more work at the University of Pennsylvania for some particular medical certification she needed for practice in Hong Kong. Horace had brought her to stay with him for a short period when there had been a lull in her workload. Our first meeting was rather strange. When she got out of Horace's car she seemed totally unnerved by my presence. He was trying to introduce us, but she was more concerned with the condition of the white mice she had brought with her than with meeting some unexpected strange woman. The four mice were in two cages and were part of some experiment she had been working on. Clutching the cages, she was unable to shake hands and looked rather frazzled as she greeted me. In the short time she was with Horace I did not get to know her at all well. She was nice enough, but was the only one of his sisters with whom I never developed any rapport.

I had met Horace's two older sisters, Ida and Margaret, when they visited us shortly after our marriage. Our house was much too small to put them up—the two of them, with their husbands, Y.K.

and P.W., stayed in a nearby hotel—but they spent all their waking hours with us. During that time all four were vocal in their praise of the way I had decorated the house, the living room drapes, the kitchen curtains, the small ornamental touches. They complimented me profusely on how immaculately I kept the house, P. W. insisting my floors were clean enough to eat from. I squired them all over Washington in Madame Koo's Cadillac during the day and cooked for them in the evening. We all seemed to enjoy each other's company and I certainly felt they approved.

Y. K. was the most talkative, regaling us with accounts of minor language mishaps during their trip. Before coming to us the four had been traveling in Europe. Y.K. himself had studied law in London and had seen much of Europe, but foreign travel was a new experience for the other three. I remember particularly Y.K. laughing uproariously while telling us of P.W.'s naivité when being measured for trousers in London's posh Saville Row. While measuring his inseam, the tailor had asked, "How do you carry yourself, sir?" P.W. had drawn a total blank. "Carry myself?" "Yes, do you carry yourself on the left or the right, sir?" It took even Horace a few moments to grasp what the tailor's question meant. I wonder how many men in America would have been equally naïve in the same circumstances. How many would have instantly grasped that custom-fitted trousers required that the correct accommodation be made for a man's genitals.

What I remember most about P.W. was his playing the violin every moment that he was not actively engaged in conversation with the rest of us. He played as he walked in and out of each room; he played while going up and down the stairs to the basement; he played in the garden. Though he was an amateur, he was a serious violinist and the proud owner of a Stradivarius. Even on their travels through Europe and the U.S. he had carried it with him, all much to Y.K.'s annoyance. Personally, I rather enjoyed the music.

I had been somewhat apprehensive about how I would get on with Ida. She was the oldest, and after the death of Horace's mother in the early forties, Ida had become kind of the matriarch of the Eng family. Horace had spoken of her often, obviously admired her. It was clear to me that for him, Ida was the model for all womanhood. I suspected that my position within the family would hang on her approval. Throughout the years of my marriage, Ida was unfailingly good to me. She was unstinting in helping us get settled in Hong Kong. If I needed anything, I went to her. If I had a problem, she was the one I turned to. However, even as I accepted her many gestures of love and goodwill, I never got over the feeling of being under her judgmental and critical eye.

With the Hong Kong assignment firm, we made plans for departure. This time was different from the last time we had left. There was an air of finality about it. We recognized that now with three children, the house was much too small for us. We put it on the market and it sold immediately at a much higher price than we had paid. It had served us well as a first home, and had also been a good investment. We were sorry to leave it and the neighbors who had become good friends.

This time, our journey was not by sea, but by air, on a Boeing Stratocruiser. We had been told well in advance about this crown jewel of the Pan American fleet. I don't believe any commercial passenger plane before or since has rivaled it in sheer luxury. This was a time when travel by air was an exotic and luxurious adventure. Men traveled in business suits, and women dressed for the occasion. We wore white gloves, and it was all-important that our shoes and purses matched. Friends came to the airport to give travelers a sendoff, often bearing a corsage in a florist's box. The plane's seats and the aisles were wide. Legroom was generous. Meals were served on a linen-covered rolling cart with an attendant doing the carving and serving. It was full-service fine dining replete with silverware, linen napkins, and tiny individual salt and pepper shakers. Eric and Kathy were enthralled with these and had more fun playing with them than with the coloring books, crayons, and other toys provided for children.

A unique feature of the Stratocruiser was that it had a lower deck fitted out elegantly as a cocktail lounge. The plane's seating configuration was two and two, which left one member of our five-person family sitting alone. That person was usually Horace. Thus, he was able to break the monotony of the flight by going down frequently to chat with other passengers and to enjoy a drink at the bar. I, on the other hand, was *tied to* the three children. This time I did feel tied, but since I was not a drinker, and also not as disposed to chatting with strangers as Horace, it was not a great hardship for me to forgo the attraction of the lower deck.

For me, and for the children, the best thing about the plane was being able to lie down full length. In first class, which was the way those in the State Department's Foreign Service traveled then, the seats, fully reclined, were converted to beds after dark; above, there were pull-down bunk beds. When the curtains were drawn, the center aisle looked like the aisle of a Pullman train. Horace and I had the lower beds, Eric and Kathy the bunk beds above. They loved climbing up the ladders and squirreling themselves behind the curtains. Unfortunately, none of us noticed that the metal arm holding Kathy's bunk was broken, and she, scrambling up into the bed, ran into the arm's jagged edge and scratched her face badly. The resulting scar remained on her cheek for several years before fading away. Despite this minor injury, having their own little cubbyholes was a thrill for both children. They couldn't resist poking their heads out of the curtains time and time again, and I had a hard time getting them to settle down. But finally they did fall asleep. Horace too retreated into his cubicle and soon there was not a sound from him. I have no recollection at all of where we put little Bean. I assume I kept him with me. I must eventually have fallen asleep, because the next thing I knew, the sun was pouring in from the window—I had forgotten to pull down the shade—and I could hear signs of life in the aisle.

When I arose the stewardesses were already restoring beds to their original seating positions. The flight had been a long one—we had been on the plane for over twenty-four hours—, and despite the luxury of beds and other amenities, it was still an exhausting flight. As soon as the pilot announced that we would soon be reaching Hong Kong, I dressed each child in turn in clean clothes, brushed their hair and washed their faces. I was so proud of how they looked, Eric in his little Eton suit, Kathy in a white ruffled dress, and Bean in a brand new outfit. I was feeling quite smug and pleased with myself that I had had the foresight to bring fresh clothes for all three children. I sat back in my seat, proud of the picture we would soon be presenting to Horace's family. Little did I know how quickly that pride would be shattered.

Chapter 9
Hong Kong, the Foreign Service

It was the summer of 1956 that we headed for Hong Kong. As we began our sharp descent into Kai Tek airport—one of the steepest and most dangerous descents in the world, I had been told—we were experiencing extreme turbulence. The plane banked so sharply that for a moment I thought I would be tipped out of my seat. Looking out the window, the mountains seemed alarmingly close. Within seconds, buildings seemed even closer, so close that I could look into the buildings' windows. It was frightening. Kathy was sitting beside me. As I leaned over to tighten her seatbelt, she whimpered, "Mommy, I don't feel good," and promptly threw up all over herself and me. We were buckled in and couldn't get to the bathroom. There was no way to clean up until we landed. Then, as other passengers were crowding down the aisle, the stewardess brought us wet towels and did her best to clean us up, but when we disembarked, Kathy and I definitely did not look our best. It was not the picture- perfect arrival I had envisioned.

Horace's four sisters and their husbands were all at the airport to meet us. I was the only one aware of the bits of vomit still clinging to Kathy's ruffles. I was the only one conscious of the odor of her upheaval on my dress. I was the only one who cared about the stains on my clothing. To the others our appearance couldn't have mattered less. The children and I could have been in potato sacks and no one would have cared. Their attention was riveted on Horace. They were

Horace and four sisters

all so glad to have their brother among them. It had been years since the family had all been together and it was good cause for rejoicing.

When all the greetings were over and I had been introduced to those of the family I had not already met, our entire group headed for the ferry that would take us across the harbor. What a wonderful introduction to Hong Kong the Star Ferry was! The trip took not more than twenty minutes, and seated on the upper deck, with a cool breeze blowing off the water, we had a spectacular view of Hong Kong's city skyline and of the tiers of homes that dotted the mountainside above. To the left and right of us other boats plied the harbor, and along the shoreline, sleek pleasure craft of the modern world were tethered side by side with small hand-manned *sampans* of an older culture. In the distance we could see a wooden junk in full sail, a romantic picture of the East.

On reaching the Hong Kong side we were thrust immediately into the hustle and bustle of the city. Taxis zig-zagged up the hill to Ida and Y.K's house at "mid-level" on the hillside. Horace's father was waiting there to greet us. He was small and mild mannered, and to my relief, not in the least intimidating. He told me how pleased he had been when he first learned his son was marrying the daughter of an old schoolmate—he and my father had attended Harvard at the same time. Ida and Y.K.'s three children, older than our three, were there to greet us, their *Kao Fu* (Cantonese for uncle, specifically, mother's brother), and their new *Kam Mo* (Cantonese for aunt, specifically, mother's brother's wife). The servants were told I was their new *Kam Nai*, a title that indicated my position as the wife of the mistress's brother.

We stayed with Horace's sister Ida and her husband Y. K. for a full month while waiting for our household shipment to arrive from America. Three luxurious apartment buildings, the Repulse Bay Mansions, had just gone up on the south side of the island. Horace's brother-in-law P.W. Chiu—the husband of Horace's sister Margaret—was the developer, and an apartment was available for us if we wanted it, which of course we did. We chose one on the third floor in the center building of the three. It was large, and had a wide balcony overlooking the bay and the beach below. Two houses the size of our little suburban house in America would have fit comfortably into our personal living space alone, not to mention the additional servants quarters, kitchen, laundry area and extra balcony at the rear.

And so, for Horace and me, began a new lifestyle in a new world. In America we had been no more than average middle class citizens. In our first tour in Japan and the Philippines, we had still been merely middle class visitors to a foreign country. Now, as representatives of the United States government, we were suddenly elevated to a higher class, a class of Hong Kong's social elite.

Horace's status was further enhanced by his relationship to Y.K. Before coming to Hong Kong we had had no idea of the important position Y.K. held within the community, not only through his family, but in his own right. His father was founder of the Bank of East Asia, and through the marriages of his fourteen children, the family was tied into all the wealth and prestige of *old Hong Kong*. Many had invested in real estate long before Hong Kong had become an international free trade port and now owned large swaths of the island's prime real estate. Others were prominent figures in the financial world. Y.K. himself, a lawyer, was a partner in the city's leading law firm, serving successively on the Colony's Urban, Legislative and Executive Councils. The very mention of the name Y.K. Kan, and waiters and storekeepers would start to bow and scrape in homage.

Added to this new-found status was the additional respect Horace received from being the first and only ethnic Chinese to be assigned to the U.S. Consulate. In the eyes of local Chinese residents, he had actually broken an unspoken barrier by achieving "white man" status. During the period we were in Hong Kong, from 1957 to 1961, the island was still very much a British colony, and British colonialism still ruled. Racial walls were coming down, but among the local Chinese population there was still the pervasive feeling that the white man was king. The Ladies Recreation Club still did not admit Chinese to its membership, and it was only the year before our arrival that Y. K. had been the first Chinese admitted to the exclusive Jockey Club. Horace recognized the still existing racial barrier and adjusted accordingly. He learned early on that he could not stop in at the office on a Saturday in a sport shirt as the Caucasian officers did. If he was not in a suit, he was invariably taken for part of the cleaning crew. He was also well aware that any local Chinese coming in with a problem or an appeal of some kind, always assumed that the Caucasian colleague with whom Horace shared an office was the person in authority. Horace always enjoyed seeing the surprise, and even awe, on the visitor's face when the Caucasian officer would turn to Horace for advice or a decision.

Though we both accepted these perceptions of white superiority, it was still a surprise to me when for the only time in my life I felt personally the painful sting of overt racial discrimination. When our oldest child Eric reached school age we applied to the British school nearby for admission. Other newly arrived American children were being admitted speedily, but still we received no notice that our application had been accepted. I made an appointment to see the principal. She made one excuse after another, each of which I countered. Finally, she announced, "Mrs. Eng, I'm not obliged to give you any further explanation. Your son cannot be admitted." With that, she stood, dismissing me with finality as if I were some recalcitrant student.

At dinner that evening I told the family of the humiliating experience. Y.K. was irate, *and* indignant. "We'll just see about that," he muttered. Barely two days later we received notice that Eric was admitted. Another Chinese-American child, who had been experiencing the same rejection as we, also received notice of admission. I don't know what steps had been taken or how much pressure had been exerted to bring about this change. I know only how fortunate we were to have had the right connections. It seemed ironic, though, that despite never having experienced any racial discrimination in predominantly white America, it was in a Chinese city, albeit a British colony, where our Chinese race was held against us.

While Horace was adjusting to his new position as a political officer at the consulate, I dived in to the role of a Foreign Service wife. After making my obligatory courtesy call on the wife of our Consul General, we were swept into the diplomatic social circuit. During the day it was bridge, or coffees, lunches, or teas. In the evenings, cocktail parties and dinners. The social life was hectic. Most of the Consular corps were on two-year rotational assignments. With every departure there was a round of farewell parties, these followed by welcome parties for their replacements. During the summer months when most of these rotations took place, it was not unusual for us to attend two cocktail parties and a dinner in the same evening. Added to this frenzy of partying was the never-ending stream of visitors who had to be wined and dined and taken on shopping and sightseeing trips. Many of these were VIPs at the highest levels. When Vice President and Mrs. Johnson visited Hong Kong, I was assigned to take a sub-Cabinet member shopping. I cannot remember his name but noted that he did not hesitate to buy items from Communist China though it was strictly prohibited. At the time, all Chinese items, particularly artifacts, had to be accompanied by a Certificate of Origin proving they did not come from Communist China. As we shopped, I had the temerity to remind him of this fact. His response, with a smile: "Well, we won't worry about that, will we." We both knew that the VIP plane on which he was traveling would not be subject to U.S. customs inspection or the regulations that applied to ordinary mortals.

For Horace and me, in addition to the social life within the various Consular groups, the foreign business community, and the local Hong Kong elite, we also had our own frequent family gatherings. Horace and I did a great deal of entertaining, probably more than most of our colleagues. Though our round dining table could seat ten for Chinese food, for western food, since western settings take more space, it seated only eight. We supplemented this with two bridge tables, and regularly hosted groups of sixteen.

All this entertaining required an efficient staff, and therein lay many problems. Since I spoke no Cantonese, I was happy to find a couple from North China with excellent references who spoke Mandarin. Male servants always commanded higher salaries than women, and Northern Chinese usually asked for more than local Cantonese. Nonetheless, we were prepared to pay the higher fee for a cook who came so highly recommended. He submitted his accounting weekly, and for the first month, being unfamiliar with Hong Kong prices, I accepted his figures without question. Even though his accounting for the next month showed a definite upward creep, I tolerated the increase. In past years in China, my mother had told me that it was expected and accepted that a cook would make a 10% "squeeze" on his purchases, but not more than that. However, when our cook charged us for fourteen pounds of butter in one month (the only meal at which we used butter was breakfast), I knew it was time for him to go. Thereafter, we employed Cantonese *amah*s (maids), one to take care of the children, one to do the cleaning and the laundry, and a cook. This was a challenge for me because, though they could understand my Mandarin, at least for the first year or two I had a hard time understanding their Cantonese.

Most of the servants hired by Americans spoke some English. Ours did not and had never worked for foreigners. Thus their salaries were on a local scale and lower than the salaries received by English-speaking servants. This seemed like a great savings for us, but we did not realize that all kinds of extras were expected. For instance, at Chinese New Year, they expected an extra month's pay. Likewise if there was a death in the employer's household. And when their jobs came to an end, an extra month's pay was expected for every year of employment. We did go along with the some of the extras that our *amah*s claimed were their due, but not all. As in so many other instances, Ida helped us in the negotiating of a reasonable amount.

I was now a lady of leisure and free to take on whatever pursuits I was interested in. Chief of these was shopping. I had thought that Japan was a shopper's heaven. Now I found that Hong Kong was paradise twofold and more. When my mother, Jeannie, and I had left China right after the war we had had only twenty-four hours notice to board the American Navy evacuation ship. All the beautiful Chinese things we had once owned had been left behind. Now I had the chance to replace those lost objects from my cultural past. A favorite haunt, known as Cat Street, was jammed full of Chinese artifacts, many, antiques of great value; others, copies, but undetectable as such to the novice antique hunter. I was never concerned with the antique value of my purchases, buying only the things I liked. Years later, after I retired, I took my purchases down to the Freer Gallery in Washington for authentication, and, surprisingly, found that many were in fact genuine antiques and of considerable value. Today, except for the few items that belonged to Horace's family or to mine, almost all the decorative items I own and treasure today were bought in Hong Kong. But apart from Chinese artifacts, I also bought beautiful hand-embroidered linens, tablecloths, place mats, napkins, and enough monogrammed handkerchiefs to last a lifetime. From England I bought wool blankets and beautiful dress fabrics, fine wools, linens, and lawns. And gorgeous silks from Italy, Thailand, and India. Jewelry too. Mikimoto pearls were cheaper than in Japan. Gold jewelry was cheaper than in America. It would seem that all these things would have been a strain on our finances, but they were acquired over a four-year period and at prices that could not be matched in the U.S. On our departure from Hong Kong, we also ordered rosewood furniture that cost no more than our starter maple furniture had cost in America.

Apart from shopping, I also had time for other pursuits. In China, most young Chinese girls of good family took up painting. My maternal grandmother was noted for her paintings of flowers in the *kung pi* style, in which each petal, leaf, or stem is painstakingly outlined and then filled in with color. My father too was a painter. He specialized in landscapes. During the four years we were in Hong Kong I studied with three different teachers, finally settling on one famous for his flowers and birds. He painted in the bolder *yi pi* style where each leaf or petal is made with a single stroke of the brush. Like most Chinese painting teachers, he taught by demonstrating; we students learned by copying, on the premise that, once the technique was mastered, we would then create original paintings of our own. I proved to be a great copier, but found I had little creative talent, never producing any good original work of my own. Still, I do have many quite pretty pictures to show for my efforts, and despite their not being original, my children are happy to have their mother's work hanging on the walls of their homes.

My painting of two peonies

But while we were enjoying the high life of our new status, we were not unaware of the difficulties the colony was facing. Hong

Kong was being inundated with refugees from China's Communist mainland. Its pre-war population of four hundred and fifty thousand had mushroomed to three million. The hillside overlooking *Wan Chai*, one of the island's busiest commercial areas, was massed with makeshift squatters' huts. When we arrived, in the summer of 1957, Hong Kong's water reservoirs were totally inadequate to provide for the burgeoning population. Water was restricted to four hours *every other day*, two hours in the morning, and two hours in the early evening. For us and the well-to-do, this was an inconvenience, but no more than that. Bathtubs were kept filled with water for us to use at will, and we simply adjusted our bathing schedules to the hours of availability. We also had large earthenware crocks in both kitchen and laundry areas. But for the squatters on the hillside it was an unimaginable hardship. The Hong Kong government was doing its best to build low-cost housing in Kowloon to accommodate the new settlers, and had made the decision not to pipe water up the hill to avoid attracting additional squatters to the hillside. We couldn't avoid seeing the long lines of mostly women and children waiting for their turn at the water spigots in the sweltering heat of summers and the chilling cold of winter. The sight of tiny tots staggering back up the hillside under the weight of heavy containers of water was heartbreaking. Fortunately, by the time we left Hong Kong in 1961, the water situation had improved somewhat. Water was still restricted, but was available for four hours *every day* rather than every other day. The population problem, however, was still present and refugees continued to pour into the city. Among those trying to gain entry into Hong Kong was my father.

We had hardly gotten settled in our new apartment when the father, whom I had hardly known as an adult, re-entered my life. In the twenty year period since the Sino-Japanese war began in1937 and the family had been separated—he fleeing to China's interior with the government, we remaining in Peking—I had seen him for only a few months in 1947 when he had come to America to attend my graduation from Smith. Now it was 1957. A surprise phone call from an old family friend informed me that the exit permit from China that my father had been denied for so many years had finally been granted and that he was already in Kowloon. Friends were making plans to smuggle him into Hong Kong. The very thought was appalling, but immigration restrictions were stringent and they saw no way he could gain legal admittance. Here, once again, Y.K. stepped in. With him as guarantor, restrictions were waived and my father was admitted legally. The Consulate processed his visa in record time, and within the week he was off to join my mother in America.

My father

During the few days he was with us in Hong Kong we had hardly had time to get acquainted, but I found almost instantaneously that I liked him as I had when I was a child. I had been only twelve years old when we had been separated—now I was thirty-two—but I remembered him as a loving father. Now, he was almost a stranger. In later years I saw him only during the short periods we were on home leave. When I came back to America permanently, he was already gone, the father whom I barely knew.

Chapter 10
Hong Kong, the Family

We were in Hong Kong for a total of four years, from the summers of 1957 to 1961. During those years Horace's family was ever present. Immediately after our arrival Ida and Y.K. hosted a lavish dinner for us at a Chinese restaurant to introduce us to all the family and to close friends. There were four tables, seating ten people at each. Our common language was English, and all those present spoke English to me, but it was unavoidable that they would lapse into their native Cantonese when talking with each other. I often lost track of what was going on around me and felt awkward much of the time. Different people kept raising their glasses to Horace and me in welcome. Ida reminded us that we should toast those at the other tables. I had no idea how to go about this; it was all so new to me. But Horace seemed to be an old hand at this kind of thing. I followed his lead. We rose and went to each table in turn to toast the other guests. We had been married for over six years, but I felt very much as if the occasion was a welcome to the new bride and groom. And in these circumstances I felt like a very insecure young bride being inspected by the groom's family.

In the months that followed, many family members and friends invited us to their homes. I quickly became aware of the wealth and prestige that surrounded us. Evidence of it was everywhere. Y.K.'s sixty-four foot yacht; P. W.'s Stradivarius, the Rolls Royce of his brother P. P. And also their homes. All the houses were large, all opulent. The house of Y.K.'s sister Ivy in Repulse Bay—not far from our apartment—was the most stunning I have ever seen, with a swimming pool cantilevered out over the bay. I remember one evening at a dinner party at her home, a guest had asked how many bedrooms the house had. Ivy went through the motions of counting, and finally, giggling, replied, "I'm not sure how many bedrooms, but we have nine bathrooms." This was when the average middle class American was happy to have two. P. P.'s house also had a swimming pool where our children spent many happy hours, but as I look back, I wonder how the pools were justified or allowed when water was so scarce.

But the wealth was not confined to just family. Among Horace's friends was an old grade school classmate from their early years in Canton. Jieh KaiJu was now the head of the Hong Kong branch of the Bank of China, the Communist bank. He had a collection of almost two hundred Bonsai trees that Bonsai societies from all over the world came periodically to view. Of course he maintained a gardening staff to tend these trees. He kept twenty-three thoroughbred dogs of different breeds, again tended by a full staff. I have no idea how it was that a person of such wealth could be a representative of Communist China. When our tours in Hong Kong came to an end, his farewell gift to me was a gold Rolex watch.

And then there were Y.K.'s law partners Sir M.K.Lo and Sir M.W. Lo. Both had been knighted some time before our arrival in Hong Kong, and both were wealthy of course. They kept three grass tennis courts, beautifully maintained, with play on two courts only, while the third rested. So, Horace and I enjoyed the luxury of playing on lush grass as well as other courts. Both the Los were excellent tennis players and were sponsors of the Davis Cup matches when played in Hong Kong. For us, being connected to them through Y.K. provided an extra bonus in that we not only had choice seats at Davis Cup matches, but were also included in post-match social gatherings with some of the tennis greats.

During the four years we were in Hong Kong not a week passed that we were not at the home of one sister or another. Many weekends we were out on Y.K.'s yacht, sometimes with just the family, and other times with groups of friends. The sixty-four foot yacht was manned by a two-man crew and I believe could sleep six. We never overnighted on it, but enjoyed many outings to nearby bays, with lavish picnic fare served on board by the servants who were brought on board. Y.K. offered us the use of the yacht to entertain our friends any time we wished. However, we took advantage of his offer only once, as after tipping the crew and preparing the food, we found it was a much too expensive form of entertaining.

Sundays were reserved for *mahjong* games with Horace's father. In some ways *mahjong* is like rummy, but it is a gambling game, and it is not the one who goes *out* who wins, but the one who amasses the biggest score. Certain sequences score higher than others, and the draw of a single card/tile can change the value of a hand in an instant. It is a lightening fast game, cards drawn and discarded instantaneously, requiring a quick brain, facility with numbers, and intense concentration. Going *out* is luck, but *scoring* big is skill. I was not a skilled player and regarded my consistent weekly losses simply as contributions to family unity.

It was during a *mahjong* game at our apartment that Horace's father complained, in Cantonese, "I don't know why, but I feel a kind of ache in my back." Weiping, usually the least vocal of the family, spoke up immediately. "You need to lie down." And to the rest of us in a quiet voice, "It's a massive." With that, she went down to her car to get her medical kit. I led Horace's father to Kathy's room and had him lie down on her bed. I had hardly turned around when he seemed to have fallen asleep. I told the others, "He's fine. He's gone to sleep." His mouth was open and he was taking deep rhythmic breaths, but Moping, also a doctor, was instantly in the room. "Get a spoon," she said to me quickly, "and press his tongue down. We don't want him to swallow it." I was still sitting by the bed pressing firmly on his tongue when his breathing stopped. When Weiping returned with her medical kit he was already gone. It had happened so quickly. It didn't occur to any of us at the time to look at the *mahjong* hand he held, but I always hoped that his last hand had been a good one, and that his final waking moments were of a phenomenal *mahjong* score.

With the death of Horace's father, traditional Chinese custom took hold. The very next day our tailors had produced black cotton clothing for all the family. For the next hundred days the women in the family could wear only rough black cotton. Even a black-on-black design was not permissible. No nylon stockings, only cotton. No patent leather shoes, only plain leather. No jewelry of any kind. And for one hundred days we could not indulge in any form of public entertainment. Movies, concerts, sporting events, all were taboo. For one hundred days we could not enter the homes of even the closest friends. That would have brought our association with death into their homes. I don't know from what roots this hundred-day tradition had sprung, whether it was associated in some way with religious belief—Horace's family were all Christians, not Buddhist, Taoist, or even Confucianist—or a custom unique to Hong Kong. I only know that it was strictly observed. Near the last few of our hundred days of mourning we stopped at the home of a close Chinese family friend. We knew they were home, but the servants denied us entrance, saying they were out.

Though I was almost glad to have a reprieve from our hectic social life, the hundred days of family togetherness was confining. However, it did give me a chance to get to know each individual member of the family well. Y.K., whom I liked tremendously, could be insufferable at times. He was demanding and overbearing with the servants. He often made others the butt of his jokes. He was condescending to the two less affluent of Ida's sisters. He was scornful of others who had achieved lesser knighthoods than he, referring to their *pitiful* Knights Bachelor honors in comparison to his own Knight Grand Cross title, the same rank as Prince Philip. Through the years, as head of Hong Kong's Trade Development Council, he had played a large part in building up Hong Kong's trade with the rest of the world, had met with any number of world leaders, and had received numerous honors by them in return. But despite his bluster and his brashness, Y.K. had a big heart, and if any of the many he often derided had been in need of help, he would have been the first to give it. Besides, he will always have a warm place in my heart, because in later crucial years in my life he was the only one who spoke up in my defense when others found me lacking.

Ida was the complete antithesis to Y. K. She was modest and unassuming. When Y.K. criticized her in the presence of others, or made a joke at her expense, she never retaliated, never defended herself. She just smiled. At the many social functions they attended, other women of the Colony's social elite were beautifully turned out. They wore lovely fabrics. They were coiffed, manicured and bejeweled, their accessories in the latest fashion. Ida, on the other hand, always dressed in muted tones, a simple brown wren among brightly hued fine-feathered birds. I don't recall ever seeing her in a colorful print. Her hair she pulled back into a bun. She wore almost no makeup and little jewelry, possibly a simple strand of pearls around her neck. She was a handsome woman, the most attractive of the four sisters, and I often wondered why she chose this kind of self-effacement, especially since Y.K. would so often joke delightedly and quite unkindly after each incident when she was taken for his mother. Ida was highly regarded by all who knew her. For some, she had achieved sainthood merely for putting up with Y.K.

Margaret was totally different from Ida. There was a lot of vanity in her. She was proud of her trim figure and took great pains with her appearance. P.W., her husband, was wealthy, perhaps with family money, or perhaps from his brother P.P.'s lucrative medical practice. P.W. was probably the sweetest man I have ever known. He was modest and unassuming. He was kind and considerate of others. He was generous to a fault. His servants were devoted to him. He saw good in every person, excused even the most egregious faults in others. And he tolerated Y.K.'s occasional jabs with good humor. He dabbled in a number of business ventures, among them land development, Repulse Bay Mansions where we lived being his prize. He was also much involved in the exporting business, though I'm not sure in what capacity. I know that Horace and I attended many dinner parties for visiting business contacts at his home, and several times I visited showrooms where Hong Kong products were on display. Y.K. was, however, scornful of these business ventures, often claiming that P.W. had never worked a day in his life.

Weiping, Horace's third sister, and her husband Kingho were the only two of Horace's immediate family with whom I never developed any rapport. She had her own gynecological practice; Kingho, also a doctor, held a senior position in the Colony's health department. For some reason, we saw less of them than of the others. I suspect Kingho looked for excuses to avoid Y.K.'s condescension.

Of the four sisters, I felt closest to Moping, the youngest, possibly because she was the nearest to me in age, but also because her forthrightness and down to earth, no-nonsense manner reminded me of my Peking friends. She too was a doctor, an obstetrician. Both she and Weiping had probably been much influenced in their choice of professions by their mother, who, according to the family, had been China's first female obstetrician. Moping had undergone her medical training at the Peking Union Medical College, which was funded entirely by the Rockefeller Foundation and was at the time the pre-eminent medical school in China. It was probably during Moping's years at the PUMC that she had acquired these qualities that so often distinguished the girls of Peking.

I also liked her Moping's husband Ed, who was an internist, also trained in Peking at the PUMC. He had a good practice, but I know it was a sore point with him that Y.K.'s sister Ivy and brother Y.H. would send their servants to him for their medical care, but would themselves go to more socially prominent physicians. Ed, like me, was a Northern Chinese, and to the rest of the family, all of whom were Cantonese, we were *lao soong,* outsiders. They accepted us, but much as, to a diehard southerner in the U.S., a Yankee will always be a Yankee, to them we would always be *lao sung,* not quite one of them. That provided an extra bond between us, but I think it was also because Ed and Moping were nearer to us in economic status. I never felt overwhelmed by their wealth and position

   Both Ida and Y. K. and Margaret and P.W. couldn't have been more generous to us. Whenever we were with them, we were never allowed to pay for anything,—not restaurant meals, taxi fares, tickets to events, or even hair cuts. If we were with them, they paid. Ida insisted on making us a gift of the beautiful 9 x 12 Tientsin rug that is still in our home and is much admired today. Gifts to Horace from Margaret and P.W. included a Rolex watch one year—not an ordinary Rolex, but the much prized Oyster Perpetual. Later, an Omega, both gold of course. They gave me a Rolex, and pearl earrings—of natural, not cultured pearls—set with diamonds. Also, through the years, lesser gifts like suit-lengths of fine British wool for Horace, cashmere sweaters, fabrics, perfumes for me. We reaped enormous benefits from their generosity, and I couldn't have been more appreciative, but with all the largesse that was showered upon us, plus all the wealth that surrounded us, I couldn't help feeling like a poor relation during our entire time in Hong Kong. Horace was a senior officer at the Consulate; he had a good salary by U.S. standards. We were not poor, and I did not like feeling poor when we were not. But there was no way we could reciprocate. What does one give people who have everything? Once in a while, when the Consulate's small commissary received a shipment of beef from America, we were able to give them a large cut of prime rib. This particular cut was not available in Hong Kong and it was a real treat for them. On home leave we looked for the latest gadgets that might not yet have reached Hong Kong. I occasionally made brownies and took them when we visited. It was hardly an even exchange.

   I am sure Horace's two younger sisters must have shared our feelings. They were comfortable financially, but all too often must have felt the vast difference in their circumstances. Though they did not drown us in gifts, they were good to us in other ways, and each of them had joined the other two in presenting me with a beautiful piece of jade shortly after our arrival in Hong Kong. Though Horace and I had already been married for over seven years, these were in effect "bridal gifts" from the family. One is a ring, a circle of jade needing no setting. The others I had set myself into a pair of earrings, a pendant, and a bar pin. They will one day go to my children, and from them, I hope, to theirs.

We departed Hong Kong in the summer of 1961 amid a flurry of almost daily farewell parties. Our last month we had only two evenings at home with the children. It had been a wonderful four years. It had given us a taste of the high life that we otherwise would not have known. We had acquired beautiful things for our home. Horace had had the enviable chance to be with his family even on a foreign assignment, and for me, I had found a new family to whom I felt closer than to my own.

Chapter 11
Taipei

After Hong Kong we had a two month home leave before embarking on our next overseas tour in the summer of 1961. This time it was Taipei, the capital of Taiwan, home of the Chinese Nationalist government since being ousted from China by the Communists in 1949. The Sino American Mutual Defense Treaty, signed in 1954, committed the United States to her defense, and consequently there was a large American military presence on the island. The U.S. Army, Navy, and Air Force were all well represented, and the Navy's Taiwan Defense Command (TDC) was headquartered in Taipei. Likewise, the Army's Military Assistance Advisory Group (MAAG). The Thirteenth Air Force had a smaller unit. The Naval Auxiliary Communications Center (NACC), for which Horace was now working, had its own compound of offices, including its own clubhouse, but used all the other MAAG and TDC facilities. Then there was of course the American Embassy staff, plus a smattering of private citizens. The PX, commissary, a movie theatre, swimming pool, and Protestant church were all located within the MAAG compound. The Naval hospital provided medical care for the American community, though NACC had its own medical offices and staff.

Unfortunately, our first days in Taipei did not go well. A young security officer met us at the airport and took us to the house that had been assigned to us. Upon our arrival it was immediately apparent that the house was not ready for ocupancy. Furniture was not in place and workers were still moving additional pieces into it. We were hot and exhausted from the long trip, but there was not even drinking water in the refrigerator. The young security officer who had met us apologized profusely for the lack of preparation, but soon departed leaving us to cope as best we could. If it had not been for the young Embassy wife who lived around the corner from our house, we would have felt totally lost. Donna Randolph appeared even before the workmen had departed to introduce herself and to offer whatever help we needed. She was horrified that we had not been supplied with drinking water or basic groceries and immediately brought over supplies from her own kitchen. Other than the security officer who had met us and brought us to the house, no other NACC person called or dropped by to welcome us.

Even more disheartening was the way we were received at the party held at our club the weekend after our arrival. Given that it was billed as a "hail and farewell party," we assumed it was to welcome new arrivals such as ourselves and to bid goodbye to departees. When we arrived, the club was already filling up, but there were still several empty tables. We sat down at one, only to be told that the table was taken. We found another and were told by new arrivals that it too was taken. And then another. Finally, the waiters, who saw our plight and were as embarrassed by the situation as we were, squeezed a small table and two chairs into the hallway, which at least gave us a place to sit. Soon, Ray C., our Station Chief, arrived with a group of Chinese guests. I don't believe he saw us. There was music; there was dancing. Ray gave a short speech bidding farewell to those who would soon be departing and welcoming the new arrivals. No individuals were asked to stand and be recognized. No names were mentioned. Everyone seemed to be having a fine time. Other than a few people who looked at us rather curiously, probably wondering why a strange Chinese couple were at their party, Horace and I were totally ignored. This was not the type of welcome we had expected. In Japan we had been greeted personally by the Chief of Station. In the Philippines we had been invited by the Chief of Admin to share his house. In Hong Kong we had been embraced by Horace's family. But here, there didn't appear to be any interest whatsoever in our arrival. It was depressing.

We later learned that NACC's Deputy Chief, George M. and his wife were to have been our sponsors and were the ones who should have made all the preparations for our arrival, including making some arrangement for our attendance at the hail and farewell occasion. When we arrived in Taipei, they had been away on a two-week excursion to the southern part of the island. In their absence, the job should have been delegated to others, but evidently someone somewhere had slipped up. We never knew who was responsible for this lapse, and saw no point in voicing our disappointment after the fact at the poor reception we had received.

The house assigned to us was rather nondescript. It had a few oriental touches such as the two stone lions that flanked the front doorway Chinese style, and a Japanese *tatami* room above the dining room. Also, here and there were some sliding doors, Japanese style. Otherwise, it was basically a western style one-story house with a western kitchen equipped with an electric range and refrigerator. Behind the house, however, detached from the house proper, there was a Chinese kitchen with two large gas burners, plus separate rooms for the servants.

The location of the house couldn't have been better for Horace. It was only a mile and a half from the NACC compound, and on the few occasions when for whatever reason he did not drive himself, he enjoyed the short ride in a pedicab or taxi. It was, however, a handicap for our children. Most NACC personnel lived either in a small housing area in the city, or in the much larger housing area on Yang Ming Shan, the hillside to the north. Our house was one of the few that was not within either housing area, and was not on NACC's normal bus route that ended at the NACC office compound. Our children could not visit their friends, or their friends them, without either walking or taking a pedicab to our house.

When we first learned of the Taipei assignment, both Horace and I thought it would be a wonderful opportunity for the children to learn Chinese. One of the first things I did on our arrival was to go to the local Chinese school to discuss enrolling our children. I had assumed that the school would make some accommodation for their not speaking Chinese and asked if our children could be enrolled in some kind of "special student" status, as were a few American children attending the school, at least until their Chinese improved. Unfortunately, that was not to be. The principal's rejection was almost as bad as the blatant racial discrimination we had experienced at the British school in Hong Kong. Here, it was a perverse kind of racial discrimination. But again, it was *because we were Chinese*—to the Chinese principal we were not *really* American—that our children could not be given the consideration that Americans received. She seemed to resent a Chinese claiming to be American. Our children would be expected to keep up with the regular Chinese students at every level. With Eric already at the third grade level we knew this would be an impossible situation, and given the principal's uncompromising attitude, we resigned ourselves to the children not attending Chinese school. Instead, we arranged for a tutor to come to the house to give them Chinese lessons. I wrote to my father thinking he would be pleased, and was so disappointed when he replied, "it's a waste of time." Of course he was right. The children hated the extra daily Chinese lessons after school, and they hated having to come home after school instead of joining their schoolmates at one home or another. At the end of our eight years in Taipei, though their Chinese accents and pronunciation were perfect, their reading and writing did not stay with them.

Despite the initially poor reception we had received on our arrival in Taipei, both Horace and I were soon well integrated into the Taiwan scene. In this assignment as Special Assistant to the Station Chief, Horace was part of "the front office," which included the Chief, the Deputy Chief, and the Chief of Admin. Horace got on well with all of them and was soon absorbed in his new responsibilities. While he was adjusting to his new assignment, it was my job to take care of the home front. The first order of business was to hire servants. The children were now of an age where a baby amah was no longer needed, but we did need a cook and a housemaid. I was delighted with the young girl the office service group sent me. Ah Lin was nicely dressed, and very well spoken. Most important, she spoke excellent Mandarin, the Chinese national dialect, and I found it surprising that her speech was that of an educated person rather than that of the working class. The children seemed to like her, and she them. I was ecstatic. What did it matter that they couldn't attend Chinese school? It would soon be their daily language at home. But on the third day that Ah Lin was with us I returned from a shopping trip to find the house in an uproar. Ah Lin was sitting astride one of the stone lions in front of the house with nothing on but her underpants and a thin thing that passed for a bra. The caretaker, who had been in the house when we arrived, and whom we had kept on until we could find a replacement, was trying desperately to cover her with a towel, but she kept batting him away and throwing the towel off. The children were delighted with the whole episode and were laughing and yelling, "Mom, she's crazy, she's got to be crazy!" I immediately called Security, and two local staffers came over within minutes on motorcycles. They were reluctant to handle her barely clad body, but finally, by tempting her with a ride on a motorcycle, were able to get her off the stone lion and onto one of the motorcycles behind one of the men. That was the last we saw of her.

During the nine years we were in Taipei we went through a series of servants, each one bringing a separate story. Our next was a couple, a man and wife from North China. Again, they spoke excellent Mandarin. Lao Shu did not cook western food, but was a terrific Chinese cook, especially with anything that involved the use of flour—North China was after all wheat country. He could make hand-made noodles; he could make all kinds of flatbreads, some with scallions, some with meat stuffings. Best of all, he could whip up hundreds of *chiao tzes* or *bao tzes* (meat-filled dumplings) in no time at all. For me, being from Peking, this was a pleasure I hadn't had in years. Unfortunately, it couldn't last. Within a month we found that he was smoking opium in his room. That, we couldn't allow, so that was the end of Lao Shu and his delicious meals.

Next came Lao Kwan who had been a cook in the Taiwanese army. His cooking was about what one could expect at an army mess hall. At the same time we hired Ah Ming, a young Taiwanese girl who was very likable, and an excellent worker. However, I soon noticed that things were disappearing. I would buy socks for the children, and soon six pairs of socks would dwindle to four. I would be unable to find a shirt of Eric's or a new toy I had bought for Bean. New boxes of Kleenex would be almost empty within a few days. Likewise my hand lotions and colognes. She had to go. Neither did we keep Lao Kwan as he was really not satisfactory as a cook.

After them came the Old Battle Axe. That is how the children referred to her. She was a good solid cook for Chinese food, but had an erratic disposition. When in good spirits we were one big happy family, but when displeased by one thing or another she was insolent, rude, and confrontational, and would totally ignore me while I was speaking. We put up with her for a full year, but inevitably there was a blowup. On Christmas morning, she deemed our gift to her inadequate and hurled it at my feet, yelling, "You can take back your crummy gift! I don't want it," and stormed off to the kitchen. That was more than I could take. I told her to be out of the house by the next morning. I gave her an extra month's salary. She was stunned, but I think knew she had overstepped. Our Christmas was somewhat dampened by her outburst, but none of us was sorry to see her go.

After the Old Battle Axe we were fortunate to find a cook, Ah Ting, whom the whole family was happy with and who stayed with us for the rest of our tour in Taipei. Ah Ting, was modest and bashful. I had a hard time getting her to look at me instead of at her feet. She was not very bright, but she was eager to please. She was always trying to do better, the complete opposite of the Old Battle Axe in every way. When she came to us she already had a good repertoire of Chinese dishes, but during the years she worked for us she became even better. I had had numerous cooking lessons with a variety of teachers, one of them being Pei Mei, totally unknown at the time, but later to publish a two-volume set of Chinese cookbooks, acknowledged by our Chinese friends to be the best ever written. I passed all these recipes on to Ah Ting, and described the cooking process, and she, through many many trials and failures and much correction on my part, eventually got them right. But even after perfecting the dish, she would go off track again and I would have to remind her, "You've left out the five spice seasoning," or "you've let the oil get too hot," or some other thing she'd forgotten. In the end, she became an excellent Chinese cook, and the meals we served to our Chinese guests were consistently praised. When I told her one day that some friends in the Chinese Ministry of Foreign Affairs wanted to "borrow" her for a dinner party, a blush spread over her face and as usual, she looked at her feet, but I couldn't fail to see the broad smile she was trying to hide. This honor, plus later an even greater honor, cooking a meal for Chiang Ching Kuo, the son of the President, on his wedding anniversary, must have made her very proud, but within our household she remained as modest as always.

Along with Ah Ting, for a short while we had Ah Bi, a beautiful girl whom the whole family liked, but it always bothered me that she did not seem to know "her place." Her past employment had always been with Americans, who had apparently been unaware that in China servants simply did not *sit* in the presence of their

Ah Bi, center, with our friends Jake and Ann Brandt

employers. During the few months she worked for us I found it awkward when she would sit down on the couch beside me, but I never could bring myself to tell her that this was not appropriate. I cannot remember why she left us, but we parted amicably and we were sorry to lose her. She came back several times to visit and to see how the children were doing. On those occasions she was always attractively dressed—definitely no longer in the uniforms we provided—and looked like any other guest of ours might have looked. She seemed to find it perfectly natural to sit down and be served tea by Ah Ting who had been her former coworker. I know that Ah Ting found this awkward too. By standards of those days, which were very rigid, the more appropriate behavior for a maid visiting her past mistress would have been to stand until invited by the mistress to sit. After that, if she were served tea by the present maid, she would have risen and insisted on taking the tea from her. Following a few courtesy sips, she would then have excused herself from the mistress's presence and retired to the servants quarters to continue her visit with the other servants. Given these standards to which I was accustomed, Ah Bi's visits were disconcerting.

After Ah Bi left we found Ah Jen, who, like Ah Ting, stayed with us throughout the rest of our tour in Taipei. She too was a great success. Efficient, a good worker, and a pleasant disposition. Both were scrupulously honest and our household ran smoothly. Many evenings, when the day's chores were done, the two would join the family on the back porch to watch TV, Horace and I on the couch, the children and the two maids on the floor beside us. Often in the winter months Ah Ting would have sweet potatoes roasting in the ashes of the fireplace, and family and maids would enjoy them together. We were a happy family. Life was good.

A happy family

Chapter 12
Taipei, continued

The years we spent in Taipei, from 1961 to 1969, were good years. Horace seldom had to work late, and he did not spend long hours at the office on weekends. Saturday mornings, both summer and winter, the whole family went to the movies in the MAAG compound. Most of the time it was to see a Roy Rogers film. From there to the PX for shopping, and then on to the NACC club for a western lunch. At home our regular meals, except for breakfast, were usually Chinese. Sunday mornings we almost always went to the MAAG Officers Club for coffee and free doughnuts. In warm weather we spent many hours at the Grand Hotel by the tennis courts or the swimming pool. I ferried Eric to Little League, and all three children to tennis lessons and swimming lessons. I took up golf, playing regularly twice a week. When, after only a few weeks of lessons, I shot a forty-two on the nine-hole course, the pro convinced me I had great potential. Unfortunately, as with most of my efforts in other areas, that potential was never realized. I reached the stage where I was breaking one hundred fairly regularly, but never went beyond that. But regardless of the scores, I enjoyed golf tremendously in Taipei. With the luxury of caddies to carry our clubs, we played in rain or shine. The caddies held umbrellas over us as we walked down the fairways, emerging from under cover only for the brief moments it took to make our drives or our putts. Years later, on the very few occasions that I played in America, I found that without a caddy to carry my clubs, to locate my ball, to tell me the distance to the green, and to tell me which club to use, golf was not the game it had been in Taipei.

Professionally, this Taipei assignment was one that we had really been looking forward to. Horace, from his war years as Aide to various China Theatre Commanders, was already known to many Chinese government officials, including President Chiang Kai Shek himself and Madame Chiang. Also, many of the Chinese Embassy staff whom we had known when we were living in Washington were now in Taipei in senior government positions. We were excited at the prospect of getting back in touch. I had no expectations of meeting either the President or Madame Chiang, but shortly after our arrival I was pleasantly surprised to receive an invitation to a ladies' reception welcoming the wives of newly arrived American officers. As I passed through the receiving line I did not expect Madame Chiang to remember me, the young girl who had failed to stand when first introduced to her so many years ago at the Chinese Embassy in Washington, but I did wonder if she would recognize Horace's name. I need not have wondered. When I was introduced as "Mrs. Horace Eng," her first words were, "And how is Horace?" and added that she looked forward to seeing him again.

In the eight years we were in Taipei we never did see her or the President again. However, we did have frequent contact with the

Horace and Chiang Ching Kuo

President's eldest son Chiang Ching Kuo, and also occasionally saw the younger son Chiang Wei Kuo, whom we had known in Washington. Ching Kuo was at the time Deputy Defense Minister, but would later become President himself many years after we had departed Taipei. NACC already had an established relationship with Ching Kuo, but our personal association with him soon moved well beyond mere official contact to a more personal level. We were included often in family affairs such as their grandchild's birthday parties or their own birthdays. Three couples, friends from our Washington days, were close to Ching Kuo and his Russian wife Faina. Joseph Ku, who had been Press Secretary in Washington, was now Chief of Protocol. I Fu En, then a Colonel, had been Air Attaché, and was now a General. He and his wife Lillian were godparents to Ching Kuo's only daughter Amy. S.K. Hu had been Military Attaché in Washington and was now also a General and close to Ching Kuo. These old friends welcomed us into their close-knit circle, and the ten of us shared many evenings of good food, much laughter, and a great deal of drinking, much of it done while playing at the finger game. Not being a drinker, I did not play, but this was a fun game to watch as each challenger and opponent threw out a number of fingers, at the same time calling out the total. Fingers flew in rapid succession to a steady beat, and whenever one called the right total, the other had to drink. It was always *kan pei,* bottoms up, so it didn't take long for spirits to get high.

One of Ching Kuo's wedding anniversaries was celebrated at our house. Ching Kuo insisted that he wanted home cooking and not some fancy catered affair. Our cook Ah Ting was a bundle of nerves, but managed to produce an excellent meal. I Fu En had brought a long string of *bien p'ao* firecrackers to celebrate the event. After dinner, Ching Kuo insisted on tying the string of firecrackers himself onto the basketball hoop in our front yard using his own handkerchief as the tie. As he climbed up onto a rickety kitchen chair, the servants were in a panic lest he fall and they be held in some way responsible for an injury to the son of the president. However, the firecrackers went off in a prolonged ear-splitting burst with no damage done. The next time we saw Ching Kuo, I gave him back his handkerchief, freshly laundered. He insisted on giving me a dollar in return. I don't know what the custom was that required this.

Due to Ching Kuo's encouragement I started painting lessons once again. He had seen one of my paintings at our house, had admired my strokes as "bold." He insisted that I take lessons from his teacher KaoYi Hung, who was famous for both his painting and his calligraphy. He then made the arrangements personally for me to join one of KaoYi Hung's classes. Once I had started painting with KaoYi Hung, that became another tie with Ching Kuo. We were then included in gatherings he hosted for his painting buddies.

It was on one of these occasions when we were talking about painting techniques that Ching Kuo's wife Faina told me how discouraged Ching Kuo was that he could no longer stand while doing his painting. (This was important to painters, as only by standing could one get the freedom of arm movement that brought *pi li,* brush power, to one's painting strokes.) When I mentioned it casually to Horace, he was immediately alert to its importance. The state of health of the President's son, who would be in line for the succession, would be of key interest to U.S. intelligence. Ching Kuo was known to be a diabetic, but the fact that he was unable to stand for any length of time was an important indicator of how far his diabetes had progressed. The information was immediately cabled to Washington.

Though Horace and our Station Chief, Bill N., worked well together, I suspect that Bill must have been often frustrated that he did not have the contact with Ching Kuo that Horace and I had. At social occasions we were often in the awkward situation of receiving more attention from Ching Kuo and Faina than Bill and his wife Pat. After the initial exchange of greetings, we would always back away to clear the way for them, but since both Ching Kuo anad Faina were more comfortable in Chinese than in English, it was inevitable that they would gravitate toward us. At official dinners too, the customary Chinese seating protocol was that guests of honor sat across from the hosts rather than beside them. This always put Horace and me, the lowest ranking, beside Ching Kuo and Faina. Thus, it was with us that Ching Kuo and Faina conversed most often through dinner.

Despite being included in so many occasions hosted by Ching Kuo, I never felt our relationship was anything more than social. I never felt it was a real personal friendship. Friends though we were, none of us called Ching Kuo by his given name, instead always addressing him by his title, *Fu Bu Chang,* Deputy Defense Minister, and a few years later when he became Defense Minister, *Bu Chang.* His wife Faina, however, we did call by her given name. For me, there was always the unavoidable deferential factor. To the best of my knowledge, I Fu En and his wife Lillian, godparents to their daughter, were Ching Kuo and Faina's closest friends. Yet, during the last two years of our Taipei tour, Ching Kuo did not hesitate to have Fu En put under house arrest. Whatever Fu En's infraction, I do not know. I know only that very late one night Lillian came knocking at our door, and that she and Horace were in deep discussion for almost an hour. When she left, it was apparent that her visit had been made in secret. She had not driven her own car, and she wouldn't let Horace call a taxi or a pedicab. She walked in the dark to the main street. Horace explained nothing to me.

Unfortunately, Bill N. was never able to achieve the degree of rapport with Ching Kuo that his predecessor Ray C. had or that Horace had. In fact, there were frequent confrontations in which Horace was invariably the moderating influence. At one meeting Bill clashed so badly with Ching Kuo that Ching Kuo pounded on the table and refused to deal further with Bill. For me this was hearsay information, obtained from Horace but corroborated by others who had attended the meeting. Following this fiasco, Horace was the one who smoothed things over. He hosted what all involved called a "Bury the Hatchet Party" and relations were grudgingly restored. Bill N. eventually became Director of CIA's Operations Directorate, but a participant at that party claimed that he would never have risen to that post if Horace had not rescued the Station's relationship with Ching Kuo.

While Horace was coping with these and other problems at work, I was proceeding with my painting and other activities. Lessons with Kao Yi Hung turned out to be totally different from what I had experienced in the past. At my first class, four other women, all Chinese, each with a roll of paintings in her hands, gathered around him as he sat at his painting table. Each in turn produced her paintings. He went through them one by one, commenting on the good strokes and the bad. Then, while we looked on, he made several different paintings, all of the same subject, such as chrysanthemums, or bamboo, and handed each student one painting. We were to take them home and make copies. These we were to bring to our next class for his inspection. We did not paint at all in his presence. He did not see how we held our brushes, or how we applied the ink. We were expected to learn from watching him.

At our next lesson he reviewed my paintings first. He criticized a stroke here and another there, but I was generally relieved that he seemed to approve. However, I was chagrined when after going through the six copies I had produced, he asked, "where are the rest?" I had thought six was quite an achievement. I had not noted at the previous class that others had presented ten or more. I continued my painting lessons throughout our Taiwan tour, though I never got as much satisfaction from it as I should have. First of all, I never really liked Kao Yi Hung's work. He did paint in the free-flowing *yi pi* style that I liked, but there was a remarkable sameness to all his paintings. For me, copying was more work than pleasure. I was being taught to master a technique rather than to create something of my own. I do, however, have one product from these lessons that I prize greatly today. It is a painting done jointly with Chiang Ching Kuo one evening at our house after dinner. Ching Kuo had asked how I was coming along with my

**Joint painting
with Ching Kuo**

painting and wanted to see what I had done lately. I led him to the back porch and showed him some of my orchid paintings, my strongest suit, whereupon he suggested that we do a painting together. I was to go first with orchids. I was nervous, and with him watching managed to copy Kao Yi Hung's latest demonstration painting reasonably well, making only one really poor stroke. Ching Kuo then sat down and added bamboo, *his* strong suit, to my work. At my next class I showed the painting to Kao Yi Hung, who instantly recognized the bamboo as Ching Kuo's. He then added to the painting in his own hand the Chinese characters for, "Orchids painted by Chien Jung Huan (my Chinese name); Bamboo added by Chiang Ching Kuo; Calligraphy by Kao Yi Hung," and affixed all three of our Chinese seals.

Today, as I look at the many paintings on my daughter's walls as well as on my own, I see many attractive, and very decorative, but poorly executed paintings done during my lessons in Hong Kong. I see also the paintings done under the tutelage of Kao Yi Hung. They are still not my favorite paintings, but I can't help noting the progress I had made in mastering the technique. My children hang my works proudly on their walls where they are duly admired, but I deplore the fact that every painting is a copy, not a single one original.

While I did enjoy some minor success with my painting, it was in a totally different area that I came into my own. It was midway in our eight years in Taipei that I underwent a complete metamorphosis. In the early years of my marriage I had been the insecure young bride trying to stay abreast of Horace's older and more sophisticated friends. Then, in our tours abroad my role had been that of a supportive wife, making sure our home ran smoothly and taking care of the children. Now, suddenly, I was catapulted onto center stage.

It all began late one evening after dinner at a friend's house. Someone had started us off singing old favorites. Even though I had been brought up in China, I knew them all. I had been raised hearing my American mother singing those songs. A Station party was scheduled a few weeks later for St. Patrick's Day. At all our parties one group or another always arranged a performance of some kind. This time, someone said, "Get Marguerite to get up there. She has a nice voice." That was the beginning. At the party I did get up and sing a few Irish songs. After that, it was a given that I would be part of every party performance. Also, many evenings at the Grand Hotel I would be urged to get up and sing. And at the Officers Club too. The band leader's wife Lorna was the band's vocalist, but if Andy, the leader, spotted me, he would often call on me to get up and sing. And when he and the other musicians gave me an emphatic thumbs up as I left the stage I knew I had delivered well.

Somewhere along the line I was also included in the monthly jazz sessions organized by a MAAG Colonel in his home. These were made up of musicians from Taipei's three American service clubs: the Officers Club, the NCO Club, and the Thirteenth Air Force Club. They were informal affairs. Sometimes only five or six showed up; other times there would be twelve or more. Different musicians would take their turn at soloing. When I was given a nod, it was my queue to pick up the vocal. All this was a new world to me, and I loved being part of it. The real breakthrough, however, came when I learned to play the guitar.

On one of our visits to Hong Kong, Horace's sister Ida had given son Eric a guitar. I arranged for lessons for him, but the day before classes were to begin Eric burned his hand badly and could not make the lessons. A Chinese neighbor's son, a few years older than Eric, had brought him some phosphorus in a tube of water. Knowing that the element glowed in the dark, Eric and a friend took it into our dark, windowless storeroom and were painting on the trunks and the walls when the phosphorus ignited in Eric's hand. The two boys were able to put out the fire, but it was a frightening experience that left Eric with keloid scars on his palm that he still has today. Since I had already paid for Eric's guitar lessons, I joined the class in his stead. Five children, ages eight to ten, and I, learned to play three chords. For me, those three chords opened a new vista. I found that an incredible number of songs could be played with only three chords. As the years went by I added more, but never progressed beyond simple chording. It didn't seem to matter. Now I could accompany myself. I could do my own timing, set my own pace. I could phrase as the lyrics moved me. And what to do with my hands was no longer a concern. Now I had my guitar to hold, my security blanket. Yet, on stage, when I climbed up on that stool behind the mike, with the first notes, my fingers would tremble so badly I could hardly find the guitar strings. But soon, with the spotlight zeroed in on me, and the blinding light fading the audience into darkness, I was in my own private zone. The room was hushed, and I was lost in the sound of my own voice filling the silent void. It was the applause that followed that brought me back to the world around me.

Me, performing

All this was heady stuff, and I basked in all the compliments. A perfect stranger came up to me after one performance and said, "That was the best rendition of *Freight Train* I have *ever* heard." Someone else told me that the person devouring a steak at the table adjacent to his had totally stopped chewing and hadn't taken another bite until I had finished my performance. On another occasion a woman was heard to say, "It's a crying shame that someone like that doesn't have a chance to go to America." Comments like "You can hear a pin drop when Marguerite is singing" were commonplace.

In those years in Taipei I developed quite a fan base. As the request of Taiwan's Information Bureau I did the English language narration of a documentary on Taiwan. I was also asked to record a Chinese popular song which I did in Chinese. But more gratifying than the fans I acquired in Taipei was a letter I received from Mildred Jeremiah, a MAAG wife whom I had known only slightly when she and her husband had been stationed in Taipei. She wrote that she had lined up three people to listen to me. She asked me to make a tape and to send it to her as quickly as possible together with a photo of me with my guitar sitting on a stool in a Chinese *ch'i p'ao*. The head

Studio portrait

of the Armed Forces Radio Station, whose name I can't remember, was one of my fans and had already asked me if he could record me, so it was a perfect time to make the tape. The resulting product was amateurish and I didn't think it would lead to anything, but I mailed it together with a studio photograph. Several months later—in June 1968—I heard from her again, saying that those who had listened to my recording had been enthusiastic, and that she had had six copies made from my original. They were already in circulation to contacts in the entertainment world, among them Ed Sullivan. I was incredulous that anyone would think I was good enough to interest someone at that level. However, I thought it quite ridiculous that any of her contacts, least of all Ed Sullivan, would even think of taking on a singer whom they had neither seen nor heard personally. When we left Taiwan a few months later I had not heard from her again, but I was not surprised or even disappointed. I had had no real expectations.

Later, a much improved recording was made by José Villanueva, the Dominican Ambassador. He was perhaps my biggest fan of all. Drew McConnaughy, the daughter of then U.S. Ambassador Walter McConnaughy happened to be visiting from America. She played the twelve-string guitar and had brought it with her. Together, doing only a single practice run, with both of us on guitar, and Drew singing harmony to my melody, we sat down and taped a few songs in the Villanueva's sound proof music room. I was familiar with two of the songs Drew had suggested but did not know the words. I remember her hastily scribbling them out and propping them up on the bookcase beside the mike. The recording was not bad, but in many places the guitars drowned out the vocals. José was not satisfied and later requested I make another tape with just me accompanying myself. I still have that tape today, the only reminder I have of once having had a voice at all.

Today, as I look back on what I think of as my glory years, I often find it hard to believe that I ever could have been that good. I did not have a strong voice, and I had no range to speak of. I knew my voice was sweet and true, but I often wondered what else it had to make it so appealing to so many. I must have had something. I don't know what it was, but for those few years I was on the most glorious high, feeling for the first time in my life that others found me good, really good, at something. But more important to me than all the public acclaim I received was something else. In the years of our marriage Horace was accustomed to hearing me singing around the house, in the garden, and at length while soaking in the bathtub, but I don't believe he had ever thought a thing of it. Now he was so proud. And I was proud that he was proud. Friends said that when I was performing they loved watching *him*, that his face simply beamed with devotion and pride. During those last years in Taipei, Horace was not well. When he was tired and lay down to rest, "Sing to me," he would say, and it meant so much to me that that was what he wanted. Horace is now long gone, but so often when I think of him, it is those moments that keep coming back again and again, when he would say, "Sing to me," and I would sing to him the songs he loved as he slowly drifted off to sleep.

Chapter 13
Widowed

Horace died on January 24, 1969 at 7:30 AM, just a month before his fifty-sixth birthday.

I had known for some time that Horace would not live a normal life span. During the years we had lived in Hong Kong and Taipei, he had been hospitalized three times. Each time he had been diagnosed with extreme hypertension. The first time was in Hong Kong, in 1960. It started with a simple nosebleed, but the bleeding would not stop. I took him to the hospital. There, they brought the bleeding to a halt, but wanted to keep him for observation. Other than an elevated blood pressure, they found no other problems. Horace claimed he felt fine. The hospital was very relaxed about visitors. Not only was I permitted to spend the nights with him, but we were allowed to have food brought in—no doubt loaded with salt—from a nearby Chinese restaurant. Two of Horace's sisters joined us for delicious meals, and the whole episode seemed no more than a pleasant interlude from Horace's usual work week. There didn't seem to be any cause for alarm.

The second time he was hospitalized was in Taipei. Again, they found his blood pressure was elevated, but after the readjustment of his medications he was released. It was the third time that was so frightening. It was 1964 and we were still in Taipei. Horace had had a slight cold and cough, but this time, when he coughed, the hand covering his mouth was colored with blood. It was dripping through his fingers. As he held a blood-soaked cloth to his mouth and a bowl to catch the flow, I managed to get him to the hospital. There, they were able to stop the bleeding, but his blood pressure readings were alarmingly high. Our two NACC doctors, both surgeons, decided he would be better served at the military hospital in Okinawa where he could be examined by a qualified internist. He was packed off to Okinawa on the next flight out.

There, within hours of his admission to the hospital he was visited by the Base Commandant, a General who had known Horace well during the war. When the hospital staff learned that Horace was a personal friend of the Commandant, he received royal treatment. During his stay, he was under constant observation. Even something as unrelated to him personally as bad news in the newspaper would send his blood pressure into the stratosphere. Yet, at other times it would be at acceptable norms. Fortunately, his system seemed to have tolerated these wild swings, and at that time there had been no damage to either his heart or his kidneys. After two weeks he was released with a revised medical regimen.

For the next five years Horace seemed to be functioning quite normally. He was monitored regularly by our own doctors, and I took his blood pressure twice daily at home. It wasn't until the last two years that his heart showed a slight enlargement and his kidneys were affected. He was also tiring more easily. On the morning of his death, he had already gotten up to wake the children, but had returned to bed for a last few minutes of rest. I was dressing when I saw him wince as if in pain. With some effort he said, "I think you'd better call an ambulance. I need to get to the hospital." I picked up the phone immediately, and while I was still waiting for someone to answer, Horace's face contorted and his whole body went taut. It couldn't have been more than three or four seconds, and then suddenly, his body slackened. I knew then that he was gone. I put the phone down— still unanswered—and felt for a pulse. There was none.

Still getting no answer from the hospital, I called our Chief of Station Dan A. He was at the house in minutes. Together with his driver and another man from Security, they lifted Horace into Dan's car. The driver said at the time, "For no other man than Mr. Eng would I carry the dead." When the children and I were dressed and fed, we too went to the hospital. There, I found Jack and Judy Chew waiting for us. Jack, Admiral Jack Chew, was the head of TDC (Taiwan Defense Command), and it meant a lot to me that he and Judy had made the effort to get to the hospital so early in the morning. They stayed with me until Dan reappeared to tell me that the children and I could go in to see Horace for a last time. With the children I entered the room where Horace's body, covered in a white sheet, lay on a gurney. Up until that moment, I had not shed a tear. I had been totally composed. I had thanked Dan for his help, had thanked the men who had carried Horace's body, and had thanked the Chews for their support, all completely dry-eyed. But when I walked into that room and saw Horace's lifeless body—he looked so very very dead—the tears poured out in a torrent. I have a vague recollection of saying to the children, "Say goodbye to Daddy. Give him a kiss." Today, they remember only that his face was cold.

In the days that followed plans had to be made for a funeral. The Protestant church within the MAAG compound would be too small and it would be a problem for Chinese guests to enter without the passes required. However, the church's minister would perform the service. It was decided that the service could be held in the much larger St. Christophers Catholic Church across the way. At the service, all the religious objects exclusive to the Catholic faith were removed. A table at the entrance held a large photograph of Horace and two books for guests to sign, one for Chinese signatures, the other for English. Eulogies were delivered in both Chinese and English, the Chinese eulogy by an old friend, General Wen Ha-hsiung, the English by David Dean, a State Department friend from our Hong Kong days. Rather surprisingly, I did not cry. Instead, during the eulogies, I tried to blank out my mind and to tune out all the words that would bring memories of Horace to the surface.

Later, when tears were no longer visible to public eyes, I read the words of these two old friends. Both spoke glowingly of his distinguished military record and the role he played in promoting Chinese/American relations. But it was David's words about Horace's personal attributes that brought back memories of the kind of man that Horace was. We had not been married long when I discovered how thoughtful and caring he could be. During my pregnancy, when I was having trouble sleeping, he didn't just roll over and bury himself in his pillow, but instead stayed awake to keep me company. When I complained of my mouth feeling dry, he would be up, unasked, to get me a glass of water. A friend once told me how envious she had been of my having a husband like Horace. On a chilly evening, she had seen him leave the room silently and return with a sweater, which he then draped over my shoulders.

Horace at age fifty-five

His thoughtfulness extended not just to me, but to others, particularly those who were less fortunate. He often took a pedicab to work rather than the more convenient taxi, just to give the pedicab driver a much-needed fare. He then paid the driver far beyond the normal fare because he recognized that need. When I would haggle with a street vendor over a few cents, a practice that was common and expected practice when shopping in Asian countries, he would admonish me, "Come on, Marguerite, the man has to make a living, and a few cents means nothing to you." I always felt somewhat chagrined at his reproof.

Horace loved people and was so naturally affable that people could not help liking him in return He had a warm personality that drew others into his orbit, and laughter came easily to him, even when directed at himself. He had always been popular with women, but was especially so on the dance floor. The hostesses in Shanghai's dance halls, from whom he had learned to dance while a student in Shanghai, had taught him well. He had a natural sense of rhythm and he was smooth on the dance floor.

Horace's sense of right and wrong was immutable. The favors requested by friends of an officer assigned to his country of origin are often difficult to refuse and often carry the risk of losing a friend. If asked by a Chinese friend to buy a refrigerator at the PX, Horace would not do it. A request like this was particularly hard to refuse as it was well known that others in similar positions were not only equipping the kitchens of friends and family with appliances from the PX, but also filling their larders with American food items from the commissary with complete impunity. On the other hand, if the requested items were small, Horace would agree to make the purchase, but would give them as gifts afterwards. This ensured that no future requests were made.

In David's eulogy, his words about Horace's "sartorial elegance" brought a smile to my face. I would not have chosen the word "elegance," but there was no question that Horace always looked impeccable in whatever he wore. He was a small man, only 5' 7", but he was well built and wore his clothes well. None of the men to whom I later passed on his many suits wore them with anything approaching Horace's panache. His hair was prematurely gray, which added to his distinction. The few extra years it added to his appearance did not concern him, and in fact he was delighted when he was occasionally taken for my father. He was not a vain man, but he *was* disturbed, however, over his thinning hair. Unfortunately, when we were in Hong Kong in the sixties, the overhead ceiling fans in the old colonial buildings could dismantle even the most artfully arranged coifs. How Horace hated those fans! In this one trace of vanity, he always carried a comb. Each time he emerged from under an offending fan, he was forced to whip it out to re-comb his thinning wind-blown hair.

A long-time friend once told me that she had asked Bean when he was a small child, "What do you want to be when you grow up?" Bean, then only three or four, without hesitation had answered, "I want to be a gentleman, like my Daddy." I had thought, even then, that that was a worthy goal, to be a gentleman, like his father. For Horace *was* a gentleman in every sense of the word. He was a man of honor, unfailingly kind, thoughtful, and courteous. He was also a *gentle* man; but he had a quick temper, and when Eric was a child I have known Horace to literally pick him up by the collar in fury. Yet, he could also be extraordinarily gentle. When Kathy, at five or six years old, in her frequent bouts of rebellion against me, would be lying on the floor beating her little fists and screaming at me, "I hate you. I hate you," Horace would lift her up gently, draw her to him, and say quietly in Cantonese, "Kathy, you mustn't talk that way to Mommy." His soft words would end her tirade, and she would become begrudgingly contrite. Other times, when she was misbehaving, he would simply look at her and without raising his voice a single iota, say, "Kathee-ee." The tone of his voice and the look of reproof in his face, were enough to set her straight.

Horace was very much a family man. He loved his children. Having been raised in China in the old fashioned Chinese way, he was not the kind of father who played catch with them in the yard, or taught them to hunt and fish, but he loved just being with them, and with me. Though he thrived on being with people and enjoyed the company of his many many friends, he was happiest when surrounded by his family. Taking the children to the movies, watching them swim and cavort at the swimming pool, or simply sitting on the couch at home with the children at his feet, these were the moments that gave him the greatest pleasure. The family was his world.

At the service for Horace, the church was packed with probably five hundred or more people, with many others forced to stand outside the church. President and Madame Chiang Kai Shek were not present, but all the rest of the royal family were there, Ching Kuo, his brother Wei Kuo, and their families. Also present were Supreme Court justices, a battery of Chinese Generals and lesser officers, many Chinese friends, and of course a large contingent of American military and Embassy officials. Chinese Archbishop Paul Yu-pin was also present. But more important to me than all of these people of importance were the numbers of local NACC employees who took time off from work to attend: the waiters at the club, the car-washers, the security guards, our own servants, and also the servants who worked for many of our American friends. All these were people who had come to know and respect Horace during the years we had been in Taiwan. Unfortunately, none of Horace's family were present. Horace's two older sisters Ida and Margaret were expected, but were unfortunately unable to obtain their visas into Taiwan in time, and didn't arrive until the day after the service. They brought with them a beautiful bronze urn to hold Horace's ashes. At their insistence we went together to the crematorium to view Horace's body. Again, he was on a gurney, but this time he lay fully dressed and shod. His feet stuck up vertically and I recall how shiny his shoes were. I wished that my last image of Horace, the one that I carry with me to this day, had not been this one, of him lying there, very dead, with his shiny black shoes sticking up in the air.

Ida and Margaret stayed with me for only three days. It was after they left that Horace's ashes were delivered to me in the bronze urn. I placed it on Horace's dresser in our bedroom. In the days that followed, I received many visitors, among them Archbishop Paul Yu-pin. Looking back, I often wondered if he had come as a personal friend—we had known him socially—or, the service for Horace having been in the Catholic church, if he thought we were part of his Catholic flock. Rather unexpected were the visits from several Chinese Generals who had been Horace's working counterparts. Each came, however, not to offer condolences to me, but to pay respects to Horace's ashes. When I led them to the bedroom and showed them the urn, each stood at attention facing the urn and bowed three times in respect. I was unaware of this Chinese custom. In retrospect, I believe I should have moved the urn to a place of prominence in the living room. Somehow it seemed so incongruous having these men perform a formal rite in the intimate setting of our bedroom.

Another unexpected development relating to Horace's ashes was that our cook Ah Ting felt she could not live in a house that contained the ashes of the dead. She came to me one morning, with head bowed, visibly contrite. "Tai Tai, I am so sorry I have to leave you," she said. "I am so afraid of the Master's ghost." I had to reassure her. "Ah Ting, tell me, did you believe that Master was a good man?" "Oh, yes, yes," she replied. "He was the best master I have ever had." "Then, if he was a good man when he was alive, do you really think his ghost could become a bad ghost?" "No, I suppose not," she said, but she still seemed unsure. I went on. "Well then, you must believe that the Master's ghost is a good spirit that will watch over this household and keep us all safe from harm." Ah Ting still seemed skeptical, but she spoke no more of leaving. She stayed with us until we left Taipei that summer.

In the weeks that followed letters of condolence started pouring in. Somehow the news of Horace's death had been broadcast. I don't recall writing an obituary myself, but possibly someone else must have put one together and posted it in the Washington papers. Many of the letters came from friends and people I knew, but many came from people I had never even heard of, people who had known Horace during the war years. Some were brief; others recounted stories of shared experiences or told of fine qualities in Horace that they remembered. Each letter I read brought forth a river of tears. Every word I read was a reminder of the wonderful person I had lost. I was mired in my own sorrow; I was drowning in my own tears. I thought only of my own loss. I was a wife who had lost a husband. I had forgotten that I was a mother too, a mother of three young children who had lost a father. How had they been coping? I did not even know.

Eventually, however, I got hold of myself. This is not to say that tears were not renewed afresh with each letter of condolence that arrived, but at least the outward semblance of the person I had once been reemerged. I personally answered each and every one of the letters received, over two hundred letters written in long-hand. I took stock of our family situation. U.S. government regulations stipulated that on the death of an officer while stationed overseas, the surviving family members could remain in place for six weeks, after which they were required to return to the United States. That meant we would have to leave by mid-March. I requested permission to remain in Taipei through the school year. But well before we knew that permission would be granted, MAAG chief, General Cicollela, had said to me, "Marguerite, if your office doesn't grant your request, let me know, and *I* will give you a job that will allow you to stay until the children are out of school." It was gestures like these that made my heart brim over.

Now I had to think about the future. Horace's paychecks stopped immediately and were now replaced by a survivor's annuity for me. My monthly income was now only a quarter of what we had received in the past. I would, however, receive an allowance for each child. While we were in Taipei, our housing was covered by the government, but on return to America that would be an added expense. There was no question I would have to find a job. But what? I had a college degree, had worked as a private and social secretary; I could type. That did not seem like an impressive resumé. Friends offered suggestions. One suggested teaching English as a foreign language. That held no appeal for me. Another suggested interior design. That would have required taking courses and would not have brought in an immediate income. Yet another said that I should not overlook temping, that temporary jobs often provided inside pictures of job possibilities within a company. The best advice, however, came from a colleague of Horace's. "The CIA will definitely give you a job," he said. "There are all kinds of jobs within the Agency, and once you are in, you can find a niche that suits you." His advice was sound.

It was also the easiest path, and it was a bird in hand. That is where I would start.

The next few months went by quickly. Before I knew it the children's school year had come to an end and we were preparing for departure. At the airport, Dan A. had reserved the VIP room. I believe he had made the reservation on the off chance that Chiang Ching Kuo and Faina might be among those coming to see me off. However, in this he was disappointed. Faina and her daughter-in-law Nancy had come to the house a few days earlier to say their farewells, as had several of Horace's official military contacts and their wives. They did not come to the airport. However, more than a hundred well-wishers jammed the room and others spilled out into the public areas. A friend of Kathy's leaving on the same flight, questioned, "What's going on with all that crowd in there?" Kathy, unaware that this was at all unusual, said to her, "Oh they're just here to see my mother off."

It was truly a grand sendoff, one that I would remember for a long time. It was not until we boarded the plane that I had time to reflect on the years we had spent in Taipei. We had had eight good years there, had forged friendships that would last a lifetime. And even though I had lost Horace, I had had more support than any widow could have hoped for. I was sorry to be leaving for I was leaving behind a major chapter of my life. But my feelings were mixed. On the one hand, I was eager to get on with my life; on the other, apprehensive about what the future held. From now on I would be on my own, with three children, ages twelve, fourteen, and sixteen, to bring up. I thought about my mother and how she had raised me and my brothers and sisters alone. And she had done it under far worse circumstances than those I was facing. I reminded myself of one of the most important things she had taught me, that "life, whatever it brings our way, is what *we* make it." I told myself, "Whatever lies ahead, it's going to be up to *me* to make a life for myself and for my children." My mother had done it, and so would I.

Chapter 14
Resettlement in America

We left Taipei the first week in June 1969. On arriving in America I received an unbelievably heartwarming reception. Nancy and Charlie Hall, who had been our best friends while in Taipei, met us at the airport and were to have driven us to General Wedemeyer's home where we would be staying temporarily. But instead, they took us to their home, where a whole contingent of old friends gathered for a welcome home party. I was so overcome at this outpouring of friendship that with each hug the tears that had been fairly well under control for the last few months came pouring out again. After an hour or more of renewing old ties, the Halls then drove us out to Friends Advice, the Wedemeyers' home in Poolesville, Maryland. I don't know how the Wedemeyers had learned of Horace's death. I don't remember informing them myself. However, a letter from General Wedemeyer had been among the early letters of condolence that I received. In his letter he had invited me and the children to stay at their home until we were established with a place of our own. It was a generous and welcome invitation, and we accepted it gratefully.

Friends Advice was a beautiful estate and was an officially designated historic site. A large stone house built in the early nineteenth century as a plantation house sat at its center. It had originally been owned by Mrs.Wedemeyer's father, General Embick, but whatever the amount of land that had surrounded it at that time, General Wedemeyer had added to it, and it was now surrounded by seven hundred and fifty acres of prime property. I had been to Friends

Advice only once before, in 1945, when General Wedemeyer had *thought* he was introducing me to Horace, his wartime aide, for the first time, and I had forgotten how impressive the estate was.

Mrs. Wedemeyer showed us through the house and told us her plans for our stay. The two boys, Eric and Bean, would sleep in bedrooms on the third floor of the main house, and Kathy and I would stay in what had once been the carriage house. Now, part of it had been converted to a garage, but on one end was a tiny seating area and kitchen, and above, a spacious studio apartment. Mrs. Wedemeyer said that she would like us to have dinner with them every night, but hoped we didn't mind fending for ourselves during the day. I was delighted with the arrangement as I had been concerned that too much togetherness would be hard on both the Wedemeyers and ourselves. As it was, I fixed breakfast for the children and myself each morning, and then we were off house-hunting.

Finding a house was our first priority. We had been referred to a real estate agent, and each morning for that first week the realtor drove us to house after house. I'm afraid we were difficult clients, as not having lived in the U.S. for fifteen years, we had only the vaguest idea what we were looking for, and had not even decided on a suitable price range. After a week of looking, and finding nothing that suited us, I started looking in the paper's real estate section at new housing developments. Some looked appealing, but without a realtor to drive us around, we would have to get to them ourselves. The Wedemeyers, who now insisted that we call them Uncle Al and Aunt Dade, lent us a car and we embarked on our house-hunting mission on our own. I tackled the driving with some trepidation. For the past fifteen years I had not driven at speeds over thirty-five miles an hour, and I was not looking forward to driving on high-speed roads. It was the most stressful experience I had been subjected to in years. I desperately hugged the right lane as other cars hurtled past me. Added to my frayed nerves was the pressure from my children. "Mom, you're driving too slowly. Mom, speed it up. Mom, you're holding up the traffic." I was doing the best I could, but I was scared to death. Navigating the beltway, which had not even existed when we first went overseas in 1954, was an indescribable nightmare. Several times I took wrong exits, had to re-enter and start again. At the end of each harrowing day, I returned to Friends Advice exhausted, my knees weak from tension and nervousness.

After a few days I became accustomed to driving at higher speeds and actually found my way without too much trouble to the various new housing developments that looked interesting. However, here I had to cope with the vying opinions of three teenagers. What one liked, the other two objected to. One liked the large family room; another preferred the bigger bedrooms. And so it went. But I was gradually getting a feel for prices, locations, and the varying house styles. By the end of our second week I had found a split-level house in Vienna, Virginia, that pleased us all and we agreed on a settlement date.

While all this house-hunting was going on, we were enjoying our stay with the Wedemeyers. There was a swimming pool on the property, and each day when we came home, hot and tired—the car was not air conditioned—we would go down to the swimming pool with Uncle Al. There was a well stocked man-made lake on the property, and sometimes the children would go fishing with him. For the two boys, however, it was not all fun and games. Uncle Al set them to painting the fence that separated Friends Advice from the neighboring property, a small price to pay for the generous welcome we were receiving. He also asked for the boys' help at other times. Through the years, the General's portrait had been painted by several distinguished artists. One sat above the mantel in the living room. Two others remained in the basement. I remember particularly the day one of the artists called to say he was in the area and would like to drop by for a visit. Panic followed, as Uncle Al quickly went down to the basement to find the portrait painted by the visiting artist. The boys were useful in hauling it up the basement stairs and hanging it up in place of the one then on display. I often wondered how Uncle Al would have managed if the boys had not been there to help.

Dinners with Uncle Al and Aunt Dade in the evening were pleasant affairs. The meals, prepared by Alberta, the cook, were plain but good, almost always ending with ice cream. The children and I all remember having either squash or zucchini daily, served up in varying styles and always loaded with butter. I was delighted that the children actually put into practice the table manners I had drilled into them through the years. They remembered their pleases and thank-yous, sat up straight in their chairs, and kept their elbows off the table. I could tell that the Wedemeyers approved.

I do believe it gave Uncle Al and Aunt Dade pleasure having us stay with them. They were always eager to hear of our days' experiences, wanting to know all about the houses we had looked at and the one we finally decided upon. Where was it located? Was it in a good neighborhood? What was the school like? They seemed genuinely concerned about our welfare, particularly with regard to our financial situation. Uncle Al was always careful not to be intrusive, but I was more than happy to have someone with whom to share my problems and spoke to him quite freely about our financial status. I know that he was much relieved to know that, unlike many widows, I was quite capable of handling our family's finances. Though he was a bit dismayed to learn that my monthly survivor's annuity was only a quarter of Horace's past salary, he was glad to hear that during the sixteen years we had been overseas, with our housing provided, we had a substantial amount in savings.

Throughout our marriage, other than earning an income to support the family, Horace had never taken any interest in our finances. That had been my department. Early on I had started investing in the stock market, and most of our assets were held by Merrill Lynch. Unfortunately, after Horace's death, even though the account had been held in our joint names "with right of survivorship," I had been unable to get access to the account. The CIA had referred me to a Washington lawyer, who was to have handled the matter, but other than informing me by mail that the account could not be released to me without a Federal Transfer Certificate, I had had no further word from him. I contacted him immediately on our return to Washington and was told that he had written to Merryll Lynch's lawyers for clarification on the specific requirements, but was awaiting their reply. When Uncle Al learned that the lawyer had done no more than write a single letter in the month since I had first retained him, he said to me, "If I had a lawyer who in a month's time had done no more than that, I would discontinue his services." I took his advice, and did just that. Instead, Uncle Al put his very competent secretary to work. Elaine Hill had been his secretary for many years and now lived in a small apartment on the Wedemeyers' estate. It took her only a few days to get the information that the high-paid lawyer had failed to obtain in a month. She found that the Transfer Certificate was issued by the IRS and could not be issued until Estate and Death taxes had been paid. Within days, Uncle Al, through Elaine, had set up an appointment for me with the IRS's Director of International Operations. The Director himself greeted me on my arrival at the IRS office—as a courtesy to General Wedemeyer's four stars, I'm sure—and assigned an officer to take care of me. The officer guided me line by line through the estate tax forms, I filed the tax form and submitted the appropriate estate tax, and the Federal Transfer Certificate was issued. Merrill Lynch released the account to my sole name. All this was accomplished during the short time we spent with the Wedemeyers. Once again, I felt so fortunate in knowing the right people, people who were in a position to help.

By the first week in July 1969, exactly a month after we had returned to the U.S., the children and I had moved into our new home in Vienna. We had enjoyed our stay with the Wedemeyers, and through the years that followed we returned to visit them regularly, visits that continued even after they had moved from Friends Advice to a retirement community in Alexandria, Virginia. Being in a home of our own was a heady experience for us all. I, of course, had known the joy of home ownership when Horace and I were first married, but for the children this was new and exciting. Having been brought up abroad with servants, they had never wielded a hammer, banged a nail, or used a shovel, but together we worked hard on our suburban home. Once again, we were lucky. The Dahls, our immediate neighbors, were childless, and practically adopted my children. Norman Dahl was as handy a man as I have ever known, and Eric was as apt a pupil as Norman could have found anywhere. The two of them partitioned the basement, Norman instructing Eric on how to install two-by-fours and plaster board, and on plastering techniques. Eric and Bean together put up additional shelving in the closets. Norman's wife Ruth was an avid

Our house in Vienna, 9903 Madrigal Way

gardener, and her enthusiasm rubbed off on me. The children and I shopped for shrubs and flowers and added to the minimal landscaping provided by the builder. Our back yard was deep, and we created an island of azaleas and hosta under the trees that stood midway between the house and our rear lot line. We started a vegetable garden too. In our 8 x 10 foot plot we planted four tomato plants, two peppers, and two zucchinis. We had enough tomatoes for spaghetti sauce that fed our family of four for the full year. Our pride in our home and garden was immense.

For me, however, the pride and joy in our new home was accompanied by an acute awareness of what was missing: a husband, a father. I had thought that time would ease the pain of losing Horace. During those last few months in Taiwan I thought I was becoming accustomed to being without him, but now, each time I sat back to admire some small part of our new home, I thought of Horace and how he was not here to see it. He was not here to see how the many beautiful things we had purchased abroad looked in place. He was not here to see the first blooms on our newly planted rosebushes; he was not here to share our pride in the boys' carpentry. He was not here to admire the drapes and curtains I had made. All I could think of was that he was not here to enjoy all the things we had planned to enjoy one day together. When the children were out and I was alone, the tears would well up often and unexpectedly. The loss of Horace was still very much a part of me.

Rather strangely, I thought, the loss of their father was not as traumatic for the children as I had expected. Nor did the absence of a father in the following years seem to have an adverse affect on their lives. Horace had always been a loving father, and even a doting one, but our lifestyle while overseas had not given him a major role in their lives. Now, they adjusted well to having only a single parent. In September Eric and Kathy started at nearby James Madison High School. Bean attended Thoreau Junior High for a year before joining Eric and Kathy at James Madison. It was not easy for them to break into new schools where friendships had already been made, but being in a brand new housing development, they were able to find friends among the other newcomers to the area. I had had some concerns about the possibility of their facing some racial discrimination, but on that score, I need not have worried. Though they were among the very few Asian faces at the school, none of them encountered a single experience where their being Chinese was an issue.

What *was* troubling, however, was that for the first time, they became aware of the deep racial divide existing in America between blacks and whites. Up until this time their schooling had been for the most part in the American school in Taipei. Its student body was largely made up of the children of American military families, blacks and whites well integrated. Now, both boys told me of their discomfort when walking past a gathering of black boys in the school hallways. Rather than be confronted with hostile looks and snide comments as they passed, they would take another hallway. Kathy echoed their feelings and said she would back out of the girls' bathroom if she found a group of black girls inside. "But why?" I asked. "What do they do that's so bad?" "It's not what they do. It's their belligerent attitude and the way they look at you. As if they're thinking, "Who the hell do you think you are!" I found it so sad, that my children, who had had both black and white friends in Taipei, with no thought of their racial differences, now had it thrust upon them, that in America, there *was* a difference.

Apart from adjusting to the new school environment, the children were also adjusting to the do-it-yourself culture of America. Having never lived without servants to do the menial chores, they were not accustomed to manual labor. Now, on weekends I put them all to work, ruling the household with an iron hand. Saturday mornings was cleaning day. Each of the children was responsible for one floor of our split-level house. These we rotated, as some floors were more work than others. Sundays we worked together in the garden. To this day they remember how I *forced* them to dig up buckets of crab grass instead of allowing them to use weed killer.

Among their unwelcome memories of those early days is my serving them Spam for dinner. I was then afflicted with what my husband of later years called "widow's syndrome." I had always been a frugal person, but now, with a reduced income and the heavy expense of setting up a new home, I had become even more cautious about spending any of our savings. Apart from serving Spam, which the children hated (they insist I served it almost daily, whereas actually it was only on a few rare occasions), I took to buying the more expensive items of clothing in thrift shops. Spam, and having to wear someone else's castoff winter clothing, was an unbearable indignity for the children, and I soon got over those excessive efforts at thrift. However, I still put a limit on how much the children could spend for clothing. Living for so many years in the Far East with access to PXs and inexpensive locally-made clothing, I was unprepared for U.S. prices. Kathy was unable to find anything within the price ranges I set. When, after hours of shopping, she reported that jeans at under

$5.00 or blouses at under $6.00 simply did not exist in America, I was forced to raise my pricing limits

In Taipei I had tried to teach Kathy to sew, and she had fought me every step of the way. Time and time again, when I had insisted she redo something that she had done badly, she would sulk and never finish the project. But now, suddenly, in desperation, she resorted to the sewing she had resisted so stubbornly in the past. Soon she was frequenting fabric stores and plowing through pattern books. She would buy dress patterns and three pieces of fabric at a time, cutting them out in one evening, and two weeks later, proudly sporting three items of new clothing. For her high school graduation I gave her a top-of-the-line Elna sewing machine—though I was tightfisted on many things, I knew better than to stint on the important things where quality counted. The Elna Lotus was a small compact machine, one of the best models Elna ever produced. It is over forty years since I bought it for Kathy, and it is still serving her well today.

My thrift with the children extended to their allowances too; I wanted them to earn some of their own spending money. The man whom I would later marry, declared jokingly that I thought I was building character by expecting them to work. Eric did not have to look far for a job. The CIA regularly allowed children over the age of sixteen, whose parent were Agency employees, to work at Headquarters during the summer months. As soon as we were settled in our house in Vienna, I enrolled Eric, and it was then that he learned for the first time, much to his surprise, that his father had worked for the Agency. He learned too of other CIA employees. In the evenings he would report to me with some excitement, "Guess what, Mom. I ran into Mr. X (or Mrs. Y) in the hallway. I didn't know they worked for the CIA." I thought at the time how ill-advised it was that teenage children were now privy to the identities of Agency employees.

Most of the children were given mundane clerical jobs, but when a contact of mine in the Science and Technology Division learned that Eric had taken drafting at school, Eric was assigned to a drafting job instead. When his exceptional skill was noted, he was given a permanent slot as a part-time employee at the GS-4 level. He was paid accordingly for whatever hours he was available, whether evenings, weekends, or during his vacations. Eric worked there during his free time for four years, covering his own spending money during that period. I no longer gave him an allowance.

Kathy, only fifteen when we returned to America, did the usual baby-sitting—the going price was fifty cents an hour at the time—regardless of the number of children involved. But she was soon looking for better paid work and took on a variety of jobs. At Woodie's Department Store she worked as a salesgirl at the hosiery counter; she did some telemarketing, selling local magazines and newspapers; and she also worked as a waitress both after school, and on weekends. At one of her waitressing jobs, Kathy learned of another source of income. A male diner, who had unsuccessfully been trying to stop her each time she passed by his table, finally thrust his card upon her. On it he had written the words, "I'll give you $100 to spend the night with me." Kathy showed the card to the restaurant manager, whereupon he, with the card in hand, marched up to the man and said one word, "Out!" To the man's claim that he had not yet had his lunch, the manager, with thumb directed firmly toward the door, repeated, "Out!" He was gone. As Kathy repeated this story to me, she observed, "Just think, Mom, I could have made a lot of money." She was sixteen, and a very young unworldly sixteen, at the time.

For a brief period, Kathy also sold Colliers encyclopedias door to door. She and other young sales recruits were dropped off by their manager at a housing development or apartment building—always in the evenings when presumably the family wage earner would be home—and were turned loose to make their sales pitches. Kathy did remarkably well at making the sales, but since the contract stipulated that customers could cancel within a seventy-two hour period, more often than not the orders were cancelled and her commission lost. When Eric calculated her earnings from this venture, he found that including the time spent on training sessions, she had made twenty-nine cents an hour. However, that particular effort was not a total loss. In later years, when Kathy was interviewing for permanent jobs, she found that prospective employers were more impressed by her having tackled door-to-door sales than by any of the other jobs she had held.

Bean too, only thirteen when we settled in Vienna, mowed lawns in the immediate neighborhood, and worked during the summer months at a nearby garden nursery. I am not sure how much character was built by my expecting the children to work, but early on they did learn the value of money, that it was not something to which they were entitled, that it had to be earned. At the time, our family of four was operating with only one car, and ferrying the children to and from their jobs was a major problem. With some major coordination we were managing, but Kathy was finding it increasingly hard to get work that fit into our driving schedule. As soon as she got her driving license, she spent her own money to buy a used Volkswagon "bug."

As for me, I was taking a hard look at our financial situation. My monthly annuity was not nearly enough to sustain our lifestyle, and from the time of Horace's death in January to the present day, we had been drawing heavily on savings. I knew I could not delay going to work much longer. I did put it off, however, until after Christmas. Christmas day, when families everywhere were gathered together, was both happy and sad for our family. It was our first Christmas in a home of our own. The tree was beautiful, the decorations glowed, and I made sure that Santa was more generous than usual to the children, but for me nothing could disguise the fact that we were absent a father. I made it through the day, however, and beyond. But in the quiet of my room, as at so many other times, the tears flowed once again.

Chapter 15
The CIA and Other Options

I began work at the CIA immediately after Christmas 1969. I had decided to work part time, Mondays, Wednesdays, and Fridays. Once I had made the decision to work there, things moved along quickly. I had heard that the application process and the required security clearances could take as long as two years, but somehow doors opened for me at every step. Application forms were obtained and brought to me in person by old friend Hal F., one of our Chiefs of Station while we were in Taipei. Pages and pages of questions had to be answered. All foreign contacts for the past umpteen years had to be accounted for, and names and addresses and reasons for contact included. Though I was unable to provide complete details, I assume my answers were adequate for it was not long before I was scheduled for a meeting with the Agency's Chief of Personnel. I doubt that meeting with someone at that level was the norm for most applicants, but for me it did not seem surprising since that position was now held by Bob W. with whom Horace and I had shared a duplex house in the Philippines in the mid fifties. It was now almost fifteen years later, and our only communication had been through yearly Christmas cards. Still, it did surprise me that our meeting was as formal as it was. Instead of it being like a reunion between longtime friends, it seemed more like a routine personnel interview. I remember clearly Bob's concluding words to me: "Marguerite, we will definitely give you a job, but we won't pay you more than you're worth."

I couldn't help wondering exactly what I *was* worth. I was a college graduate, with no work experience other than the years I spent at the Chinese Embassy as a social secretary. Somehow, I didn't think that would count for much at an intelligence agency. They had brought me in at a GS-9 level. I would be working in the Operations Directorate, within the Agency always referred to as the DDO. It was the glamor part of intelligence. It was the world of intrigue, secret agents, covert activities, and clandestine operations. My work designation was "Intelligence Assistant." I had no idea what that grade level indicated, but was told that I was lucky, that other widows had been taken on at only a GS-5 level. The assumption was that my Chinese language capability accounted for the difference.

Now, as I started the long walk from the far end of the CIA's parking lot to the main entrance, I wondered what my job would be like. Given my being an ethnic Chinese and my so-called language capability, it was natural that I would be assigned to work in China Operations. There, I would be in the Covert Action section. My first assignment was to evaluate some of the CIA's "black radio," i.e. propaganda broadcasts, that were being beamed into China. These were supposedly originating from dissident groups within the Chinese countryside and were intended to light a fire of discontent among the local populace who in turn would rise up in revolt against Communist rule.

My first day on the job was miserable. I was led to a small cubicle at the end of the hall where I sat in total isolation for the entire day with a tape recorder, a stack of tapes, and a typewriter. No one came to see how I was doing. No one told me to take time off for lunch, or even where the cafeteria was located. Totally ignored, I left for the day when I saw that others were leaving their offices. It was worse than the rejection that Horace and I had experienced on our arrival in Taipei. But then, Horace had shared that disappointment with me. Now I was so very alone, with no shoulder to cry on, no one to bolster me. With Horace, in our past assignments, I had had a position, a status. Now I had to face the fact that I was a nobody. But worse, as I played the first tape, there were words, phrases, that I did not even recognize. My formal Chinese education had been through grammar school only, plus one year in Chinese college. In social conversations, Chinese had always come to me quite naturally, but Chinese political terms were like a foreign language. The panic that swept over me was something I had never known before. I was totally out of my depth, and overwhelmed with the job that faced me. How was I going to support my children? I had become a nobody, and a nobody who was not able to do her job. When I left the office it was already dark. Walking back through the parking lot, I was drowned in despair. The tears rolled down my cheeks. They blurred my vision on the drive home. I could not stop them.

By the time I pulled into our driveway I had regained my composure somewhat. I made dinner for the children. They wanted to know what my first day at work had been like, had been excited that I would be working at the CIA. I told them that my day had been fine, but that even though I was an overt employee, it didn't mean I could talk about my work. I certainly could not tell them how worried I was about being able to do my job. That evening, in the privacy of my bedroom, I called an old friend for help. T. J. was another Chinese American and had been one of Horace's colleagues. He was able to explain the various Chinese phrases that had mystified me, and in the days that followed brought me up to speed on Chinese political terminology. By the end of the second week I had regained my confidence. I told myself firmly: "I *can* do this. If I work at it I *can*." But thankfully I did not have to. The program was being discontinued. My evaluations, all well received, had only been additional confirmation that these broadcasts were not achieving their purpose.

In the weeks and months that followed, none of the jobs I was given was as stressful as my first struggle with the Chinese tapes. I no longer felt that early panic of being unable to do the job. Suddenly it seemed that the whole of China Operations had discovered it had a new part-time body on board on whom they could thrust unwanted chores. Most of these consisted of reviewing the files of various

Chinese officials who had at one time been of interest, but had since been relegated to the back burner. The work was tedious and boring, and many an evening as I walked the one mile through the parking lot to my car, I cried all the way. I told myself, "There *has* to be more in life than this," but there seemed to be nothing brighter ahead.

Fortunately, there was an occasional reprieve from the monotonous paperwork. One of my assignments was to help with the resettlement of a recent Chinese defector. He had been part of a Chinese delegation to a Near Eastern country when he had decided he did not want to return to China. Now, he had already been debriefed and was being held in an Agency safe house in St Louis while waiting to be resettled. And though he had provided no significant intelligence, he had an inflated view of his own importance, probably because of the great lengths to which the Station had gone to get him out of the country. He had ridiculous expectations of being supported for the rest of his life and provided with a luxury apartment as well as a new luxury car (he did not know how to drive). It was my job to disabuse him of these expectations and to spell out the limits of our aid. I left him disgruntled but chastened. I was thankful that I would not have to be his handler as I anticipated he would be a problem. I have no idea what happened to him afterward.

Returning to Washington from St. Louis, I was once again confronted with files and more files. I was grateful that the Agency had given me a job, but this was not what I wanted to spend my days doing. I started scouring the classified ads in the newspaper. Nothing looked promising. Then I came upon an ad by a Bernard Haldane who was conducting a seminar on career counseling with the promise that he would identify strengths that would lead to a rewarding career. The two-day seminar was not cheap. My part-time job provided only a limited income, and I was concerned about the cost, but decided the money was less important than the possible benefits. The program turned out to be very interesting. There was extensive delving into one's past experiences, what things in one's life had given the most pleasure and satisfaction, followed by what work one had actually done. The object was to bring the two together, to seek a career that was both enjoyable and to which one could apply one's past work experience. In my case there was no question that my singing had given me the most pleasure, but there was little to say about what I had done. Other than having been a social secretary and while living abroad done a great deal of entertaining at lunches and dinners, I had little work experience. The Bernard Haldane program led to several job interviews. I went to each, full of anticipation, but all were with vacation resorts that were seeking new members or new buyers. I was to show a movie about the resort and then to host the free lunch or dinner that followed. It was basically a sales job under cover of a social event. These jobs were not what I was looking for, and I had to conclude that the money I had spent had been wasted.

"Well," I thought, "so much for that." I wondered what other possibilities were out there. I began to think of my singing and wondered if I could do anything with it at all. But I was already having doubts. In Taipei I had been floating on a cloud, but now I was in Washington, back down to earth in the real world. Maybe my success in Taipei had been nothing but a delusion fostered by supportive friends and my own ego. I wondered if I had really been any good at all. I needed someone to give me an unbiased opinion. A friend had once taken my daughter Kathy and me to one of the regular Sunday night hootenannies at The Cellar Door, a small music club in Georgetown. It had been so much fun watching the series of performers take their turns at the microphone. This was in the days before open mikes, and long before karaoke. Some performers had been incredibly good, others only marginal. I had thought at the time, "I can do better than that." Now, I wondered if The Cellar Door might be a good place to start. I called for an appointment, only to be told that the man in charge did not make appointments but would be there on a given day for auditions. With no other alternative, I showed up on the specified day. I was surprised at how many people were there—the room was packed—, all apparently there to audition. One man, sitting at the very back of the room with pen and paper in hand was obviously the club's responsible party. He stood up, introduced himself as Josh,

and said, "O.K. Let's get started. Two songs apiece. Who'll go first."
Wanting nothing more than to get out of there quickly, I raised my
hand. Someone brought out a stool and I seated myself behind the
mike. My heart was thumping so wildly I was sure others could hear
it. I started a folk song, lost my way, and had to begin again. Then
sang another. No one clapped. Josh beckoned me toward him. Before
he opened his mouth I jumped in. My words tumbled out, and all in
one breath I said, "I know I was awful. But I'm not here to audition.
I just wanted an objective opinion of whether I was good enough to
try to go professional. I guess I'm not." Josh sighed and shook his
head. "Boy, you're asking for a lot," he said. "*I* can't make a judgment
on that. You've got a nice voice and you came across pretty well.
Come to the hootenanny next Sunday. I'll give you a ten minute spot
and we'll see what kind of a reception you get." He gave me a piece
of paper with instructions and turned to call on the next performer.
I stayed to listen. He was good, but no one clapped for him either.
I guessed that applause was not the norm at auditions. I felt a little
better about my performance.

The following Sunday I was beset with misgivings. I had
never intended to audition. Should I go through with it? I wished I
had someone to support me, someone who believed I *was* good, who
would tell me I was wonderful, and to make me believe it. I had not
told anyone about my intentions. I had not even told my children.
I had been afraid people would think I had too good an opinion of
myself. I could imagine them saying, "Can you believe it? Marguerite
thought she was good enough to sing professionally." I watched the
clock as the hours of the Hootenanny came and went. I did not go. I
had lost my nerve.

But I had not completely given up. The tape that Jose
Villanueva had made at the Dominican embassy in Taipei was not
too bad. It was still very much an amateur recording, but it was much
better than the one made at the Armed Forces Radio Station that I
had sent to Mildred Jeremiah. I sent a copy to Columbia Records. I
had nothing to lose. I was not surprised when I received a form letter

expressing regret that they could not use "the enclosed material." It was signed Tom McNamee, Artist and Repertoire, Contemporary Recordings. What did surprise me was the handwritten letter that accompanied the form letter. He wrote, "I found your singing very pleasing, but these days one has to go at recording with more than just a voice—there has to be an entire, palpable identity: meaning either original material or an entirely new slant on familiar songs. I'd urge you to work toward this goal." It was still a rejection, and to have my voice called "pleasing" was not exactly a rave review, but I couldn't help being pleased that he had taken the time to write personally. As it happened, I *had* written some music for the lyrics a friend had given me. I had thought that both lyrics and melody were good, but my friend's efforts to get them on the air via a singing group he knew had gotten nowhere. Looking back at my Cellar Door experience I couldn't help feeling disappointed in myself, that I had not had the courage to appear before a *real* audience, an audience to whom I was a stranger. I was even more disappointed when I later learned that many of country and folk music's "greats" had sung at The Cellar Door, and that it was there that Mary Chapin Carpenter had gotten her start. If I had gone to the Hootenanny I would at least have been able to say I had once performed at The Cellar Door, but it was too late for recriminations.

Not too much later, however, another opportunity arose. I was invited to dinner by Anna Chennault, the widow of General Claire Chennault, who had commanded the famed Flying Tigers during World War II. Though Claire Chennault had died many years ago, in 1958, Anna was still very much a public figure, active in both Washington's social and political scenes. Anna had asked if I would bring my guitar and if I would be willing to sing after dinner. I believe she had heard me on one of her frequent visits to Taipei. The dinner was held at her apartment in the Watergate complex and was the most unusual affair I had ever attended. A Chinese banquet was served at three round tables, each seating ten guests. While the cold dishes customarily served as a first course at Chinese banquets were waiting to be tasted, Anna asked each guest in turn to stand and introduce himself. This was an amazing display and I marveled at how each guest seemed pleased in his own way with the process. The prominent guests had the opportunity to declare their importance; the lesser guests, such as myself, to be thrilled at finding themselves in such exalted company. The guests included Washington Post writer Sally Quinn, later to marry Ben Bradlee, Editor of the Post; Hope Rydings Miller, Society editor of the Times Herald; the Vice President of Northrop Aviation; the Vice President of Columbia Pictures; Ray Cline, our once Chief of Station in Taipei; General Cicollela, who had been MAAG chief in Taipei; several Chinese Generals already known to me; and others whom I cannot remember. When it was my turn to introduce myself, Anna followed my words by announcing that I had "graciously agreed to sing for us later in the evening."

The dinner was sumptuous, and at its end I was hoisted up onto the grand piano by Ray Cline and "Chick" Cicollela. I was not even particularly nervous since there were old friends among those present who I knew would be supportive. I sang a few songs, winding up with *Lily Marlene*. The applause that followed was enthusiastic and I felt I had done well. I was even more pleased, when after dinner the ladies retired to the bedroom to "powder their noses" (that was the custom in those days), and Hope Rydings Miller asked if I had ever considered singing professionally. I suspected that Anna Chennault might have told her that I had recently lost my husband and was still pondering what to do with my life. I did not mention my brief attempts at entering the professional world. I confessed to her, "I would like that more than anything but don't know if I'm good enough," whereupon she replied, "I think I know someone who can be the judge of that." A few days later, she called to tell me that she had talked to Howard Devron, orchestra leader at the Shoreham Hotel's Blue Room and that he had already agreed to listen to me. I could hardly believe that someone I barely knew had gone to so much trouble on my behalf.

Howard Devron was rehearsing with the orchestra when I arrived at the Shoreham, but excused himself and took me into an empty reception room. He was nice. "Now, sing for me," he said. And I did. I wasn't nervous. I felt that he had liked me. He said. "You needn't have any doubts about yourself. You're good. I'd use you myself if I could, but I'm tied to union musicians." "But I think I know just the place for you," he added. He then explained that the Georgetown Club was a small private club, intimate, and very exclusive. He thought it would be a perfect setting for me, and to me it sounded too good to be true. Maybe it would lead to something, but I hardly dared hope. On the spot Howard Devron wrote a note of introduction to the manager of the club, Norman Larsen, describing me as "an amateur, but one who sings like a professional."

A few days later I met with Norman Larsen. I sang for him, and he was more excited than I was about the prospect of having me sing at the club. "Let's definitely give it a try," he said. "When can you come?" We set a date, and when I showed up, he had a microphone and amplifiers already set up in the center of the clubroom. But even as we were discussing how we should proceed, an Asian man appeared, clearly unhappy with what he was seeing. He took Larsen aside and in harsh tones asked what was going on. Larsen's explanation that he thought some entertainment would be a welcome addition to the club was not being well received. The man was the owner of the club, and he clearly objected to any kind of performance at all. To Larsen he said, "As long as she's already here, she can go ahead, but you are *not* to announce her, and you are to move her to the back of the room where she will be *background music only*. Understand? And you are to turn the sound down low." Though he was speaking in hushed tones to Larsen alone, I could hear every word. I was embarrassed on Larsen's behalf. He had clearly overstepped his authority by taking me on.

It was an awkward situation for me. In the end, I sang, but as background music only. It was a quiet night and there was only one rather large group of guests in the far corner of the room enjoying pre-dinner drinks. I don't believe they were even aware of my presence. The club's owner, however, sat at a small table with a drink in his hand, listening. When I had sung one round of songs he invited me to join him and introduced himself as Tongsun Park. He was extremely gracious. He apologized for forcing a change in plans. Explained that he regarded all members of his club as personal guests, and that they in turn considered the club as an extension of their own living rooms, not a public place with commercial entertainment. He sounded quite sincere when he said he had enjoyed my singing. I later learned that Tongsun Park was a wealthy Korean businessman whose name had figured largely in the Watergate scandals. My disappointing experience at the Georgetown Club brought my attempts to sing professionally to a close. I lost the will to keep trying.

Chapter 16
Clandestine Ops

Having tried the singing route, I resigned myself to desk work at the CIA. But things had gradually started looking up. At least I had now been assigned office space, and actually had an inbox, so that I was seeing some of the reports and cable traffic that came through our section. Soon I was being asked to respond to some incoming cables from the field, those with relatively simple requests. However, reading and summarizing files on Chinese officials of interest still occupied most of my time. Some of the files had no more than a few sheets of paper in them. Others were quite thick, full of bits of miscellaneous information on the subjects collected over a number of years. Suddenly, one of these officials, Hu Yoping (not a true name), an official with the New China News Agency, became a target of interest. Headquarters wanted someone to meet him, to consolidate all we knew about him, and to make a judgment on whether he was worth pursuing. I had just read his file; knew more about him than anyone else. I was "it." The official was located in Bonn, Germany. I was to go to Bonn to meet him. False documentation was prepared for me. A date was set for the proposed meeting. Bonn Station had arranged for a "cutout" to put me in the subject's orbit at a social function. After that I would be on my own.

I can't begin to describe the exhilaration I felt at being given this assignment. I was still only a part-time employee with no training or experience in clandestine work. This was definitely a chance to prove that I was good for more than reading and summarizing files.

But, unfortunately, the mission did not get off to a good start. At Dulles Airport my outgoing flight was delayed. There was no way I could make the connecting flight to Bonn at Heathrow in London. I called Headquarters immediately to report the problem and was instructed by the responsible officer to pick up a flight to Dusseldorf instead, that they would arrange with Bonn Station to have someone meet me there and get me to Bonn in time for the scheduled meeting. I was to look for a man with white hair and glasses. This unexpected change was a bit disconcerting, but I had no doubts about being met as promised. After all, this was the CIA. Surely a change in plan like this must be routine and would be handled without problem. At Heathrow, I had no trouble getting a flight to Dusseldorf, but when I disembarked, there was no sign of a man with white hair and glasses. At the time, I was not particularly concerned as I felt sure someone would soon appear. However, when an hour had passed with no sign of my contact, I began to worry. I had not been told his name, whether he was young or old, tall or short, fat or thin. Through the next hour I approached every man with white, or even gray hair, and glasses, asking if he could tell me the time, a stupid question as there was a large clock plainly visible on the wall. None of them was my contact. Finally, I called a USIA officer, a personal friend, in Bonn and asked him to tell Henry W., our Bonn Station Chief, that I was waiting at the airport in Dusseldorf. Eventually, much to my relief, someone came to pick me up and drove me to the W's house in Bonn. Immediately after welcoming me, Henry informed me that the meeting was off, that the cutout had gotten cold feet and didn't want any part in the operation. I was so disappointed. This was my first chance to be actively involved in any kind of ongoing operation and I felt a real letdown. Henry, however, didn't seem particularly perturbed. "Don't let it bother you," he said. "These things happen all the time. Let's just relax and enjoy ourselves. You've come at a perfect time." It *was* a perfect time, for the annual celebration of Oktoberfest was in full swing. That evening Henry and his wife took me out into the streets to enjoy the festivities. While living in Taipei, I had once taken part in an Oktoberfest celebration when the Station had put on a party for the annual German holiday. In fact, it was then that I had sung "Lily Marlene"—in German—and had also learned the words to many German songs. Now, as we made our way through the crowded streets, there was music everywhere and I was in my element singing along with the joyous throngs.

The next morning, Henry and I discussed the aborted meeting. The original plan had been that I would play the role of a freelance writer, who, on meeting the Chinese official, would ask for an interview. I hated the thought that I'd come all this way and accomplished nothing. "I don't see why we can't still carry out the plan, with me going in "cold" instead of via a third person," I ventured.

"How do you mean "cold"? he asked.

"I'll just knock on his door and introduce myself." I made it sound so easy.

"And if he turns you away?"

"So what have we lost? I think," I said, "that he, being a Chinese in a foreign country, when he sees another Chinese face, he'll at least be polite. I can work up some story and talk my way in."

John was still skeptical, but in the end agreed that we had nothing to lose. "OK. Go to it, if you feel you can carry it off."

The next day, as I stood in front of Hu's door, I did not feel nearly as confident as I had sounded the day before. It seemed an eternity before anyone answered my knock, but finally the door was opened by a Chinese man who turned out to be Hu himself. From that moment, the whole exercise proved easier than I could possibly have imagined. I introduced myself (in alias) as an American, a freelance writer. I explained that a friend whom I was visiting in the neighborhood had mentioned that a Chinese official lived nearby, and that I had immediately seen this as a rare opportunity to interview a Chinese official. This was 1971, before Nixon's China visit had normalized U.S./China relations, and there being no Communist China representation in America, my eagerness for an interview not possible in America was quite plausible. Far from looking skeptical, Hu was expansive and invited me in. His wife brought us tea, and I took the opportunity to ask if she could join us, explaining that I thought an article on the role of women in today's China would be well received by American readers. Both Hu and his wife were extremely receptive and more than eager to talk, always pushing the party line. They gave me so many examples of women's achievements in the new China that I had more than enough material for an article if I chose to write one.

In my single meeting with Hu and his wife, both seemed secure in their jobs with the New China News Agency and had seemed proud of China's position in the world. I had not seen any reason why they would be susceptible to recruitment. In later years, Hu moved up to become the head of the New China News Agency, evidence that his career had been on an upward track with no cause for disenchantment with his work status. Although my opinion alone, based on one meeting, would not be enough to determine whether a target was worth pursuing, I do know, that combined with other factors, it did cause the Station to shift its focus to other potential targets. That I had undertaken the meeting with Hu without outside help, however, earned me lots of points with both the Station and with Headquarters.

In the years that followed I was called upon again and again to participate in operations abroad. I was dispatched on so many TDYs (temporary duty assignments) that several co-workers were concerned that I was being over-exposed. These trips included Rome, Paris, Beirut, Brussels, Mexico City, and Kingston, Jamaica. Some of these assignments were only for a few days, for a single meeting, others extended over several weeks. In meeting with Chinese officials I always used an alias, and in most cases was provided with full alias documentation to back up my cover story. I was in Brussels for six weeks working against a Chinese couple. It was a particularly interesting operation as we had audio coverage of the targets' bedroom and we could later replay their conversations of our meetings. On a tape of our first meeting, the most crucial in establishing one's bona fides, the couple are discussing my visit. The woman says, "she certainly is an attractive woman." (I was tickled by this.) And he replies, "Maybe this is a case of *Mei Jen Chi*." (*Mei Jen Chi* is a true story of seduction and intrigue in which a beautiful young girl is the major figure in a plot to bring down a contender for power during the final years of the Han dynasty.) To this, the woman responds, "Don't think you're so important, you silly old goat. It's me she's interested in, not you." I got quite a kick out of hearing this replay. Despite his initial *Mei jen Chi* comment, their conversations that followed showed that they had accepted my cover story.

Another operation in which we had audio coverage was in Beirut where I stayed for two weeks. This had started as a sexually oriented case. A female agent had been installed in an apartment adjoining that of the target official. She had established an ongoing sexual relationship with the target, but thus far it was yielding no useful information. I was brought into the picture as merely a visiting friend from America. My job again was to make an assessment of possible vulnerabilities that would make him susceptible to recruitment and to determine whether continued pursuit was warranted. Getting to know the official proved to be quite easy. He was delighted to meet Maria's Chinese-American friend and in the course of my visit I spent many evenings in Maria's apartment chatting with our Chinese target. Unfortunately, in this case, our audio technicians had done a very poor job of concealing the audio device. They had placed the "bug" under one of the cushions on the couch. At our first meeting I noticed with some apprehension that the target had the nervous habit of running his fingers down the sides of the cushion and sliding them back and forth. I held my breath every time his fingers curled under the cushion. He was much too close to the bug for comfort. The next day I had to ask the Station to have the audio equipment removed. We lost the benefits of audio coverage.

Maria was not the only woman who was targeted with sexual intent against Chinese officials. Despite the fact that up to this time sexual operations had not been productive, there was always some senior officer who was convinced they were worth a try. Apart from Maria, who was Yugoslavian, I was involved with the handling of two others, both Asians. Neither one was a prostitute, but, like Maria, was willing to oblige if required. While these operations were in play, I often wondered what my children would have thought of their straight-laced mother and the "guidance" she was providing to the women who became known up and down the halls of China Operations and beyond as "Marguerite's stable."

One of the Asian women played a role in my TDY to Kingston, Jamaica. The Chinese official we were targeting was there for some conference. She was staying at the same hotel and they had already become friendly. Sex did not enter into the relationship. I stayed at the same hotel for a week, ostensibly just vacationing. Actually it was a nice respite from the office. I met the Chinese official by the pool and spent several evenings chatting with him. The trip was unproductive, as he showed no signs of being disenchanted with the direction China had taken or with his own circumstances. However, for me this trip was memorable for the conditions under which I was sent. At the time, Jamaica was in a state of local unrest and there had been several unsettling incidents. I had been told not to rent a car on arrival and never to get into a taxi or any car in which I didn't know the driver. What I had *not* been told was that the week before my trip, an American woman had been raped in the elevator of the Hilton Hotel, and that two of our own communications officers had been mugged in the hotel's parking lot. I was not told of these incidents until my return, but to my remonstrations, the reply I received was only, "We were afraid you'd back out if you knew." It rankled that to the Headquarters officers the operation had been more important than my safety.

Throughout the seventeen years I worked for the CIA I was never involved in any operations that were dangerous. There were, however, several incidents that could have put me in an awkward position. One of these was in Brussels. My husband John, also a CIA officer (I had remarried by then), was returning from a trip to

Kenya where he had been training the local police on interrogation techniques. He planned to join me in Brussels for a few days. It was late at night and I was waiting for him in a shopping alcove near my hotel. For some inexplicable reason the Station had put me in a hotel in a red light district, and I could see several women trolling the street. Suddenly, a police van pulled up, and two men in plain clothes jumped out, grabbed the women unceremoniously, and herded them quite roughly into the van. I retreated as far back into the alcove as I could and escaped unnoticed. However, if they had picked me up too, it would have been more than awkward for me, as my passport did not match the alias name under which I had checked in at the hotel. Looking back, I find it hard to understand why the hotel desk had not required me to surrender my passport at the time I checked in.

Another operation that could have been awkward was to take place in Karachi. I was to be part of a husband and wife team targeted against a Chinese couple. We would be living for a projected three-month period in an apartment adjacent to that of the Chinese. David H, a recently widowed Chinese-American, whom I knew only slightly, was to be my husband. At this time, I had just remarried and my husband John understandably was unhappy with the idea of my sharing quarters with another man for three months. I reluctantly withdrew and David continued the case as a single. The operation, however, never got off the ground. There was an attempted hijacking of the plane carrying David to Karachi, and although the hijacker was caught when the plane landed at the Karachi airport, the newspaper carried the names of all passengers. The Station decided to abort the operation. David was lucky that the Pakistan authorities did not check the passengers' passports as he was carrying two alias passports, not a good situation in which to caught. I imagine he must have had some nervous moments. I was glad I had not been with him.

While these TDY assignments added a new and interesting dimension to my job, I was also making steady progress as a Headquarters officer. After three years as a part-time contract employee, in 1972 I had been converted to staff and had begun working full time. As I assumed more and more responsibilities, I was promoted from my original Intelligence Assistant category to that of Operations Officer. In this capacity I provided guidance to field stations on the China target, and also played a key role in China Operations training courses. The course included the study of the Chinese personality and Chinese culture in addition to presenting case studies of past operations against the China target. I also made presentations to other Divisions within the Agency and briefed outgoing Military Attachés from the Defense Department.

In addition to the above activities, as the only ethnic Chinese woman in China Operations, I was called upon on occasion to participate in experimental programs. Being bicultural (Chinese *and* American) I was in essence a two-dimensional guinea pig. In fact, I was a three-dimensional guinea pig because I was female at a time when there were few women actively involved in clandestine operations. One of these programs was a sensitivity session, referred to by some skeptics as "touchy feely sessions." These were quite popular at the time and were also being employed in the business world. (My brother Luther, who worked for DuPont, participated in a similar program.) They were supposed to make you more aware of yourself, your impact on others, and their reaction to you.

Our group was composed of five men and three women, plus the psychologist running the program and the senior officer who was promoting it. We were housed together at a training site for a full week of total togetherness. All our waking hours were spent together. Our ages ranged from twenty-two to fifty-five. Grade levels were from GS-7 to GS-16. None of us had known each other previously. We were not to talk about our pasts and were to keep always within the bounds of the here-and-now. We engaged in several exercises that seemed almost childish, but taken as a whole, proved surprisingly revealing. One exercise was to pretend to be an animal. It was amazing how in most cases a person's choice mimicked so closely his personality, i.e., the tiger was aggressive; the dog was friendly. I chose to be a doe. I wondered what that said about me. Another exercise was to describe what we thought another person had been like as a child. In almost every case we were right on. I was always described as a good little girl. There was also an exercise in which each of us was to identify our own façades and to describe the others in a few short words. I was dismayed to find that every description of me contained the word "lady." "A real lady," "very ladylike," "a perfect lady." One even said he could imagine me presiding at the White House. These perceptions of me were the more surprising to me since here at the training site I was wearing tee shirts and jeans. Those present had never seen me in the high heels and the slim Chinese *ch'i p'ao* I habitually wore at the office. Throughout my childhood, all my mother's training had been geared toward making me into a lady. It seems she had been successful for I had apparently achieved a "lady" façade. But in a working environment being seen as a "lady" was not what I aspired to. To me, the word put a degree of separation between me and my working colleagues, whereas I wanted nothing more than to be one of *them*

Many times we sat in a circle on the floor. Sometimes Jim, our psychologist leader, led us in some exercise. Other times we sat in silence with no instructions given. As the moments wore on, someone would pipe up with, "What's the purpose of this?" or, "This is really stupid. Are we supposed to be learning something?" These round circle sessions continued throughout the program. At first, they were stilted and awkward with most of us having little inclination to speak up. Occasionally someone would offer some comment, which, however banal, would usually release the pent-up opinions of others in the group. We were encouraged to take risks, to put aside fears of rejection. We were to verbalize our immediate reactions to persons, to situations, and to air our feelings, whether good or bad. Some of our words, particularly about others, were harshly critical, others less so. Several times I found myself in tears. But what I found so amazing was that somehow Jim our psychologist had instilled in us this love for one another, so that our criticisms, some occasionally hurtful, were given and accepted not as judgments, but as supportive observations by people who cared and wanted to help. And gradually, as the week progressed, within the round circles of which we had been so derisive at the beginning of the week, we found ourselves divulging more and more about ourselves and sharing confidences and thoughts we had not shared even with our spouses.

On one occasion, toward the end of the week, Jim asked for a volunteer to sit at the center of the circle. Rick, one of the younger men in the group, volunteered. As usual, there was a long silence, and then suddenly a shock, as Rick blurted out, "I love Marguerite." I was quite sure his words had not been a declaration of romantic love. Since by now they all knew, that despite my outward show of confidence, I was often plagued with insecurity and the fear of not being well liked, I felt that Rick was reassuring me that I *was* liked *and* loved. It was some twenty years later that I learned that Rick was one and the same as Aldrich Ames, the spy and traitor who had knowingly brought about the deaths of many of our agents. To this day I find it hard to believe that someone who had once been a caring, loving person could have changed so much that the lives of others meant nothing to him.

For me, the entire program was a definite plus. I learned a great deal about myself, and for the first time I learned how I came across to other people. I learned that a façade can be protective, but that it can also be a handicap. I learned to shed some of the reticence that was part of my "lady" image. I know I was better liked at the end of the session than I had been at the beginning. I also learned to look at other people differently, to try to see beyond the surface to what lay beyond. But while I found the program beneficial, that was not the case with everyone. The youngest participant in our group suffered a nervous breakdown immediately after the session. Among us she had been the least vocal, and I don't recall any particularly harsh criticisms being heaped upon her that might have been the cause, but as a result of her breakdown the Agency did not conduct any further sessions.

It is now over forty years since I participated in this program, and I still cannot understand how Jim, in one short week, had managed create this all-encompassing love and caring in all of us. I know only that at the conclusion of the course I returned to Headquarters full of love, not only for those in our group, but for everyone around me, for the whole human race. When I was told that I had received a promotion, I was ecstatic. When I asked who I should be thanking, I was told I could start with Bill N. Bill, our one-time Station Chief in Taipei, was now Chief of the East Asian Division, and he was the one who would have given the final seal of approval to my promotion. But once in his office, instead of a few simple words of gratitude, I wrapped my arms around him, poured out my thanks, and told him how much I loved him. This was in the early seventies when only hippies were into the loving thing. It was long before hugs had become the norm for meeting and greeting friends, and it was certainly rather unbridled behavior for the Marguerite that Bill had known in Taipei. Coming straight from the sensitivity session, the physical display had come quite naturally to me, but as all that love in me gradually wore off, I often wondered what Bill had thought, if it had been too much. Many many years later, when all of us had retired—he to the Mid west—he returned to Washington for a visit and we met by chance at a dinner party at the home of mutual friends. It was he who brought up the subject. Reminding me of that incident, he said, "That was one of the most moving things that ever happened to me." I realized then that expressions of love are never too much.

Chapter 17
The Not-so-merry Widow

By early 1972 I had switched from part-time to full time work. My job at the CIA was moving along nicely and had definitely become more interesting. At home, both house and garden were looking good, and the hard work the children and I had put in the first year was bearing fruit. A good relationship with the local Mobile station ensured that my car was well taken care of. The manager of the local hardware store, learning that the two newly arrived young Chinese boys were without a father, became friend and advisor to Eric and Bean. We were on a first name basis with the manager and tellers of the local bank, and the grocery store clerks welcomed us as regulars. We were comfortably settled in our new home and our suburban community.

My personal life, in many ways, however, was at a virtual standstill. My friends did not neglect me. The husbands went out of their way to be helpful. One brought us inflatable mattresses to use before our own furniture had been delivered. Another brought plantings from his garden to add to ours. Yet another, unasked, delivered mulch to my garden when picking up his own orders. He also supplied us with wooden boards for shelving and came to help the boys put them up. At the office, one or another would occasionally stop by my desk at noon. "Have you had lunch?" If I had not, we would go down together to the cafeteria. On a rare occasion, one would suggest, "Let's live it up for a change and go out." In only one of these instances was there an untoward advance. That, I put an immediate and emphatic stop to. He was chagrined, but we remained friends.

Again, I was never a neglected widow and was always included in the dinner parties and gatherings of my friends. In turn, I made a point of hosting dinners and an occasional cocktail party. I had a busy social life, but I was a single in a couple's world. Horace had died just before my forty-fourth birthday. I was young and considered attractive. I think most people assumed I would soon marry again, but no likely men appeared on my horizon. Except for the one instance above, no male, married or otherwise, had shown a romantic interest in me. In two years, no one had asked me for a date. At the time I was working closely with two psychologists. I asked one, "What's wrong with me? I thought widows and divorcees were supposed to be fair game, but men don't even make passes at me." He just laughed and said, "Marguerite, you are not the type of woman men make passes at. A man might fantasize about you, but he will *not* make a pass." That was consoling in a way. Perhaps I appeared unapproachable, but the fact remained, I was not an object of romantic interest to anyone.

In the years that I was single, there were few venues in which to meet the opposite sex. Many met through their churches, but I was not a churchgoer. Others met through groups called Parents Without Partners, but I had heard that these meetings were heavy on women and that the few men who attended often bragged about having their pick of the many available women. I did not attend any of their meetings. As time went by, three men who had been in our past circle of contacts lost their wives. The first, I had never liked. The second was among those with whom I occasionally had lunch at the office. After his wife's death he invited me to dinner on what was clearly intended as a "date," but did not follow up with another invitation. While I had not had the slightest interest in either of these two men as romantic partners, still, it was deflating that neither had they shown any interest in me.

The third was in California, and during the years he and his wife had lived in Washington we had been close friends as couples. Dick came to Washington occasionally on business. He always looked me up, took me to dinner, and during his stay picked me up to join him and his friends in their activities. Dick was Chinese-American, and all my Chinese-American friends thought we would make a perfect match. We had always gotten along well together, and he had often said, that unlike many Chinese women, I was someone he could talk to. We were good friends, but there was never a look or glance on his part that indicated any interest in moving our relationship to a different level. For my part, I had never thought of Dick as any more than a platonic friend, but still, it was disappointing. I was convinced there was something lacking in me. I got on well with men. They liked me, but I simply did not evoke in them any romantic feelings. I had no sex appeal.

The only singles affair that I attended in my almost six years as a widow was at the Colombian Embassy. Several foreign embassies hosted parties from time to time to give their young single staff members a chance to meet other singles. The affairs were open to select groups, among them the CIA. I had been persuaded to go by two single friends and had agreed more out of curiosity than with the expectation of meeting a promising male. The party was well attended, but by a very young crowd. I was well into my forties but had always been told that I looked younger than my age. Soon, there was music and dancing, but no one asked me to dance. I felt very much a wallflower. Left standing alone, I wandered into the living room. An older couple were sitting on the couch with drinks in hand, and on seeing me, the man immediately rose and introduced himself as the Colombian Ambassador. He introduced his wife, and I spent the rest of the evening in pleasant conversation with the two. This was the milieu that I was accustomed to and in which I was comfortable, but I had definitely not been a success at my one and only venture into the singles world.

Surprisingly, however, several weeks later, I received an unexpected phone call at the office. The caller asked, "Is this Marguerite Eng?" And when I said it was, he immediately launched into a tirade. "Do you have any idea how much trouble I've had tracking you down? I've been passed from one office to another and back again with no one seeming to have any idea what they're doing." I interrupted. "Wait a minute. Wait a minute. Who *is* this?" He then calmed down. "Sorry, it's Ron Castle. We met at the Colombian Embassy party and I remembered your saying you worked at the CIA. I've been trying to track you down ever since." Ron said he'd like to get together. I remembered him vaguely as a pleasant young man and agreed on a date for dinner. Ron worked on the Hill in the office of Texas Senator Lloyd Bentsen. He was fifteen years younger than I, but declared that older women had always appealed to him more than women his own age. We went out for dinner a few times, and he invited me several times to small parties in his Georgetown apartment and also once to a lavish home that he was house-sitting at the time. (House-sitting was evidently a much coveted job among young singles on the Hill, and Ron, with excellent references as a reliable house-sitter, had developed a regular clientele.) But despite his having gone through layers of bureaucracy to find me, he made no romantic overtures, and there was not a hint of anything more than a friendly interest. It confirmed for me that I was simply not the kind of woman who stirred a man's libido

However, despite what I concluded was my lack of sex appeal, I was not totally without male attention. Unfortunately, those to whom I appealed did not appeal to me. But then there was John. John was also with the Agency, and he and his wife Bette had become good friends from our years in Taipei. Both had been very good to me after John's death, frequently having me over for lunch or dinner at their home in Bethesda, Maryland. Recently, Bette had developed some heart problems and John took early retirement to take care of her. Returning from my first temporary duty assignment overseas at the end of November 1972, I had hardly gotten out of the taxi when all three children came rushing out of the house to tell me, "Mom, Mrs. Church died." It was a shock. I was saddened by the news. She had been a good friend and I was going to miss her.

In the days and weeks that followed Bette's death, John leaned on me heavily, and I was glad that I was there to be leaned upon. He called me often, wanting to talk. Conversations went on endlessly. Soon he was coming to the house on weekends. If it was close to lunchtime I would give him a sandwich. I didn't feel the need to put aside other things to entertain him. If I had to shop for groceries, he came with me. If I was working in the garden, he picked up a trowel and helped in the digging. If I was hanging out the laundry, he carried the laundry basket. I was comfortable with him.

Soon Eric was off to college at Virginia Polytech. Kathy left the next year for Duke. With two children gone and only Bean at home, John filled the gap. In those days two-for-one coupon booklets were a popular marketing tool for many commercial activities: restaurants, shows, sporting events, and even stores. John and I would thumb through the coupons, picking the ones that appealed. It wasn't as if we were out on dates; as far as I was concerned we were simply friends taking advantage of these freebie offers. One of these coupons was for a very posh and expensive restaurant. The meal was delicious, but it was far too much food. When the dessert came, chocolate éclaires filled with custard, neither of us could eat another bite. This was a time when it had not yet become acceptable to request a doggie bag, especially in a high-class restaurant. But, not about to let our desserts go to waste, I whipped a plastic bag from my purse and slid the two chocolate éclaires inside. John was mightily impressed with my resourcefulness and especially with my being unabashed by the surprised waiter standing by. Later, at the Shakespeare theatre, under cover of darkness, we ate those somewhat squished desserts as gleefully as a couple of school kids sneaking a forbidden beer.

John and I had a good time together and he was fun to be with. His friends were still trying to set him up with single women, and he had been persuaded to attend several sessions of Parents Without Partners. He told me about the dates his friends had set him up with. None of these had interested him. It was me he wanted to be with. I was well aware that his feelings for me, unlike mine for him, were more than platonic. In later years, he confessed that even when Bette was alive he had been attracted to me, but had the good sense to curb any wild impulses. While other husbands were inviting me to lunch, he had never done the same. "I was not about to go down that road," he said. "Bette and I had a good solid marriage, and I was not going to jeopardize it, even for you." At the time I thought that was an

John and me

admirable trait in John, and in later years, as I saw another husband, a good friend, tempted into an affair that ended in the break-up of his family, I admired John even more for his constancy.

Our relationship continued on its friendly way for a long long time before it moved beyond mere friendship. John was doggedly persistent in his courtship. He courted me not only by his constant presence, but also through the mail. When I was away on an extended trips, letters would be waiting at my destination, letters that were funny and entertaining, and though they were not love letters per se, between the lines love shone through. John had always been a prolific writer. Ever since his college days, he and his two closest friends had exchanged two or three messages a week. Some were long introspective letters; others, just postcards often with no more than a line about the current weather or a comment on some current news. Now, even though John and I were so often together, I found myself looking forward to the mail each day to see if it might bring something from John. Sometimes it was a poem, for John was also a poet. Though I found much of his poetry far too deep for my understanding, for me he wrote at a level I could grasp. Most of these poems were humorous, but some were ardent, and others were on occasion even erotic. John later said he had never known anyone who was as affected by the written word, and indeed that played a large part in moving my feelings for him beyond the bounds of friendship.

John was slowly seducing me by his written words, but mostly by his just being there for me. When I needed someone to talk to, he was there to listen. When I was discouraged, he was there to encourage. When I needed someone to lean on, he was there. But most important, when I needed love, he was there to love me. Yet, I still steadfastly believed that I was not *in* love. It was not until another woman's apparent interest in John surfaced, or rather, *his* apparent interest in another woman, that I was forced to rethink our relationship.

John and I were on a tour of the Washington National Cathedral. The lines were long and I had sat down on a bench while John stood and kept our place in line. Soon, I noticed he and the redheaded woman behind him were engaged in an animated conversation. That was followed by their both getting out pen and paper and apparently exchanging phone numbers. I found this so annoying that it was all I could do to keep from taking the car keys and driving home without him. However, I did nothing as he introduced me to the woman. Her name was Shirley Acton. She was Australian, a travel agent, and quite attractive. A week or so later I called him one evening as I often did. It was probably about nine-thirty. He was not home, but his daughter Annie, who was staying with him at the time, answered the phone. I said, "What on earth is he doing out at this hour?" She hemmed and hawed, but when prodded, finally divulged that he was out on a date with Shirley Acton, and that it was not for the first time.

On learning that John had been going out with Shirley, I gave some serious thought to our relationship. John had always told me about his other dates, but he had not mentioned Shirley's name since our one meeting. I thought his silence was telling. For the first time I realized that I had no right to keep him tied to me forever as *just a friend*. I had taken up almost two years of his life. Now I felt that in fairness to him

I either had to marry him or let him go to find happiness with someone else. It was not an easy decision. He had become a part of my life and I would miss him. Also, there was the financial consideration. I was a government employee, a civil servant, and government rules at that time stipulated that if a widow remarried before the age of sixty, she would give up her survivor's annuity. I was not yet fifty. If I married John, I would forfeit the annuity Horace had worked for twenty-six years to earn. I toyed with the idea of just living together, without benefit of marriage. I thought that surely friends and family, knowing us, would accept this as a marriage-like commitment and not a casual dalliance. But in the end I found I could not do it. Even if friends in America could accept it, I could not subject Horace's sisters to the knowledge that their brother's widow was "living in sin" with a man to whom she was not married. And then, there was still that nagging feeling that I was not *in* love. But how important was that? I knew him so well, and knew we were compatible. There was no question that in recent years, my happiest moments had been when John was with me. Surely, that fact alone augured well for a good marriage.

When Bean left for college at St. Lawrence University in the fall of 1974 I was left alone. I found out all too soon that I was not cut out for the single life. I hated coming home to an empty house, hated cooking for myself, hated sitting down for dinner alone. I wanted someone to enjoy the meals I cooked, to appreciate the house I kept, to admire the flowers I raised, someone with whom to share my life. I had thought I would try living as a single for a year, but barely two months after Bean left I decided to marry John. I thought, "I'll give it a try. If it doesn't work, we can always get a divorce." And with that cavalier attitude I entered into my second marriage.

Chapter 18
Remarriage

John and I were married in the St.Mary's Chapel of the Washington National Cathedral on November 2, 1974. It was six years after Horace's death, and four years after Bette's. It was not the wedding we had planned. As two middle-aged people, both on second marriages, we had intended a quiet wedding with only my children Eric and Bean as witnesses (Kathy was in Vienna, Austria, on her Junior year abroad). Arrangements had already been made to meet with the minister at one of the smaller chapels at the Cathedral. We had planned a party at my house two days later to announce our marriage. However, the best-laid plans have been known to go awry, as ours did. Two days before the wedding, I received a surprise phone call from Horace's brother-in-law Y.K., who happened to be visiting his daughter Patsy in New York. The week before, I had written Horace's sister Ida in Hong Kong to tell her that I was getting married again. She, in turn, had relayed the information to Y.K. in New York. Now, Y.K. informed me, that though he was scheduled to return to Hong Kong the next day, he was delaying his departure to come to my wedding. Hearing Y.K.'s words, I tried hastily to explain, "Y.K., we're not having a formal wedding, only a quiet ceremony with Eric and Bean as witnesses," to which he responded indignantly, "You mean you don't want me at your wedding?" I was at a loss. What was I to say? I could not bring myself to refuse him. Reluctantly, I said, "Why of course I do, if you really want to come." I gave him the time and place.

Now a hasty reconnoitering with John. How could we have Horace's brother-in-law and not our own families? Frantic phone calls to my brother Luther and sister Jeannie. Also my birth sister Eva, who lived in the area. John called his son Jocko and daughter Annie, and his oldest friend Frank Bliss. Disgruntlement from some for not having been included in original plans, but despite only one day's notice, all made it to our wedding. I did not dress up for the occasion. I wore a daytime suit, and did not carry a bouquet, or even wear a corsage. But the organist played the Cathedral's full organ, as the Verger, in full regalia, with mace held high, solemnly preceded our whole group of fifteen into the Chapel. John and I said our vows before the altar. Afterward, a sumptuous dinner at a Chinese restaurant. It was done. We were married.

I spent the better part of our wedding night and the next day preparing for the party at which we would make the announcement of our marriage. The wedding was on November second; the party was on the fourth. I had invited a hundred people for cocktails, the invitations extended very informally by phone. I prepared the food. Bean and one of his friends tended bar. In later years John delighted in telling friends I had spent our wedding night making meatballs. Midway in the party, when all the guests had arrived, I stood on the steps and announced our marriage. To some it came as a great shock. To others it was something they had come to expect. To all it was cause for celebration. It was a great party. The food was devoured; the liquor flowed. It wasn't until all the guests had gone that I felt the wedding was over, that I was really married.

The first few years that followed were not always easy. John's children were already married and had homes of their own. Mine, though all in college, still needed a place to call home. We had decided that John would move into my house in Vienna rather than his in Bethesda, Maryland. Though the children were away in college most of the time, to me, it always felt awkward when they were home. They had no objection to my marrying again, and John was already well known to them, but we had been an established household, and somehow he was an intrusion. He was a guest in *our* house. Kathy and Bean accepted his presence, but for Eric, then twenty-one, it was hard. He had to make room for John in what had been *his* workspace; he had to move *his* tools to accommodate John's. Also, four-letter words had recently found a way into his vocabulary, and John's attempts to curb their use *in your mother's presence* didn't go down well with him. His resentment, though never verbalized, was smoldering beneath the surface, and was all too evident in his behavior toward John. It is a wonder to me that John was able to show the restraint he did, especially during the times I was away on temporary assignments abroad and the two were left alone together. It took a long time, but eventually Eric was ready for a truce in this one-sided battle. By then, Eric had graduated from college and had moved to an apartment of his own, and my job had taken us to Australia. John was surprised to receive one day a beautifully written letter from Eric with a moving apology for his past behavior. Eric also wrote that if he had behaved that way when his father had been alive, he would have been kicked out of the house. Finally, John had gained full acceptance into our family.

While John finally felt he was a part of my family, I had already been welcomed into his. I had met his mother several times when Bette was still alive, and we had taken an instant liking to each other. After Bette's death, even before John was showing a romantic interest in me, John said she had been urging him, "Don't let that one get away." After our marriage, Memo, which is what we called her, spent a month every year with us, and I enjoyed every minute of her stay. Like John, she was comfortable and fun to be with. She made herself at home and I never felt I had to entertain her. She, like John, was a wonderful correspondent. Her letters, unlike those of my own mother, did not speak of what she had done yesterday, or whom she was seeing tomorrow, but instead were full of her thoughts, her feelings. In her correspondence she gave much of herself, and her written words allowed me to know her better. When she died at eighty-five, I felt her loss as much as I had that of my own mother. I missed her letters.

Me with Memo and the twins

I had also met John's twin brothers when we made a trip to Oregon shortly before our marriage. We got along famously. Neither had been to college. Bob was the grounds-keeper at the local high school, and Jim was a postal clerk. But despite their modest employment, they were highly respected in the community, much of that respect no doubt due to their also being joint

John with twin brothers Bob and Jim

owners of a five-hundred acre ranch and a thriving dairy business. Both were musicians, Bob playing the trombone, and Jim the saxophone. When the three brothers were together, they invariably had a spirited jam session with John playing the piano. And both brothers, like John, were funny and fun. They told marvelous stories of pranks played as twins throughout their lifetimes. I loved being a part of their family.

In addition to John's immediate family, I also acquired an extended family in John's three first cousins, all male, and all living in the Washington area. Al Church, a retired Navy Captain, had been headed for an Admiralty until in a moment of inattention he drove his ship into a pier. Dick Church was a much-decorated Marine Colonel, also retired. The most notable of the three was Frank Church, then U.S. Senator from Idaho. I never really liked Frank. I found it annoying that at cocktail parties, while he was supposedly conversing with me, I would find his eyes wandering over my shoulder looking for someone of greater interest. Also, though he never failed to ask about my children, I am quite sure that till the day he died he never knew how many I had. My greatest problem with Frank, however, was what I perceived as the damage he was doing to the CIA. In 1975 the Agency was under heavy fire from Congress. It was a time when the new leadership was placing greater value on technically acquired intelligence than that obtained by human efforts. Frank headed up the Senate's Intelligence Committee, and I blamed him for almost single handedly decimating the Agency of its most experienced officers. Also, in 1976 he made a brief run for the Presidency, and I felt he was using the high visibility of his CIA investigations as a stepping stone for his presidential bid. All that said, Frank never failed to make time for Church family gatherings, and whenever Memo was visiting he always had us for lunch at the Senate dining room. And for me, despite my criticism of Frank, it was rather nice being able to claim a U.S. Senator as a relative.

With my marriage to John came adjustments. First, we had to get rid of some of our belongings. When John moved into my house, it was not only his tools that came with him, it was also many of the things he and Bette had accumulated during their years overseas. Most of his furniture and household items had either been sold or claimed by his children when he sold *his* house in Bethesda, but what remained now filled the basement. Both Bette and I had been acquisitive shoppers, and many of the local crafts of the Far East that we had scooped up so zealously on our first arrival in those countries had now lost their appeal. We had to find a way to dispose of not only John's excess belongings, but also my own. We decided to go the flea market route. In the following weeks we made systematic trips to all the flea markets advertised in the Sunday papers to determine which one would be the most suitable for our things. Some were too junky, others too high-end. The one in the newly developed town of Columbia in Maryland was just right. It was held in a covered parking lot, and even in bad weather, in fact especially in bad weather, it would draw customers.

We reserved a two-car space in the parking garage and started sorting things for sale. This was hard work as everything had to be packed well enough to survive the long drive, and then unpacked at the site. People flocked to our tables filled with Asian crafts. Wood carvings, baskets, opera masks, Chinese scrolls, soapstone figures, coolie hats, and more. Plus of course the usual pots, pans, sheets, towels and just plain *stuff*. We were a compact version of Pier One Imports or World Market. We sold everything we brought, and made much more than expected. John started talking about our *next sale*. I said, "You're out of your mind. We don't have enough to go again," but he insisted that we did. Sure enough, after going through what was left in the basement, we started looking in our closets for things we never used. We also manufactured art work, cutting up old Chinese wall calendars—the paintings quite beautiful—and putting them in cheap black frames that had once held diplomas, citations, and old family pictures. In our selling zeal, we also almost sold several items that later became prized possessions. A carved fisherman with a fish dangling from a rod was one of these. When a customer asked if it was ivory, realizing with shock that it could well be, we hastily withdrew it. Today, when asking my children and grandchildren which of my possessions they would like me to leave them, they, one and all, want the fisherman. We also almost sold a pair of pewter candlesticks, which, though antiques, I had dismissed as rather crudely made and not worth keeping. However, once retrieved, I looked at them in a new light, and with candles lit each night, they became a regular part of our evening dinners. We went to the flea market three more times, each time disposing of most of what we had brought, and making several thousand dollars in the process.

The best thing about our flea-marketing experience was the good time we had doing it. Even on our first time out, other dealers, seeing that we seemed to specialize in oriental artifacts, started bringing us anything they had with an oriental flavor to ask our opinion. By the second time, they were sharing with us stories of their own experiences at working the flea markets. To most of them, flea-marketing was a way of life and they went from one city to another on a regular route. By the third time we were there, they were urging us to join them at their next stop. It was such fun getting to know these people from a different walk of life. We almost hated the thought they would be moving on without us.

Apart from his belongings, John brought with him his many talents, some of which were unknown to me. I already knew that he had a wonderful sense of humor, and that he was incomparable raconteur with an endless supply of good stories. I knew that he loved good food and that he was passionate about the theatre and about travel. I knew he was a musician. He had often pounded out popular songs "Chicago style" on the piano in our family room. From his many letters to me, I knew him also to be a beautiful writer. What I didn't know was how good he was in the kitchen. I had heard many times of how at the frat house where he lived in his college days he had been promoted from dishwasher to head cook. According to John, this promotion came about when someone had dropped off some windfall apples at the house and he had promptly baked six apple pies. I had always thought this was one of John's somewhat embellished stories and was absolutely delighted when I found a hot apple pie waiting for me one day when I got home from work. John had also worked at some point in his young life as a short order cook and was a whiz or at throwing together a hamburger or a BLT on short notice. These were always served up with the proper garnish, a toothpick piercing the sandwich with an olive or pearl onion, and some lettuce and tomato on the side.

Another thing I hadn't known before our marriage was the breadth and depth of John's scholarship. For he was a scholar, a perennial student, with an insatiable thirst for knowledge. He had a reserved carrel at the Library of Congress where he spent many hours researching any subject that captured his interest, from hagiography to the sex life of bees. He was a fount of knowledge, and for me it was like having a living, breathing encyclopedia always at my fingertips.

John brought so much into my life, and as I look back on our wedding day, I find myself wondering at the cavalier and irreverent attitude with which I had entered into our marriage. The words, "For better or worse. Till death do us part," had meant nothing to me at the time. They were words spoken, without intent. Yet, in the many years that followed, the thought of separation from John never once entered my mind. I could not imagine a life without him. Our marriage was long and happy.

Chapter 19
Discrimination and Frustration

While I was steadily moving forward in my career at the Agency, I was aware that further advancement would be difficult without an overseas assignment. At that time there were two career tracks within the Operations Directorate. One was as a reports officer whose duties were to analyze and evaluate foreign intelligence reports. This was basically a headquarters job. The other was as a case officer whose job it was to recruit and handle the foreign agents who could provide that intelligence. This could only be accomplished in the field. It was now 1976. Up until this time, with one child still in high school I had been happy to remain at headquarters, but now my youngest child had left for college and I was ready for an assignment overseas. I had no idea of the obstacles I would face.

During the next two years I sat at my desk supporting operations in the field and watching an assortment of case officers come in from their overseas assignments, serve as desk officers for a year or less, and then be reassigned to another station abroad. Few officers wanted to remain at Headquarters, for one could not recruit a foreign agent on U.S. soil (the domain of the FBI), and it was recruitments that were all-important for a case officer's advancement. Never mind how productive those recruited agents were; it was a numbers game. The more recruitments, the better one's record. In my case, though called upon again and again to go on TDYs to assist in given operations, and though I was a key part of the China Operations course given to outgoing officers, as well as regularly giving "guidance" to field stations on operations against Chinese targets, I was deemed to have "no operational experience."

While I was waiting patiently to be assigned abroad, I had to cope with the condescension of longtime friends, now risen in rank, who had once been Horace's colleagues. It was infuriating that to them I was still "Horace's wife," a social friend just dabbling at a job to keep busy. On one occasion, when I became quite emotional over what I considered unfair treatment, Bob C, then Chief of China Operations, actually said to me, "Marguerite, why don't you give this up and go home and take care of your children?" At the time I was so over-wrought that I did not think to ask him, "And who do you think will support my children and pay for their education?" Also, at meetings in which I was a participant, the then Chief of the East Asia Division, also a longtime personal friend, was consistently dismissive of my opinions. I would leave with the feeling that I had been patted on the head and told, "Run along now. That's a good girl."

It was during Bob C's reign as Chief of China Operations that I had first made the request for an overseas assignment. And it was under his aegis that I started compiling a list of my grievances for possible submission to the Inspector General. Slot after slot would open up in various overseas Stations and I was not even considered for the position. On other occasions, when an opening was available, I was asked to "prove myself" *before* being considered for the job. In Mexico City, I was sent on a TDY to demonstrate that I could make contact with Chinese officials. As in past TDY situations, I did this successfully, *proving* that I was capable of establishing contact. But that proof was not enough. I was taken out of consideration, ostensibly because I had been in correspondence with one of the Station's NOC officers (i.e. an officer under non-official cover), which, per the Station Chief's spurious logic, could have compromised the officer's cover. It was obvious to me that he was simply not willing to take on a middle-aged female ethnic Chinese officer.

The next possible opening was in Nairobi. I was asked to do a full analysis of the Chinese official presence in Nairobi as well as of the local Chinese community. I was also to propose several cover possibilities, the means of implementing each one, and to do full estimates on the costs of setting up these proprietary covers. I did extensive research on both tasks, only to receive a memo, "Please do a little more work on the Chinese officials—*all of them.*" That meant target studies on more than twenty Chinese officials. These assignments were above and beyond my normal duties. The end result? No assignment.

After Nairobi came Paris. This time the memo I received from the Chief of China Operations read, "You must provide me with an analysis of the China target in Paris and why your presence would likely make a difference beyond current staffing there." In the discussions that followed, I was again asked to do target studies on *all* the Chinese officials in Paris. I forget how many this entailed, but the official Chinese presence there was large. Given my past disappointments at obtaining an overseas assignment, I took this as just another stalling tactic. However, when I was sent to full-time French language training I thought that it was just possible I was under serious consideration even though no promises had been made, especially when my husband John too was enrolled.

There were two "Beginning French" classes running simultaneously. John and I were put it separate classes, both "Beginning French," the consensus being that spouses should be separated. In my class, the words "beginning French" were ludicrous. The other class members were two young men in their early thirties, and the wife of an officer who was scheduled for a Paris assignment. Roger B. had had two years of high school French and another two in college, Bill P. had had six years of French, two years in high school plus another four in college. Betty M. had graduated from college with Phi Beta Kappa honors, had been stationed with her husband in French-speaking Quebec for four years. With my miserable two years of high school French over thirty years ago, I had a harrowing and stressful time keeping up with my classmates. I did, however, do exceptionally well, but despite this, was pulled out of the course six weeks before its completion. It seems the Paris slot for which I had been led to believe I was being considered had suddenly been filled by another officer. I was never given a full explanation. It was just another disappointment added to the last one.

But this time I was not about to let the five months of full-time French go to waste. I requested a month's leave without pay, which, surprisingly was granted—I suspect there was some guilt on the part of management—and John and I took off for Paris. Whatever places we visited, John always made reservations for our first night, always in low-end hotels, but always with a private bath. From there, we scouted out our next night's accommodations. In Paris, we found one charming tiny out-of-the-way hotel where we stayed for a week, but in walking around the various parts of the city, we found others even lovelier that were totally irresistible. We stayed in four different hotels, a week in each, each one more charming than the last. And we used our French. These hotels were not for American tourists. At two, they spoke no English at all, and several times the desk clerk would call on us to come to the phone to talk to would-be English-speaking customers. We also signed in immediately with the Alliance Francaise and continued our French lessons. We joined French-speaking tour groups organized by the Alliance. Though we were accustomed to traveling on the cheap, we had intended to splurge on one five-star meal while in Paris, but found the food so good even in the most unlikely looking restaurants, that we never even made it to a one-star restaurant. We had such a wonderful time in this beautiful city that it almost made up for the loss of the Paris assignment.

It was now the summer of 1978. My performance reviews declared me to be "head and shoulders above her peers" and "one of China Operations' most effective officers," but two years after putting in my request for an overseas assignment, nothing had materialized. Many in China Operations were aware of my frustrations and the difficulties I was facing. In their experience no other officers had ever been asked to *prove* they were capable of making contact with foreign targets *before* being given an assignment. No others had been asked to explain why she could do better than current staffing. No others had ever been asked to make full studies of the officials in a foreign country *before* being assigned to that country. In preparation for taking my case to the Inspector General, I started documenting all the evidences of unfair tasking that I had confronted. I recognized the risks involved, that going to the IG could be the end of my career, but believed I had a clear-cut case of discrimination. While I was embroiled in my own battles, I had not even considered the problems other women might be having. I know that shortly after I retired in 1987, a group of over twenty women filed suit against the CIA citing sexual discrimination. They won their suit and received a sum in financial compensation. As for me, if I had taken my case before the IG, I believe I would have had a rock-solid case based on three counts of discrimination: sex, race, *and* age. However, before I took my case to the IG, another overseas slot opened up, this one in New Zealand, and I thought I would give it one last try.

As soon as I heard that there was an opening at the Wellington Station I put in my request. The following week I received a call from the personnel officer in China Operations. He asked me to stop by to see him. I thought, "surely it's too early for any kind of decision." When I entered his office, he rose and closed the door behind him. "I probably shouldn't be telling you this, but I thought you had a right to know," he said. I must have looked perplexed for he continued. "Yesterday a back-channel cable went out on you from Bob W. on the Australia/New Zealand desk. I think it only fair that you should see it."

Whatever it was, I knew it couldn't be good or this young officer would not be telling me this behind closed doors. Since it had been sent "back-channel" it was obviously not intended for my eyes.

"What did it say? Was it bad?" I asked.

"You need to see it," was all he said.

"You know, if I ask to see the cable it will mean a confrontation. And what if Bob W. won't show it to me?"

"It's up to you," he said. "You can request it under the Freedom of Information Act."

I knew he was right. But how bad could the message possibly be? And what did I have to gain by seeing it? "Let me think about it," I said. I thanked him for letting me know. I knew he had put himself out on a limb for me, someone he hardly knew. As I left, his words followed me: "You need to see it."

I didn't think about it for long. After all, what *did* I have to lose? The next morning I went in to see Bob W and asked to see the cable. He frowned, and as expected, refused to show it to me. "In that case," I said, "I will file a formal request to see the document under the Freedom of Information Act." Bob heaved a sigh. "I won't show you the cable but I'll read you the relevant parts." With that, he read aloud: "This fifty-three-year-old ethnic Chinese woman is a widow of a XXXXX, (*a denigrating term for an ethnic Chinese language transcriber),* and is now married to a box operator. She has no ops experience." He refused to read further, but the wording was insulting to Horace, dismissive of John, and disparaging of me. The cable's intent had clearly been to remove me from any possible consideration for the job in Wellington. I wondered what even more pejorative words were in the cable that Bob W had been unwilling to divulge. But what I had heard was enough. I asked, "Did this go out with the approval of China Operations?" He replied, "Yes, it was approved by Bill G." (Bill G was then Chief of China Operations.) I knew where my next stop would be.

The next morning, when I walked into Bill G's office, I spoke up before he had a chance to say a word. I was calm, composed, and totally in command of myself. "Mr. G, I think you know why I am here. I just want to say that I will be terribly disappointed if you tell me that you saw and approved the outgoing message to Wellington about me." His quick response was, "No, I did not actually *see* the message, but I did approve the gist of it, which I was told stated that you were inappropriate for the job." He continued. "I have since seen the message in its entirety and find the wording unfortunate. But, Marguerite, the job is way beneath your capabilities and it is *not* an appropriate job for you. You are completely overqualified for it." To which I replied, "And why in two years have I not been given an assignment for which I *am* qualified?" To that he did not have a ready response, and I went on. "Mr. G, my performance review declared me to be "head and shoulders above her peers," yet I have been kept at Headquarters while those peers, whom I am *head and shoulders above* have been given choice assignments." I could have gone on to plead my case further, but at this point he stopped me. "Marguerite, I repeat, the Wellington job is not for you, but I will personally find you an assignment that is fitting for your qualifications. Trust me. I will find you a job."

What more could I say? Was he to be believed, or was this just another stalling tactic? I would give it a few months, and if nothing materialized I was prepared to go to the IG. I had never verbalized my intentions, but I was told by a colleague that at a personnel meeting, one of my former supervisors, speaking up forcefully on my behalf, had said, "She would be completely justified in taking her case to the IG, and if she does, she has a solid case." Meanwhile, I went about my normal duties. A few weeks after my meeting with Bill G. I was enrolled in the Senior Operations course. This was a good sign. This could be in preparation for an overseas assignment.

The Senior Ops course was a refresher course for mid-career officers. It was a one-week course held at "the farm," the Agency's principal training site. Of the twelve people in the course I was the only woman. I was also the only one who had not been through the Basic Operations course. Basic Ops was a six-week program in operational trade craft required of all career officers. They were usually enrolled soon after they began work at the Agency. For them, the Senior Ops course was merely a refresher, but for me, not having had Basic Ops, everything was new. However, though I was slower than most in completing certain tasks, and was often one of the last to leave the classroom, I acquitted myself well. I was good at all the exercises that required manual dexterity; was absolutely terrific at microchips and making keys. I did well at charting drop locations and was able to make several successful "drops" without being detected. The one thing I could not do, even after many attempts, was to throw an object out of a fast-moving car at a given spot. Any agent trying to retrieve a message or object thrown by me would have had a hard time locating it.

This course was memorable for me, not only because I now felt I was really in the James Bond spy world, but also because of one particular incident. It was a training exercise in evading surveillance. Our group was divided into pairs and sent off in separate cars. Since you were never to let the surveillants know you were aware of being followed, it was important to behave in as natural a way as possible. My partner and I were the only boy/girl team and it seemed natural to behave as a couple on a date. We were driving along the parkway and pulled into a scenic outlook where we parked for about half an hour. There was no sign of anyone following us. We were pretty sure we had lost them, but continuing as a couple might normally do, we went into town and spent about an hour and a half at a small snack bar. Still no sign of anyone following us. We were quite pleased with ourselves, thinking we had completed our mission of evading surveillance successfully. We then went back to our individual quarters for a good night's sleep. The next morning, however, instead of being congratulated for our success, we were met by three disgruntled training officers. They had been trailing us in three separate cars. When they lost us on the Parkway, each car in turn had made a u-turn across the median strip, and each one had been picked up by the local police. They were not happy, blaming us for their misfortune instead of their own stupidity.

A few weeks later—it was now early November 1978—I was summoned to the office of the Chief of China Operations. As I entered, Bill G was all smiles. "Marguerite, I've found you a slot I think you'll be happy with," he said. I waited expectantly. "It's in Sydney, Australia. You would go out as a NOC, under retiree cover. How does that sound?" Of course it sounded wonderful to me. He had said he would find me a slot and he had. I was grateful and I told him so. "There's only one problem," he added. I thought immediately, "Oh-oh, now comes the hitch." I wondered what it would be this time. "You'll have to be there before Christmas." This was a stunner. Was it intended as just another obstacle in my path? If I said I couldn't make it by then, would it be another reason for denying me the assignment? I wasn't going to let that happen. I assured him, "that's not a problem." With a few more words on processing procedures, I left Bill G's office, this time confident that I was on my way.

Chapter 20
The NOC in Sydney

Early in December 1978 John and I departed for my first overseas assignment in Sydney, Australia. I would be under non official cover, referred to within the Agency as a NOC. At the time, Australia was being viewed as a tempting retirement locale for those seeking a slower pace of life than in America. My husband and I would be ostensibly among those who had decided to make Australia our retirement home. Since John was legitimately retired and looked the part, the retiree role provided a plausible reason for our being in Sydney. It provided what in operational parlance was called "cover for status." However, the role did not provide the equally if not more important "cover for access." As a civilian retiree, I would not have the natural access to foreign government officials that was enjoyed by officers under diplomatic cover. I would have to develop those contacts on my own.

For most officers a NOC assignment was not the job of choice. NOCs lived and worked alone. They had no contact with Headquarters until the end of their tours, their only contact being through their inside officer. Neither did they have the benefit of logistical support or the social interchange with fellow Americans under official cover. Most important, if, for whatever reason, they were accused of espionage, the CIA would disclaim the connection. Many, who had begun their careers with the CIA as NOCs, discouraged by the social isolation, often requested that they be brought back into the official fold. For me, this might have been a problem if I had been in a country where

I did not speak the language, but in Australia I was quite sure that John and I could find friends among the local population. Also, I knew that I had been given the assignment under duress, and that the Sydney slot had been created expressly for me under the threat, never articulated, that I would take my case to the IG. I suspected also, despite my excellent record as a Headquarters officer, that little was expected of me in the field. Sydney was not exactly fertile ground for recruitments. Most foreign government officials, our prime targets, were located in the Capital city of Canberra.

In Sydney, the Agency had only a miniscule presence: one man, Kent L, and a secretary. I saw Kent three times shortly after our arrival. The first was purely social, when he invited John and me to his home to meet his family. The second was to provide me with logistical guidelines on getting settled in Sydney. The third was to pass on to me all the information he had on the official Chinese presence in Sydney. This was sparse. He gave me the address of the Chinese commercial office, my principal target, and the name and address of the Australian company that handled their commercial transactions. He also provided me with the name of the leading local Chinese Communist in Australia, Arthur Wang. That was the sum total of information obtained from Kent. Henceforth I would see him once a month at designated out-of-the way locales to report on my progress. All my reports would be passed to him on film. He would relay what he deemed relevant to Headquarters. I was on my own to make what I could of my assignment. I could not help noting that at no point did he indicate that the timing of my arrival in Sydney had any bearing on the job. It was apparent to me that the requirement that I be there before Christmas had been another contrived reason to deny me the assignment if I had said I couldn't manage it.

In short order John and I located a lovely apartment in Woolloomooloo, just a mile from Sydney's central business district and equally close to King's Cross, a tourist must-see area filled with restaurants, boutiques, and trendy night spots. Sydney was a beautiful city, and even if my tour of duty work-wise turned out to be a total fiasco, I knew we were going to enjoy our stay. Once we were settled, I had to get down to work. My first order of business was to get access to the Chinese Commercial Office. It was obvious to me that to do this I would have to develop some kind of commercial activity. Though ostensibly a retiree, it would be quite plausible that I could also be looking for some way to augment a limited retirement income. The cover story I decided upon was that I wanted to start a small business importing decorative items from China. As a total business novice I would seek help from the Chinese Commercial office in how to get started.

At the commercial office I was received by a Madame Chang. My story was readily accepted, and Madame Chang couldn't have been more helpful in answering my questions. First, I needed to know what offices in China I should contact. This she provided readily. I held back on other questions, and in the weeks that followed, doled out my questions piecemeal, feigning helplessness and ineptitude in order to set up reasons for further contact. The questions, however, could not go on forever. Finally, I had to proceed with placing an order. I had already decided that my first purchase would be for silk wall screens. I forwarded pictures of various screens to the appropriate Chinese government entity that handled arts and crafts. My first order was for ten wall screens. The total cost was U.S. $600. I then sat back and waited for the screens to arrive. My meetings with Madame Chang had to date been strictly business, but it was my hope that eventually they would evolve into a personal relationship.

At the same time that I was working on Madame Chang, I also visited Kemper & Co., the Australian company that handled the Chinese commercial shipments, again with questions about shipping procedures. There, I met with a young Australian-Chinese, Richard Lee, with whom I developed instant rapport. John and I later became fast friends of both Richard and his wife Marilyn and with both their families. Through Richard, we also met Australia's leading Chinese Communist, Arthur Wang. Thus, within a few months I had already gained access to two of the Chinese Commercial Office's major contacts. If there were more, I was determined to find them. I even embarked on totally unneeded acupuncture treatments when I learned from Madame Chang that she and others in her office were patients of a local Chinese acupuncturist. I used my nasal allergies as a reason for my visits. The treatments did not help my allergies, but they allowed me to develop a relationship with yet another person who might have useful information on my Chinese targets. We exchanged dinner invitations several times, but the acupuncturist did not prove to be a source of anything useful. John and I also both enrolled in Cantonese lessons in Sydney's Chinatown, with the hope that immersion in the local Chinese scene might be an additional bridge to Chinese officials. Though we made several pleasant social contacts, this proved to be another wasted effort. The officials simply did not mix with the local Chinese population. However, the familiarity we developed with this group led to our being asked to help in the casting of the movie, "A Town Called Alice," at the time being filmed in Australia. Asian faces were needed for many of the scenes and our friends and acquaintances were more than happy to participate. I would have loved to join them, but did not think it wise to draw any public attention to myself. Still, it was exciting to have been a small part of the movie scene, and for us it was quite gratifying to later see our friends in the film.

While I was working on establishing relationships with anyone with whom my targets might be in contact, John was off enjoying the benefits of being retired. He wanted to see Australia, and not long after we arrived, he signed up for a camel trip to the Outback. I would have liked to join him on this trip, and even though it would have been an acceptable activity for a supposed retiree, I was not about to have anyone later accuse me of abusing my cover status for my own pleasure. John's trip, however, proved to be more useful to me than I could possibly have hoped. In the small group with which he was traveling was a young woman, Laura Danson, who John quickly learned was the secretary to the Australia/China Friendship Society. Her family members were all confirmed socialists and strong believers in China's Communist cause. Her mother, Jane Danson, had been the first Australian to visit China after the Communist takeover in 1949, and pictures of her standing with Mao Tsetung and holding his "Little Red Book" aloft were publicized widely in the Australian press. Laura, on learning that John's wife was Chinese, wanted her family to meet me. What a marvelous stroke of luck! And I had not even had to seek them out. It was *they* who wanted to meet *me*.

When we did get together, it was again instant rapport. The Dansons were working-class people, father and two sons both doing construction work, but they had a strong intellectual bent and were extremely well read. They took particularly to John, who could more than match them in knowledge on any given subject. The Dansons' home was a frequent gathering place for students from China, and we were immediately included among them. Chinese students were not a primary target for the Agency, but they were still of definite interest, particularly if they were members of the Communist Party, or were in scientific or technological fields of study. Our friendship with the Dansons provided us with frequent access to Chinese students. Soon the students were coming to our apartment for dinner and often helping with the cooking. One seemed older and more mature than the others and was of particular operational interest because he had let drop that he was a Communist Party member. He was fascinated by our kitchen gadgets, especially the blender. When we gathered to make *chiao tze* together, he assumed almost a proprietary manner in demonstrating to newcomers how he could chop cabbage in the blender without resorting to manual effort. He was so proud that he was familiar with all these American gadgets.

Through Laura Danson we were readily admitted as members of the Australia/Chinese Friendship Society, and were thus included in all cultural interchanges between the two countries. We became a part of the social events the group routinely hosted for visiting Chinese officials. In this capacity John and I were invited, *by name*, by the Chinese government to visit China as part of a cultural exchange program. This was a huge feather in my operational cap, for to the best of my knowledge no other CIA officer under whatever cover had ever received a personal invitation from the Chinese government before.

However, I was doubtful that I would be allowed to go. Though I was an American citizen, to the Chinese I held dual nationality. Once in China, to them I was Chinese, and if for any reason, they should detain me, I would be beyond help from the U.S. government. Headquarters decided I could not go. But even if Headquarters had approved, I doubt that John would have allowed me to make the trip. And I too was reminded of the imprisonment of a family friend by the Communist government in the early fifties. She was a Chinese-American, and had been working as a secretary at the British Embassy in Beijing. Her crime? That she would not help the Communist government in breaking the British code. She had been imprisoned for seven years.

While I was busy establishing myself as a friend of China, I also had to maintain the illusion that I was in the importing business. The ten screens I had ordered arrived. All were 36" x 72" paintings on silk, mounted on wooden frames. Two were copies of the pictures I had sent, one a landscape, another a floral scene. Both copies were good. Six others were acceptable and I felt sure I could find a store that would take them if the price were right. Two, however, were of women in Mao suits overlooking fields of grain, looking very much like Communist propaganda posters. I doubted I could sell them at any price. They were a total loss, but the others I sold quite easily, at very low prices to department stores and small gift stores. The "business" had accomplished its purpose of providing contact with a Chinese official, but for all my efforts I had not been able to establish a meaningful personal relationship with Madame Chang. I had not been in a position to determine if she was in any way vulnerable to recruitment. She and her husband did, however, accept a dinner invitation to our apartment. Anticipating that she would want to know who else might be attending, I had invited Richard Lee and Arthur Wang and their wives. I felt sure that Richard, whose company handled the Chinese commercial shipments, and Arthur, already well known for his Communist ties, would be politically palatable and non-threatening to the Changs. The evening was pleasant, but uneventful. It was disappointing that the Changs did not reciprocate, but for me it was something of an achievement that they had accepted our invitations at all.

Throughout the two years I was in Sydney I typed up detailed reports of all my activities. These I stored in a concealment compartment built ingeniously into a piece of furniture provided by the Agency. Not until I was ready for my once-a-month meetings with Kent, my inside officer, did I photograph the reports and deliver them to him on a single roll of film. Other than a ridiculous-looking wig and a pair of equally ridiculous dark glasses, the concealment device was the only object of "spyware" I was provided with. All my meetings with Kent were in person in out-of-the-way restaurants. Other than the process of photographing my reports, I never had to make use of any of the tradecraft I had learned in the Senior Ops course.

In Sydney, I was working in true name, not in alias, and thus had no need for most of the alias documentation that had always been provided for my past temporary duty assignments. However, since Headquarters wanted to disassociate me from the Washington scene, I *was* given a new home address in Maryland and provided with a Maryland driving license, a local library card, and a few other miscellaneous cards tying me to my supposed city of residence. Also, I was assigned a new pseudonym. My past pseudonym, used in all cable traffic, had been so long that it stretched across the page each time I had to sign my name. This time I had requested a short one and was delighted when I was given the name Lola Jay. A bank account, into which my pay checks would be forwarded was opened in that name. Unfortunately, some inattentive finance officer made the deposit of my very first pay check to that account, not to Lola Jay, but instead to Marguerite Church. The new pseudo was considered compromised. A new one was issued, and a new account was opened in the new pseudo.

Throughout my Sydney tour I had no contact with Headquarters. As a NOC, all my activities had been reported to Headquarters through my inside officer. However, before the end of my tour I would have a single opportunity to speak on my own behalf and to submit an evaluation of my own performance, this to be transmitted verbatim by my inside officer to Headquarters. In writing my self-evaluation I did not downplay my failings, chief of which had been that I had not been able to recruit either a Chinese official or a student, or to identify any vulnerabilities that might lead to a successful recruitment. However, I stressed that on my arrival in Sydney I had almost no help from my inside officer, and none at all from Headquarters, and yet, through my own efforts was able to gain extended access to both the Chinese official presence in Sydney and to the Chinese student body. With a minimal order of ten wall screens at a miniscule cost to the U.S. government of only $600, I not only created my own cover as a business-woman/retiree, but used that cover to establish my business credentials with the Chinese Commercial office in Sydney and with the local China-friendly community. The fact that I had been invited by the Chinese government to visit China, and that Chinese officials had actually attended a dinner party at my apartment, were additional evidence of my having achieved acceptance in Chinese eyes.

The above was the gist of a lengthy submission. While working at Headquarters I had been privy to operations against Chinese targets in other parts of the world, and unless there had been significant break-throughs to this still impregnable Chinese target, I knew I had done well by comparison. If I had not recruited a Chinese official, neither had any other officer. I felt I had done particularly well in setting up my business-woman cover, and at such a low cost, especially in comparison to the enormous sums often spent in setting up entire cover businesses for other NOCs. But more important than my own opinion was that of the Australian liaison service. I had been working in Sydney for just a year when our Chief of Station, in his annual summation of Agency activities in Australia had quoted what Australian liaison had said of me. "She has accomplished more against the China target in six months than we have in six years." Those words had me floating on air for days. My exhilaration knew no bounds. Furthermore, they stated that my contact reports, routinely passed on to them, were the best they had ever read. They wanted to meet me. They invited me to their headquarters in Melbourne where they sent me roses, and wined and dined me for two days. For me, this recognition by the Australian Intelligence service was the high point of my tour. Their praise was extra sweet for me as I was reminded of the words of Bill G. when telling me I was not the right person for the job in New Zealand. "I doubt that you would be able to get along with liaison," he had said. Well, I had proved him wrong, and that I was more than able to get along with liaison services.

The tour in Sydney was a good one for me. I had done my best against the China target, but I could not see that I could do more. Also, the head of the Australia/Chinese Friendship Society, soon to retire from his job as a local bank president, was pressing me for advice on doing business with China. I had successfully led him and others to believe that I was doing a thriving business with China, but would have had a hard time maintaining this fiction. It was time to go.

Quite apart from my work, Sydney had been a great experience for both John and me. As an ostensible retiree, without having to fulfill the duties of a normal cover job, I had plenty of leisure time to enjoy Australia. We had of course seen the major tourist sights: Ayers Rock, by which I was not impressed; the Great Barrier Reef; Sydney itself, with its famed opera house, beautiful harbor, and gorgeous beaches. John had had his camel trip to the Outback, but it was a "must see" for me also. We went by train, along the way seeing signs for auto travelers that warned not to travel without carrying food and water for *three* days. That was the length of time it might be for another car to appear. We saw dead animals, so hideously bloated that they resembled huge rubber inflatables. I had never seen such dry, desolate countryside, but I was glad I had seen it. We had also taken trips to New Zealand and to Bali, where we had been lucky enough to come upon an elaborate funeral procession and to see first hand the impressive cremation ceremony. During our tour we had also been able to host John's son for a week-long visit, and also my two sons.

Once we made the decision to leave, our cover story—that we had chosen to retire in Australia—had to be rescinded. To the good friends we had made, we had to explain that much as we loved Australia, the distance from our children was a greater hardship for them and for us than we had anticipated. We were truly sorry to be leaving our two sets of good friends, the Dansons and the Lees, but we would keep in touch with them for many years. We left Sydney in the summer of 1981 with big plans for our return trip to the U.S.

Chapter 21
Disowned

For the sixteen years that Horace and I lived in Asian countries, I was always asked by friends to shop for them. Through the years I bought jewelry, porcelains, screens, and all kinds of other decorative objects for any number of friends. They always liked my purchases, and I was confident in my buying abilities. But now, having successfully sold the few screens I had ordered from China, I had also tried my hand at selling. It had not been too difficult. For years I had wanted to try my hand at business, specifically in importing decorative accessories from the Far East. Now seemed like a good time to get started. We were already in the area. We could do our buying on our return trip to the U.S. at minimal personal expense. The government would of course pay for our direct flight home, and we would only have the extra cost of the circuitous route we would be taking to the countries from which we would be buying. John was fully supportive of a business venture, as long as we would not be involved in running a store. I completely agreed. Paying for rent, utilities, and worst of all, having to be physically present to man a store was not what either of us had in mind. We would be importers only; our market would be gift stores.

John and I decided we would each put $5000 into the venture. In forming our new company we decided that a Chinese name would lend it authenticity. We decided to use my maiden name. We had business cards printed with the name of our new company, M. Chien & Co. We would do our major buying in Thailand, Taiwan, Hong

Kong, and Japan, focusing on items suitable for sale in American gift stores. We did make a brief stop in the Philippines to visit an old friend from my Peking days, but there, only the capiz shell items appealed to us. The bowls, plates, and bathroom items made of these lovely iridescent shells were beautiful to look at, but were extremely fragile. However, despite our concerns about how well they would survive in shipment, we took a gamble and placed a small order.

In each of our next stops, we went first to the Chamber of Commerce where we browsed through brochure after brochure of

Capiz shell items

local manufacturers. We then visited each factory carrying items of interest, comparing quality and prices. Having in the past always paid retail prices at gift stores, we were pleasantly surprised to find how much lower factory

prices were. In Bangkok, we bought blue and white porcelains, small black and gold lacquer boxes, pendants of porcelain shards framed in silver, brass items with rosewood handles, all these quite commonly seen in Bangkok's gift stores. What we had never seen before were the unusual animals carved of jamjuriwood, a local wood as heavy as iron. The horses, deer, geese, and others, glistening with mirror shards, or encrusted with bits of colored glass were spectacular. Shipping costs would be high, but we bought several of each.

Returning to Taipei was like old home week. We headed straight for the factories we had identified from the brochures at the Chamber of Commerce. We ordered silk wall screens and copies of antique Chinese paintings encased in acrylic. Also, cinnabar boxes and vases, copies made of some synthetic material, but indistinguishable from the real thing. Seeing Taipei after a twelve-year absence was a shock.

What had once had the feel of a small Asian town, was now a concrete jungle. The once charming Grand Hotel with its rows of single rooms, had been enlarged upward and outward into a monstrous edifice, though still with its oriental design. What was most disappointing was the disappearance of the street vendors. John had gotten up early hoping to find a vendor selling hot *shao bing*, the delicious sesame buns commonly eaten for breakfast, only to be told that the delivery truck had come and gone. Gone were the street vendors who baked and sold *shao bing* piping hot from their own carts.

Our next stop was Hong Kong. I was so looking forward to seeing Horace's family again. It had been a long time since I had seen them. We would be staying with Horace's sister Ida and her husband Y.K.in their new apartment.—their former house had been torn down and replaced with a seven-story apartment building. They both came to the airport to meet us. Y. K., who had been at our wedding and had of course met John, was effusive in his welcome. I was not surprised that Ida was more restrained. But it was when we arrived at their apartment that I became stunningly aware that something was wrong. When the apartment door opened, I was greeted by the beaming face of one of the amahs who had worked for us for two years when we had been in Hong Kong back in the fifties. She could hardly contain herself with joy at seeing me and rushed forward to greet me, addressing me as *Kam Nai*, my title in the old days, meaning mistress's brother's wife. But hardly before the words were out, Ida abruptly corrected her. *"Chiu Tai,"* she said. Whereupon, Ah Oi shamefacedly repeated, *"Chiu Tai,"* and backed away. *"Chiu Tai"* was the equivalent of "Mrs. Church." The same thing happened when the old amah, Ah Ting, who had known me since I first came to Hong Kong as barely more than a bride, came rushing out to greet me. With a big broad smile spread across her face, she greeted me with the title, *"Kam Nai,"* and once again was corrected with a frown by Ida. She too, clearly embarrassed, repeated after Ida, *"Chiu Tai,"* and backed away. In less than five minutes I knew where I stood. I was no longer a member of the family. I cannot describe the hurt I felt. I didn't know what to say to John. He would not have noticed the significance of the way the amahs had addressed me or the nature of Ida's reproofs, but he couldn't have failed to see their beaming and excited smiles on seeing me replaced so suddenly by hangdog retreats. To John I said only, "It looks like I've been disowned by the family." Ida had not only made it clear to her servants that I was no longer 'family," but had also instructed her children that they were henceforth to call me Mrs. Church instead of *Kam Mo* (aunt, specifically mother's brother's wife) as they had in the past. To this, all three children resisted. From their childhood they had known me only as *Kam Mo,* and to them, *Kam Mo* I would remain. Today, Ida and Y.K.'s daughter Patsy is the only one of the children who lives in the U.S. She lives in New York and makes a point of keeping in touch, always addressing me as *Kam Mo* even though she is now a senior citizen herself. She calls John, Uncle John.

Despite having made it abundantly clear that I was not longer family, for the rest of our visit, all the correct things were done for us. Ida and Y.K. hosted a Chinese dinner for us with all the closest relatives and friends invited. Margaret and P.W. had us over to their house for dinner. They, and the other sisters and spouses were very warm and welcoming. It was as if the incident at Ida's house had never happened. I felt a bit better. The three amahs in Margaret and P.W.'s household, like Ida's two, had come rushing out, all welcoming smiles, to greet me. They had called me *"Kam Nai"* as in the past. They had not been corrected by Margaret or P.W. I thought, "perhaps it is only Ida who was disowning me."

But that was not the case. Some time later, after we were resettled in the U.S., I learned from Patsy that Margaret and P.W. had visited New York and stayed for a full six months without so much as a phone call to me. Also, Horace's third sister Weiping and her husband had actually been in Washington and had not even called. I didn't care about Weiping, with whom I had never established much rapport, but Margaret and P.W. I had loved as if they were my own family, and I had always thought they loved me. Their failure to contact me was hurtful. Tears came to my eyes every time I thought of it. Later, when Ida and Y.K.'s son Tom and his wife Lydia came to

Washington for a visit, Lydia told me that at the family gathering to discuss my remarriage, Y.K. was the only one who had come to my defense. "She's a young woman. You can't expect her to live alone the rest of her life," he insisted. But that was exactly what the others *had* expected. To them, I had been unfaithful to their brother's memory.

Looking back, I remembered Ida's words to me when she visited me in Taipei immediately after Horace's death. "You are more than a sister to me," she had said. But I remembered too her words to me a year later when she and Y.K. had visited us in America. When I had told her how lonely life was without Horace, she had said, "But you have the children." To her, children were enough to replace a husband. But I had been so sure of the love Horace's family had for me. As his widow I remember the amazing support I received when I discovered a lump in my breast. When the lump was first discovered, I was told that the chances of its being cancerous were only one in seven, but once in the hospital I was told the chances were one in four. Then, just before the surgery, a woman came to see me to discuss prosthetics. I had been trying to think positively, but that brought home to me what I might be facing. I was worried. I had three children to raise. Seeking no more than moral support, I had confided earlier in Horace's youngest sister Moping who was then living in Santa Monica, California. When I awoke from the anaesthetic, I found both Moping and her husband Ed at my bedside. They had flown from California to be there for me in case I was diagnosed with breast cancer. Luckily, the lump in my breast was benign, but that was how much they cared for me, their brother's widow. But now, I had to accept the fact that it was their brother's *wife* they had loved, and then their brother's *widow*. Had they ever loved the person that was *me*? And if they had, how could that love have been turned off like a spigot?

Both before and after Horace's death, my point of contact with the family had always been through Ida, but following my marriage to John, my relationship with Ida and Y.K. was limited to an infrequent correspondence. Y. K., who came to New York on business frequently, always called to say hello. Also, Ida, who happened to be in New York when my daughter Kathy was married, did make a point of coming to her wedding. Of the four sisters, it was Margaret and her husband P.W., who had always heaped me with the most praise and expressed most often what I had thought was their love for me. Their rejection was the most hurtful. Moping and Ed were another story. I had always felt closest to Moping and somehow always felt that her "disowning" me was made under family pressure. John and I had one wonderful visit with them in their Santa Monica home after our marriage, at which not only I, but John too, felt we were very much a part of the family. But through the years, it has been Patsy, Ida and Y.K.'s daughter, who has kept in constant touch by phone, checking up on my welfare and reporting on news of the family. All Horace's sisters and their spouses are now gone, so it matters not what my status is or was. But the rejection so many years ago was devastating then, and even now is a painful memory.

John and I stayed in Hong Kong for a full week and continued on our buying spree. We bought many items that made use of semi-precious stones: desk sets, hand-mirrors, and stamp boxes. We also bought terra cotta figures, copies of antique porcelains, and lacquered leather "wedding boxes" in several sizes. We were well pleased with our purchases, and our successful shopping made up in some small measure for the family's rejection.

From Hong Kong we went on to Japan, stopping only for a day in Tokyo to identify the best city to go for porcelains. I cannot remember the name of the city, but there we found beautiful dishes, bowls, and vases. Unfortunately, many of the choicest designs were already under contract to Gumps, the exclusive oriental gift store in San Francisco and could not be sold to other buyers. Still, we were able to find many beautiful pieces that we liked and I was sure would sell. By now we had spent our full $10,000 on merchandise. We also had additional expenses for hotels and meals and therefore looked for inexpensive accommodations. The Chamber of Commerce in Tokyo was helpful in that regard and steered us to what they called "business hotels." The rooms, w*ith* private bath, were modular units made entirely of vinyl. They were very small, but had everything a traveler could possibly need: two single beds with bedside table in between with good lighting, two comfortable chairs flanking a table that could double as a desk, again with good lighting. In the bathroom, the washbasin, toilet, and shower were encompassed in a single modular unit also. And in the hallway, a vending machine with full, hot Japanese meals in tin boxes. So efficient, and so inexpensive compared to any hotel we had ever stayed in. We were mightily impressed. Japan was our last buying stop. Except for the painful rejection from Horace's family, it had been a good trip. We were ready to go home.

Chapter 22
The Entrepreneur

Long before we left for Sydney in November of 1978, John and I were thinking of moving to a townhouse. With the children gone, we thought we could do with less space and also dispense with taking care of the garden. Unfortunately, at the time, most townhouses within our price range did not come with garages. However, years before, while visiting an open house in a townhouse community in Mclean, we had seen four townhouses *with* garages. We liked the floor plans and kept the brochures. None of them were on the market at the time, but before leaving for Sydney, I wrote to each of the four house owners explaining that we would be interested in buying if they were ever ready to sell. We gave them the address of our lawyer, through whom they could contact us, and thought no more about it. However, just three months before we left Sydney, a letter from our lawyer informed us he had been contacted by one of the owners. They were ready to sell. Through the lawyer, negotiations were made, and we bought the house, sight unseen.

This time, on our return to the United States in the summer of 1981 there was no fanfare. John and I went straight to the Holiday Inn near our Vienna house. We were so eager to see our new house in McLean that we stopped there before even checking out the condition of our old house in Vienna. As we walked through its rooms we were both pleased that we had made the decision to buy. The house was in immaculate condition and had obviously been well cared for. We knew its layout, but had had no idea what the garden was like. Now, we stepped through the living room's French doors onto a charming shaded garden. Its center was paved, but its corners were filled with pachysandra, ajuga, and periwinkle, all no-care groundcover. We couldn't have been happier with our new home. Our pleasure, however, was short-lived when we saw the condition of our old home in Vienna. It was a disaster. We had rented it to the Spanish Naval Attaché who we assumed would be entertaining frequently and would therefore keep the house in good order. Unfortunately, we were wrong. Our tenants, no doubt having had servants in Spain, seemed to have had no experience at housecleaning. The kitchen floor and the hardwood floors on the main level looked as if they had not been cleaned in the two and a half years we had been away. The wall-to-wall carpeting in the rest of the house was badly soiled. Even worse was the garden. Weeds had taken over the flower beds, and the lawn was almost totally crabgrass. We paid a cleaning crew to do the floors, but the carpeting was beyond cleaning and had to be completely replaced. We put the house on the market as soon as it looked habitable and put it behind us. We then settled happily into our new home and I returned to work.

Once again back at Headquarters I picked up where I had left off before the Sydney tour. I was once again providing support and guidance to officers in the field working against the China target. This time I was not champing at the bit looking for another overseas assignment. The fight for the Sydney tour had been too emotionally draining for me to want to go through that again. I was willing and content to stay in a desk job, and I was looking forward to embarking on our business venture.

However, with a full time job at the Agency, I was wondering how I could handle both job and business simultaneously when I heard of an opening in the Duty Office of the Operations Directorate. It was a shift job, three shifts per day: one 8:00 AM to 4:00, one 4:00 to midnight, and one midnight to 8:00 AM. It sounded perfect. I normally did not go to bed until midnight, so on the days I had the 4:00 to midnight shift I would have a full day to do the selling. I applied for the job even though the job slot was for a GS-14—I was only a GS-13 at the time—and doubted I would even be considered. However, I was pleasantly surprised when I was asked to come up for an interview, and even more pleased to find that the head of the Duty Office was an officer with whom I had worked on a case. We had worked well together; he had confidence in me, and I was taken on.

A duty officer (DO) works a week on each shift, rotating with two other officers. The officer is accompanied by a secretary. The job is not difficult, but it is an extremely sensitive one. The files in the DO's office contain the crypts and pseudos of every officer, every foreign agent, and every operation around the world. The DO sees every single piece of precedence traffic that comes into the Agency's Operations Directorate. The officer is *never* to leave the office unattended, even for the periodic fire drills that take place throughout the Agency. In case of fire, I was told to wait until rescued by helicopter. If an incoming cable is purely administrative, requesting that the wife be informed that her husband has missed his flight, or asking that a family be notified of an illness, the DO personally takes action. In cases involving ongoing operations, the DO simply contacts the responsible desk officer, who then takes the appropriate action.

I enjoyed the first month on the job tremendously. On the day shift there was little to do. And on the evening and night shifts the reclining chair provided was comfortable, so much so that during quiet spells one could even doze off for a few minutes. And there was no work to take home. No concerns about preparing for a presentation the next day. No worries about how to handle an ongoing operation. No mental laboring through the night on how to word an outgoing message. All a DO had to do was to take care of what was immediately at hand. After going off duty there was no further responsibility. I had thought I would love the job, but after a month, it began to pall. There was no sense of a job well done, of having brought a case to fruition, of having made a successful presentation, or conducted a productive meeting. There was no sense of accomplishment at all. I would gladly have moved on, but I was committed for a year.

The year went by quickly. I did my job and had no problems except in one instance. A "flash" cable came in at 2:00 AM from a Near Eastern Station. A cable designated "flash" is high priority and calls for immediate action. I called the desk officer responsible for the case. He was not happy at being awakened from a sound sleep and said he would take care of it in the morning. From the cable's wording I felt it could not wait, but when I told him so, he irritably questioned my judgment. He maintained that he knew the case better than I, which was of course true. When he adamantly refused to come in to take care of the matter, I said I would have to go over his head to ensure that action was taken. To that, he replied, "Go ahead," and hung up on me. With some misgiving about my own judgment, I called the Division chief, and with apologies for waking him, reported the situation. He was fully supportive of my having called him, and irate about the desk officer's dismissive attitude. I don't know what the repercussions were, but they could not have been good for the desk officer, whose name the Division Chief had demanded.

A second incident that I found rather surprising occurred not in the duty officer's office, but in the adjacent Operations Center where the President's Daily Brief is prepared. I had become quite friendly with the officers in that unit and was aware that for some days there had been rumors that someone was leaking classified information. The whispered conjectures as to who it might be didn't last long. One day, one of their members no longer appeared in the office. Whoever it was had been apprehended, and work went on as usual. I don't know how the investigation was carried out, but during this episode I fully expected to be polygraphed. I had access to highly sensitive material, was in and out of the Operations Center regularly, and was ethnic Chinese, not a native- born American citizen. I had been under the impression that CIA employees underwent a polygraph exam every five years during their employment. Yet I had been polygraphed only once, when I first began work at the Agency. That I was not required to take a repeat polygraph at this time surprised me, and brought home to me how lax the Agency's security could be.

A third incident while serving as Duty Officer that I cannot resist including here was an obscene phone call. I had never received one before, and this was fascinating. Knowing that the caller could not possibly know who I was, and that there could not possibly be any follow-up to the conversation, I let him spew forth the foulest language, which alternated with lurid sexual suggestions and enticements. I dutifully entered it into the log.

While I was going about my job at the Agency, the merchandise we had ordered was starting to arrive. There was no room in our new house to store it. Nor did we want to alert our new, rather nosy, neighbors to our starting a business. We rented space in a mini storage unit in which we stacked the many boxes and crates that were pouring in. I realized that I would soon have to start making sales if the merchandise was to earn its keep. In making our plans for the business, John had been ready and willing to handle the necessary paperwork, and also do the heavy lifting, the physical labor, but wanted no part in the selling. We had done the buying together, but the selling was to be totally my responsibility. This was a bigger job than I had imagined. I had thought that the shift job would allow me to work on the business when I was not on duty, but even when I was not working the day shift, I was so tired I could not get nearly as much done as I had planned. Two jobs were more than I could handle.

In the summer of 1982 I put in a request for a year's leave without pay. Quoting directly from my memo:

"————I need the time to resolve some of my personal and business affairs, the principal of these being the launching of a small import business that I started last October. At that time I mistakenly thought that the irregular hours of my present job in the Duty Office would give me the extra daytime hours needed to embark on the private business venture. Unfortunately, I badly misjudged my own physical capabilities and have since found that I am unable to carry simultaneously what in essence amounts to almost two full time jobs. Inasmuch as I have a substantial financial investment in this new business, I badly need the requested leave if I am not to lose my entire investment. Within a year, by devoting my full time and attention to the business, I would hope to either get it established on a sound footing or at least to recoup some of my investment and get out.————————"

As requested, the leave was granted. I was now free to work full time on peddling our purchases. While my job was just beginning, John was already hard at work. He had been driving to Baltimore in a rental truck to pick up each shipment as it arrived. However, we were total neophytes in the importing business and had not given a thought to customs clearing procedures or to the added expense of import duties. Initially we had to hire a customs broker, but soon John took over that job himself. We were learning as we went along. We were surprised to find that there was almost no duty on imports from "under-developed countries." Surprisingly, only Japan was considered a developed country, and the duty as I recall was about 20%, making the end cost of our Japanese purchases considerably higher than expected. However, the others, even Hong Kong, a thriving economic center, were considered "under-developed." We also found, much to our dismay, that the capiz shell objects we had ordered from the Philippines, had to be cleared by the Fish and Wildlife Authorities, located only in the New York port. The items had to be shipped to New York and returned to Baltimore before they could be released, all this adding to our expense. Furthermore, many of the capiz items, poorly packed, were damaged in shipping, particularly the wastebaskets. Gift stores wanted total bathroom sets of tissue holder, soap dish, tumbler, and wastebasket. They would not take individual pieces, thus our capiz purchases were almost a total loss. But from all this, *we were learning.*

My work began with scouring the yellow pages for *all* the gift stores in the Greater Washington area. This was 1981, long before the internet. I then drove to each one, first to see if it was appropriate for our particular wares, and also to check prices. My next step was to set up appointments with the owners, but there was no way I could carry around samples of everything we had to offer, so we had to have pictures or some kind of catalogue. We checked out prices with professional photographers. The cost was prohibitive. We decided we could do the photography ourselves. This was truly a Mom and Pop operation like no other. There was no aspect of the business we didn't do ourselves. Item by item we photographed all our merchandise. Then I assembled the pictures into an album and was ready to go.

A few of our small gift store iems

Carrying my photo album and a few samples in one of our red leather boxes, I was off to peddle our wares. The selling was not difficult. More often than not I would find the stores' owners present in the shop. They liked what I had to offer, and I made small sales to most. I was surprised to find that most of these gift stores were owned by what in those days I regarded as little old ladies. (They were probably in their sixties, not much older than I.) Also, that they all seemed to be operating on a shoestring. Instead of buying a dozen of any object, it was two small bowls, three vases, a couple of stamp boxes, and so forth. Since we were just starting out, I didn't feel I could set a minimum order limit. All expected to put a 100% markup on anything they bought from us, so we would have to price at no more than half the retail price. I also made appointments with buyers at department stores and quickly ruled them out as prospective customers. They expected a markup of 140%, which would mean we would have to price even lower if the items were to sell. *We were learning.*

The sales had been made. Now came the real work. With sales order in hand I had to drive to the storage unit. I had to take down the carton that held the bowls, take out two, and replace the carton. Then the carton that held the vases, take out three, and replace the carton. Then the box that contained the stamp boxes. I took the items home, put a stock number on each one, made out a sales slip, and drove to the store to make the delivery. For a bowl that retailed at $10, I had charged $5. My purchase price had been $2.50 so for the miles driven, and the physical labor involved, I had made a profit of $2.50. The only things that brought in a bigger amount were the silk wall screens. Apart from those, a small sale to a single store was netting us only $50 or $60 in profit for several hours of work. But *we were learning*.

Yes, we were learning. What we had learned all too quickly was that dealing in small low-priced items was far too labor intensive and could not be cost-effective unless working with high volume. We had to reconnoiter. We decided to forget the small gift items and go for the bigger ticket things. From our earlier buying trip we had already seen exquisite large silk wall screens and standing coromandel screens. Also, handsome large porcelains. Though a few of these things were in modern designs, most were reproductions of age-old Chinese antiques and were beautifully done. In the past we had passed these up as being too large for gift stores. Now, we decided our new market would be interior designers. We would specialize in antique reproductions and sell "to the trade." We decided to make another buying trip, this time limiting our visit to Hong Kong only, where we had decided the quality was the most reliable. This time, we did not inform Horace's family, but went directly to the factories. Once again we compared prices and quality and placed our orders. Merchandise would be shipped on receipt of our letters of credit.

By this time John was handling the customs himself without benefit of the customs broker, but we were still picking up the shipments from Baltimore ourselves. Since I was no longer working at the office, I accompanied John on his pickups. Now that we were handling larger things, we decided to store them in our basement.

Though our housing area had no rules against operating a business—it was permissible as long as the business was not visible—we thought it inadvisable to be unloading in front of our new home. Instead, we parked the truck at the far end of a Safeway parking lot, unpacked the crates *inside* the truck, and transferred the items piece by piece to a small Nissan hatchback we had bought expressly for the business. We then unloaded the Nissan *inside* our garage. This involved going back and forth from the parking lot to the house several times to completely unload. It was hard work. We also had to photograph our new merchandise and prepare new photo albums. Since the items to be photographed were much larger, we turned our garage temporarily into a photo studio, setting up curtains for a backdrop, and buying stronger lighting. We produced an impressive album to show to prospective clients. These, I later reproduced in abbreviated form and sold to designers for $50.00, the amount to be credited toward their first purchase.

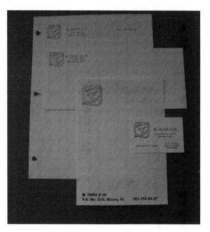

M. Chien & Co. stationery

At the same time, John was taking computer lessons and had bought a computer to keep track of our sales and inventory. Also, he was busy printing up business cards, stationery, sales slips, and billing statements for M. Chien & Co., all with a distinctive dragon logo for our company. He had had an old offset printing press for years, and in the past had enjoyed printing cards, invitations and all types of other things for friends and family. Now it was invaluable for our business.

Meanwhile, I was making cold calls to interior designers, relying completely on the yellow pages. Thankfully, in 1982, telephone answering machines had still not appeared on the scene. Calls were always answered by a live human being. My job was to talk that person into giving me an appointment. This was much harder than selling to gift stores, and I discovered quickly that I was not cut out for telemarketing. Making a cold call was one of the most difficult tasks I had ever faced. Starting off along the lines of "Hello, my name is Marguerite Church, and I am importing decorative accessories from the Far East that I hope will interest you," I was often cut off before I had finished my sentence. Or, I was told they were not interested, or already had their suppliers. If I made three cold calls without pinning down an appointment, I could not face a fourth rejection. I was through for the day. When I *did* secure an appointment, it was usually given grudgingly and I was told "Well, I can only give you a few minutes." Fortunately, once I met them in person and produced pictures of our wares, the few minutes were often extended to half an hour or more. One designer was particularly helpful and gave me a copy of the latest ASID (American Society of Interior Designers) directory. She also pointed out the local ones she thought might be interested in our products. From there I was on my way. I talked my way into a meeting with Ed Plyler, the then president of the ASID. He was a lovely man. We got along famously, and he gave me leads to other designers, the most useful of which was Bob Waldron, a well-known society designer who was probably best known for having Vice President Lyndon Johnson among his clients. Bob Waldron was willing to come to the house where we had set up a showroom in the basement. He liked what he saw, and without being asked told me I should use his name freely when contacting other designers. Being able to say, "Bob Waldron thought you might be interested in seeing what I carry" guaranteed entrée to anyone I then approached.

By the time my year of leave without pay was over, I had ready access to many designers, but despite the fact that the sale of a single porcelain fishbowl could net us $400, or an eight-panel coramendel screen $600, we were not making more than a few sales a month. It was not until we latched onto the hotel trade that M. Chien & Co. became profitable. Marriott's international headquarters was located in nearby Bethesda, Maryland, and through a referral I had managed to get an appointment with one of their interior designers. She liked the pictures of our merchandise and suggested that I bring some of the items to display in their show room. That was a big opening for M. Chien & Co. In our little Nissan hatchback, John and I, without any outside help, moved a six-panel coromandel screen, a silk wall screen, and a variety of porcelains to the show room. We were thrilled when the display drew a few orders. An even greater thrill, however, came a

Some of our porcelains

few weeks later. I was on a temporary CIA assignment in Europe when I received a long distance call from John. He could not wait for my return to give me the good news; Marriot had placed a $36,000 order. For us, this was huge. For the first time I felt, "this is going to work."

Chapter 23
The CIA, Final Years

Having gotten M. Chien & Co. off the ground, I had returned to full time work at the Agency in the fall of 1983. This time, looking for a change from working on the China target, I applied for a position in the European Division. There, I was assigned the task of monitoring the illegal acquisition of U.S. technology by unfriendly governments, known as tech transfer operations. It required becoming knowledgeable on the technical needs of enemy countries, and the infinite number of sophisticated ways they managed to secure U.S. technology to meet those needs. The required coordination with the Justice Department, Commerce Department, Defense Department, and the FBI to control these actions seemed endless. It was a tedious and demanding job, and I couldn't wait for my year in this assignment to end.

I was now fifty-nine years old. I saw no point in seeking further advancement and had decided to return to working part time until I was eligible for retirement in three years. I was assigned to the Reports Staff of the National Collection Division, responsible for the collection of intelligence reporting *within* the United States. As a part-timer I was again, as in my early years with the Agency, assigned to a job that had long needed attention, but had been put off for one reason or another. It was to devise a records–keeping system to track the Agency's response to the requirements of other U.S. Government offices. (This was before the age of computers.) While the task was strictly organizational in nature, and should have been relatively simple, it was dealing with conflicting personalities with conflicting interests that made the job more frustrating than any job I had held before. The very senior officer who was responsible for tracking these reports was a difficult man, whose sole object in life was to put every report ever written into its own little pigeon hole. Reports officers, in high-stress jobs, under the constant pressure of deadlines to be met, had little inclination to fill out the mounds of bureaucratic paper work he demanded. I was delicately balanced in the middle. By summoning all the diplomacy I could muster, constantly placating the one, and gently nudging the others into compliance, I was able to get the two parties to work together. The job was done, and I managed to earn myself a commendation for my efforts.

Though I had endured two years of tedium at the office, on another front, business was thriving. After our first big order from Marriott, others followed. Soon we were putting on displays twice a year in the Marriott show room and orders were increasing. I was also steadily gaining the trust of the design staff. When they selected something that I felt was wrong for the intended location, I would voice my opinion even though it meant the loss of a sale. I know the designers appreciated this, and they came to trust my taste and judgment. Soon they were giving me design panels of hotel décor that included swatches of the carpeting, drapes, upholstery, and wallpaper and letting me select the porcelains to complement the rest of the room. In two instances, we provided the porcelains and screens for the public areas of the entire hotels. And Marriott was generous with its referrals. Through them, we also made sales to designers from the Radisson Hotel chain.

When we started, John had incorporated us as a small business corporation, an "S" corporation, but with the hotel business, our profits moved us out of the small business category and we had to be re-qualified as a full business corporation. John read up on all the procedures in the library and did all the paperwork for these transactions without benefit of a lawyer. By this time we were no longer picking up the shipments ourselves. No longer were we unloading and unpacking our merchandise ourselves in a Safeway parking lot. We had arranged with a large trading company to have all merchandise shipped directly to its warehouse in the Virginia suburbs. There, with the company's help, we unpacked the boxes, checked the contents, and had them immediately repacked and shipped directly to the customer.

For two years, business was thriving. In addition to the hotel trade, we were still selling successfully to individual interior designers. But soon, similar merchandise started appearing from Communist China. The quality was poor and often the colors and designs bordered on garish, but the items were cheap. We would have to lower our prices to compete. At the same time, the quality of some of the merchandise from our Hong Kong suppliers was suffering. Of twelve identical silk wall screens ordered for Marriott, eight were so poorly done that I was concerned that Marriott would not accept them. I had to get out my long unused painting equipment, and one by one I laid each screen out on the basement floor and painted over the poorly done work. It was obvious to John and me that our supplier had not been able to handle the larger orders and had resorted to using unskilled painters to fill the order. The same applied to our porcelain supplier. The glazes on some of the pieces were beginning to look thick and lumpy, and the prized antique-look that had characterized our past merchandise was lost. What we badly needed was someone on the supply end (the Hong Kong end) to check the merchandise *before* it was shipped. This we did not have. Also, if we lowered our prices to compete with the imports from China, we would have to increase our volume to maintain our profit margins. That, we were not prepared to do. In 1985, just five years after the start of M. Chien & Co., we were ready to give it up. It had been a profitable business and we had done far better than we had ever imagined. Our one regret was that our porcelain supplier, unable to compete with the lower-priced merchandise from China, went out of business before we could place a final order for ourselves. Thus, in our home today there is not a single piece of the beautiful porcelains that had been the mainstay of our business for four years. Our children's homes, however, are filled with the best of our porcelains and our screens, which we had sold to them at factory costs. We were not sorry to be putting M.Chien &

Co. behind us. For us, it had been an adventure, an exhilarating and challenging one, but it had also been plain hard work. Other things in life were ahead for us.

In the spring of 1985, we moved into a new townhouse in Evans Mill Pond, a small townhouse development just a few blocks away from the one we had bought while still in Australia. We had been happy in that house, but it was small, and more confining than we had anticipated. At times I felt that if I just stretched my arms out a little farther I could touch both outer walls. Our new house was larger and L-shaped, and with exposure on all four sides, it was also a great deal brighter. The house backed onto a pond that was filled with large-mouthed bass, blue gills, and catfish. The pond was also home to a brood of mallard ducks, and an occasional blue heron could be seen picking its way across its borders. It was an idyllic setting in which we expected to live out the rest our lives.

The first two years, John and I devoted our time to working on the house. Together, we installed a brick patio in the small rear garden. We added to the minimal foundation plantings provided by the builder. We dug flower beds, and planted ground cover. After taking a county course in crown molding, we put up the molding ourselves. We also added chair rails where needed as well as other decorative touches. We decided on which walls were to be painted and which to be papered. I had never done any wall papering before, but armed with an instruction sheet, I papered the walls myself. Looking back, I find it hard to imagine that as a total novice I was able to paper the stairwell, which involved standing on a ladder propped up on a platform held up by another ladder. We painted the walls, some of them more than once. In the living room I was thinking of a dramatic brick red. I painted one wall and positioned our Chinese coromandel screen against it; it was stunning. I then painted the whole room, but what had been stunning on one wall was overpowering on the whole room. On the second try I was going for the lovely soft rose of the adobe walls of India. The color was perfect until it was hit by the afternoon sun. Then it turned a garish pink. The third try was a great success, a terra cotta with a slight salmon cast. By this time I had established a great relationship with the two young men who manned the McCormack paint store nearby, and was being given the painters' discount for all my purchases.

Apart from working on the house, we had to buy furniture to fill the extra rooms. And then there was the decorating. Drapes and bedspreads had to be made. While I tackled those myself—no easy job, for the picture windows overlooking our pond were large—John put up cornices. All this was hard work and time-consuming, but it did not occur to either of us to hire others to do the job. We were both inveterate do-it-yourselfers, and of course whatever we were capable of doing we would do ourselves. At the same time, we still had to cope with dissolving the business. I had stopped doing any active selling, but we still had some inventory to dispose of. We put everything that remained into the spare room in the basement, and as soon as we let it be known that we were selling at 20% above *our* costs, our friends became eager buyers. Only one item remained, a very large coromandel screen. It had been one of our first purchases, and both John and I had been well aware at the time that it might be difficult to sell, but it was so very beautiful, we had both been willing to take a chance on it. It was twenty feet wide and nine feet high. Not having a high enough room in our house, we had been unable to display it to interior designers. We finally did sell it, however, to the past president of the ASID (American Society of Interior Designers), who had given me so much help and encouragement when we were starting out. We were grateful that he took it off our hands, but the sale brought a handsome profit for him too. A screen that should have retailed for $20,000 we sold to him for a mere $5,000. I was told that it now sits in the lobby of Washington's prestigious Cosmos Club.

With putting so much time working on our house I was glad to be on a part-time schedule at the office. Having tried out work in other Divisions for four years with little satisfaction, I returned to a desk in China Operations. It was almost like coming home. This time I was supporting operations against Chinese targets in the U.S. rather than in foreign countries. The job was essentially a continuation of the work I had done for many years in the past and came easily to me. I was confident in my abilities, and my Branch Chief was likewise confident in me. Whenever he was called away on other temporary duty assignments, even though I was a part-timer, I was the one called upon to come in the extra days to serve as Acting Branch Chief. When I was eligible for retirement in 1987, he urged me to stay on, luring me with the promise that, as his deputy, I would be in line for promotion to Branch Chief. This was a tempting offer, but it would have required my going back to work full time. I was not prepared to do that. The Chief of China Operations, Harry S., whom I liked tremendously and had come to know well, also urged me to stay on. "Wouldn't you like another overseas assignment?" he asked. "Harry," I said. "You were not here when I was going through the battle for my last tour. You try selling me to a Station Chief." With that, he paused for a moment of reflection, but only briefly. "I see what you mean," he acknowledged. We chatted briefly, then parted with a handshake and his good wishes for me in retirement.

I retired in February 1987, shortly after my sixty-second birthday. I had had sixteen years with the Agency. What had started as a stop-gap measure, merely a holding position until I found something permanent, had ended as a full-fledged career. I was glad that my last year with the Agency had been under a man whom I both liked and respected. Two in the past had not had my respect. One, smart but slick, always reminded me of a used car salesman. I later learned that he had been fired for taking an agent (one of my "stable" of "willing" women) on a vacation in a luxury resort and charging off the expense to "development." The other was overly attentive to the female staff and was later discharged for sexual harassment. A third might have been expert at handling agents in the field, but had no idea how to navigate at Headquarters. He habitually passed on all touchy operations to me, saying, "You handle this, Marguerite. You're better at this than I am." Then there had been the bad years when I was fighting discrimination, but I had put those behind me and was ending on a high note. I had proved my worth. I knew I was valued. I was ready for retirement.

A few months later, while I was working in the garden, John called out to me that I had a phone call from the office. I couldn't imagine why they were calling, and was totally surprised when informed that I was being given an award. This was followed by a formal notification. "For what?" I wondered. I thought awards were for major achievements. I could think of nothing I had done that merited an award. However, whoever had written the citation must have gone through my file with a fine-tooth comb, for in addition to the achievements for which I felt I *did* deserve credit, he also dredged up things I had done in the past that I had totally forgotten. One of these was that I had made presentations at the Defense Intelligence School, and to a joint meeting of FBI chiefs. Also, in one case, I had spotted and passed on to the Los Angeles base a Chinese technology student whom I had met on the plane. In another, I had cultivated a friendship with a Soviet Bloc Consular official and his Chinese wife while in Australia. This friendship led to no useful information, but simply being in contact with a Soviet Bloc official was considered something of an achievement in those days. I was also given credit for my very sketchy language skills: fluent Mandarin (*but not nearly college level*), good Cantonese (*I would have said "passable"*), Shanghai dialect (*which I could barely understand*), and "usable French" (*I could speak it, poorly, but could never understand anything a French person said.*) Though the citation's wording was decidedly overblown—and indeed it was so glowing that it was almost embarrassing—based on its words, it is no wonder the Awards Committee members decided I was worth the award. That their decision was unanimous, however, was gratifying, as I understand that unanimous decisions were relatively rare.

At the official ceremony in my honor I was awarded the Intelligence Commendation Medal for my continued high performance throughout my sixteen-year career. The medal was presented by Claire G., then Deputy Director of the Operations Directorate, whom I had known when he was a young bachelor on his first overseas assignment in Hong Kong. The room was filled to capacity with many officers with whom I had worked on cases in the distant past, others who had been past supervisors, as well as my more recent day-to-day co-workers. What really surprised me was the number of the Agency's big brass who attended. I felt honored that they had taken the time to come for me, a relatively junior officer. Also present was General Wedemeyer, beaming on me as proudly as if I had been his own daughter. It was a moving and heartwarming closing of my career with the CIA.

Chapter 24
Retirement

The job was over. The business was wound up. The house was looking good. My three children, two married, each with a child, were all doing well with no need of support from me. For the first time in my adult life I had no responsibilities whatsoever. Even housework was not something I had to do; we were now splurging on biweekly housecleaning help. Of course, there was the cooking, but that was something I loved to do. And there was the garden to tend, but that too was a labor of love.

Having absolutely nothing I *had* to do was a wonderful feeling. Yet, I never thought that having nothing to do would be a permanent way of life. I am by nature an achiever, and was sure that a life without some sense of accomplishment, something to work toward, would soon become a bore. I thought a year of retirement would be fun, but a year would be enough. After that, I would go back to work of some kind. How wrong I was, and how little I knew myself. The next twenty years flew by with never a trace of boredom. John and I took up tennis. I had played during the years I lived overseas, but never had formal instruction. Now, I took lessons. John had never played before, had never been much of an athlete. He joined a county course, usually being the only man among a group of middle-aged housewives. Together we joined the county's program for senior citizens, the Golden Racquets Club, playing regularly three times a week, John even more enthusiastic than I. Tennis became a major part of our retirement years. I had never been more than an

average club player, but one year, when I was in my seventies, my
partner (not John) and I even won the gold medal, playing mixed
doubles in the Northern Virginia Senior Olympics. We went on to the
regionals in Williamsburg, but there only managed to come away with
a bronze medal.

I also joined a knitting class offered by the Smithsonian
Institution. When first asked to join the class, I had declined. I thought,
"I know how to knit. Why would I need lessons?" I had been knitting
since I was a small child. I had knit my way through college, earning
my spending money by knitting for friends and friends of friends,
and in later years I knit all my children's sweaters as well as those of
my husband. Moreover, I could knit without a pattern, something that
amazed my American friends. Growing up in China, there had been
no patterns or instruction books; all Chinese learned to knit without.
Though I was confident that I had no need of lessons, my friends were
persuasive. Reluctantly, I joined the class. How quickly I was brought
down to earth and disabused of all past conceits. How could I have
thought I already knew it all? I found I had so much to learn. This
was not a class of simple knitting and purling, but one of design and
structure, of combining colors and textures, of assembling an artistic
whole. It was a new experience, a new challenge, and each new article
I completed gave me as much satisfaction, or more, than making a
profitable sale of merchandise, or completing a project at the office.
At the same time, I was knitting and sewing for my grandchildren (I
now had three). Two were girls, and through the next few years it gave
me so much pleasure seeing them decked out in dresses and sweaters
I had made.

I also went back to singing. Not that I had stopped singing
around the house, in the shower and when washing the dishes, but
it had been fifteen years since I had put aside my hopes of singing
professionally, and I had given no further thought to singing again for
an audience. But one night, at a dinner party, I was again "discovered,"
much as I had been years ago in Taipei. All the guests were gathered
around the piano singing old favorites. When the one playing the

piano found that I could sing and knew the words to all the old songs, he then and there roped me into leading the sing-alongs he conducted weekly at the McLean Senior Day Care Center. There, on the first day I led the group, I saw how much pleasure we brought to that aged audience. I knew instantly that I wanted to be a part of it. The Center's manager was delighted when I volunteered to bring my guitar and to sing, separately from the sing-alongs, for those in her care. Any extra entertainment was always welcome. And so, I dusted off my guitar, and sang for senior citizens, some with Alzheimer's disease, others with some degree of dementia or physical disability. The audience was far removed from audiences of the past, but seeing the tapping of fingers and toes during a snappy song, or, during a slow one, seeing them lean back and close their eyes, almost lost in the music, or noting someone wiping a tear from a wrinkled cheek during a sad song, all this was more rewarding than the spotlight and applause of past years. I did this once a week for the next seven years, always staying through the lunch hour to help where needed. Sometimes it was to cut up food, or even to hand feed those who could not handle it themselves. I always left the Center feeling good.

While I was seeking activities to occupy my new leisure, John had never had any problem filling his days. He had been retired for fifteen years and continued with his prodigious amounts of reading, his poetry, and his various research projects. John had always had an insatiable thirst for travel and made many trips on his own while I was tied down with my office job. He had gone on several archeological digs, one to Tel Dor in Israel. He'd also walked Hadrian's Wall in England, been to the Joyce symposium in Ireland, taken trips to the Galapagos and to Papua New Guinea. The most adventurous of all his travels was going down the Amazon on a raft. But for me, the most important of his trips had been the camel safari in Australia, which led to the successful contacts made in my CIA job.

Amazon raft

For me, marriage to John opened up new horizons in the world of travel. I had visited many places during my working years at the Agency. With Horace, I had lived in different countries, and en route to and from, visited others. But we had always done things the conventional way, staying in hotels or motels and eating in restaurants. With John, on the other hand, travel was never an orthodox pursuit; it was an adventure. We rode on mules, slept in caves, in tents, in ramshackle buildings. We were fortunate that John had maintained his military reserve status, making us eligible for free travel on military planes on a space available basis. We took full advantage of these benefits.

Traveling Space A on military flights, however, was not without its problems and was always a bit nerve-wracking. We had to make the two-hour drive to Dover Air Force Base, never knowing if we would get on a flight. Often we had long waits as we watched flight after flight leave with no space for us. But once on board, these flights were a joy. They were certainly not fancy; the seats often boxed in among piles of military equipment. They were, however, more comfortable than any commercial airline. The seats were widely spaced with plenty of leg room, and some, probably remnants from the early days of airplane travel, even had adjustable foot rests. Also, not only were the flights free, but box lunches designed for two-hundred-and-fifty-pound active duty servicemen, were provided for a pittance.

Flying military Space A, we made several trips to London, staying at the officers' quarters on arrival, all free. On one of these trips we rented a car and drove up into Scotland, staying at one of the castles of Mary Queen of Scots.

Also, for five years, daughter Kathy was working for Continental Airlines, and as parents, we were eligible for free space-available travel on commercial airlines as well. On commercial lines, it was a nervous experience waiting for our names to be called, but this was before the airlines had introduced frequent flyer miles, and empty seats were always available. Not once were we unable to get on a flight of our choice. Even so, both John and I learned to travel light with only carry-on baggage, as there was always the possibility, however slight, that we would not get on. During Kathy's years with Continental, we made full use of these travel perks, making several trips to Porto Vallarta in Mexico, as well as flying to and from Elderhostel tours, the popular programs for senior citizens.

These Elderhostel programs provided not only the opportunity to see and explore a new locale, but also offered educational courses. In the late eighties they were still relatively inexpensive, the accommodations being in college dormitories with communal bathroom facilities, and the meals in the schools' cafeterias. The visit to the Oregon Shakespeare Festival in Ashland, Oregon, was a standout. John, a longtime Shakespeare buff, was in his element. Not only were we treated to three performances, but we were also taken backstage to see the workings of the theatre. We were also fortunate in capturing a rehearsal of a fight scene. This was a fascinating experience, as it brought home to us how precisely every movement of every actor had to be coordinated. The director periodically shouted, "freeze," to check out exact positions. In later years, whenever there was a fight scene at a Shakespearean performance we were attending, John would threaten to stand up and yell "freeze." Thankfully, he never followed through on this threat, though I often wondered what the results would have been if he had.

The most memorable of our Elderhostel trips was its pilot fine arts program to Moscow and St. Petersburg. I am not even attempting to describe the wonders of Russia as they are covered far better in the countless travel guides now published. But for us, this was a glorious trip. Our days were packed with visits to the major tourist sights, and every evening was filled with a performance of some kind, a circus, a puppet show, a gypsy dance group, a piano concert, a variety show, an acrobatic performance, and several ballets, every one magnificent.

What really impressed me about Russia was how steeped the people were in art and learning. The number of bookstores on every street almost rivaled the number of liquor stores. And when visiting museums I was amazed at the number of parents I saw with young children in tow, exposing them to art at an early age. However, I left Russia convinced that the people were immune to cold. The airports were cold, the theatres were cold, the museums were cold. I was cold for the entire two-week length of the tour. Even in the theatres I kept my coat over my shoulders, incurring some hostile looks and critical comments from other attendees. It seemed that coats were to be checked and not worn into either theatres or museums. This was late October, not freezing, but still cold. What surprised me also, was the ice cream and popsicles sold on every corner, whereas it seemed roasted chestnuts would have been more in order.

Apart from our Elderhostel trips, we went on scientific expeditions that required work and sweat. And though we were providing the labor, we paid a substantial amount to join these expeditions. However, the trips, since they were devoted to scientific research, were tax deductible, reducing their cost considerably. The best of these programs was run by the non-profit Earthwatch group. John had already been alone on an Earthwatch archeological dig to Israel while I was working, but together we went on an expedition to St. Croix in the Virgin Islands "to save the leatherback turtle." These giant turtles, weighing as much as 1,300 pounds, were threatened with extinction, first, because their eggs were often washed away when laid too close to the water's edge, and second, because they were highly valued for cooking and easy prey for poachers.

Every night our team of six patrolled a one-mile strip of beach where the turtles were known to nest. (They were averse to light and only came on shore after dark.) Our first night we walked that strip ten times with no sign of a turtle. For me, never a walker, each successive mile was more grueling than the last. Thankfully, on our second night we spotted a turtle, which gave us a reprieve from further walking that night. The turtle was already attempting to dig its nest, but it was so near the water line that as it dug with its back

John in foreground taking notes

flippers, the waves were washing the sand away. Our role was to help both in the digging and in packing down the sand. Only when the nest had reached a certain depth did the turtle start to lay. We then caught the eggs as they were being laid, close to a hundred, each the size of a billiard ball, counted them, measured them, and later reclocated them to a safer area. All this had to be recorded and mapped in detail. When all the eggs were laid, the turtle, exhausted, was completely inert, allowing us time to measure it and tag it. It rested a long time before dragging its enormous weight to the water's edge, but finally, buoyed by an incoming wave, it slid effortlessly into the sea. As I watched that magnificent creature leave our world and plunge into the darkness of its own, I felt the strangest sense of loss, as if a part of me was going with it.

During our two-week stint in St. Croix we were lucky enough to come across three more turtles, and each time we went through the same procedures. The remaining nights, however, we still made our patrols. It was exhausting. Our friends were incredulous. "You *paid* to do this?" Yes, we paid, but the experience was well worth it. And we did have some leisure time to see the island. Most of us slept from daybreak until about noon, but in the afternoons our leaders personally served as our guides. Among other things, they took us on a fantastic trip through an "underwater park." Neither John nor I were great swimmers, but we donned the snorkels that were provided, and guided by a rope, swam through the park seeing an amazing display of fish, plants, and coral, all properly labeled as in any on-land park. An

John at left, taking notes, me, center, looking on

added bonus on this expedition was that Earthwatch had brought in a team of photographers to record us at work. It was a source of some pride to both John and me that we are in the pictures that Earthwatch used for years on its postcards and in their advertising brochures.

On our next venture into scientific research, we were not so lucky. This was in Grenada. The dual program, one an archeological dig, the other a study of the endangered green monkey, was sponsored by some university in California. We were told that housing would be in a university dormitory, but when we arrived we were instead taken to a local grade school, which in no way resembled a grade school in the U.S. Even before entering we could see the peeling paint and the jagged glass of broken window panes. Bugs were crawling around the refuse in the stairwells. Twelve of us were ushered into a large schoolroom, where mattresses were spread on the floor. We would all, male and female, be sleeping in the one room. When dressing, the only privacy available was behind one of the two standing blackboards. As for bathroom facilities, the toilets and washbasins were adequate, but the shower consisted of a single pipe, without even a shower head. Returning from a hard day of labor, twelve of us had to line up for the meager trickle of water. This halted intermittently whenever the cook preparing our dinner turned on the kitchen tap. I cannot remember what we were served for breakfast, but lunch, in the field consisted daily of bread and large blocks of cheese. Dinners were meager, served family style, and the amount served up for our group of twelve was in my opinion only enough for half that number. Admittedly, we were provided with plenty of fruit, mostly mangoes, but even mangoes, which I love, were not enough to make up for the other sparseness.

As for our research, John joined happily in the dig, and I elected to participate in the study of the green monkey who supposedly lived in the rain forest. This was right after the rainy season and I was dismayed to find the forest floor was nothing but mud. With each step my foot sank into the slime, only to be released grudgingly with a great sucking sound. On that first day, eager to see the monkeys, I gamely slogged on. However, no monkeys appeared. On the second day—still no monkeys—I slipped and fell. I was totally covered in mud. That was enough of searching for monkeys. On the third day I joined John on the dig and was promptly attacked by fire ants. On the fourth day I gave up and flew home. That was the end of scientific research for me.

Chapter 25
Travel

Though John and I never had trouble filling our days, it seems that those early years of my retirement were filled almost entirely with travel. No sooner did we return from one trip than John would be making plans for another. Whenever possible we made our own travel arrangements, always with a reserved room for our first night at whatever destination. After that, we relied on the local travel information centers for accommodations and transport facilities. Wherever John felt capable of conquering the local roads, we rented a car. We traveled at the lowest possible end of the financial scale, our only concession to luxury being a private bathroom whenever bathrooms were available.

John was always looking for trips that were out of the ordinary. The first of these was in 1988 to the annual Pushkar Camel Fair in India. Though several travel groups offered tours, we decided to do this on our own. Getting to Pushkar was an adventure in itself. The taxis promised in guide books were nowhere to be seen. We tackled the local bus lines. We could see that getting on board a bus was not going to be easy. People were climbing on even before the bus reached its starting bay. As we stood wondering which of the many buses to take, a young Indian boy came rushing up. "Where you go? Where you go?" When we told him Pushkar, he pointed to the correct bay. As John and I were occupied getting our tickets the boy grabbed our bags and took off. We were sure that was the last we would see of him or our bags. But then, through the window of an empty bus I saw what looked like our things. But the bus was driving *away* from the bus stop. It was then that John took off like a bolt of lightening, chasing after the bus, waving his arms frantically and yelling, "Stop, stop!" It was a scene rivaling the Keystone Cops for pure slapstick comedy. Luckily, it turned out that the bus was merely circling the area to pull into the correct bay. On board, our suspected "thief," with a big gap-toothed grin on his face was waving to us. He had not only gotten our bags aboard but was holding two seats for us. Our trials, however, were not over. Arriving In Pushkar, we found ourselves at

Me, arriving in style at Pushkar

the wrong end of the town. Taxis? Of course there were none. But John commandeered a man pulling a makeshift cart who agreed to take me and our baggage aboard. Sitting among sacks of grain, I arrived in high style at the "tent hotel" where we would be lodged. This tent hotel was an amazing logistical feat. The desert sand was covered with artificial sod, and colorful tents dotted the tent city. Our "deluxe" tent held two beds, two chairs, and a single light bulb dangling from a wire, sparse, but adequate. Meals, vegetarian, were served buffet style in a large communal tent. What was truly surprising was that water had been piped in to this barren area, and wonder of wonders, there were actually flush toilets. As for the fair itself, I will not attempt to cover what is much better done in travel guides, but when I think of the Pushkar Camel Fair, it is not the thousands of camels stretched to the horizon that I see. It is the picture of John running after the bus, his arms flailing wildly, and madly shouting "Stop, stop!" that sticks in my memory.

John and me in front of our tent

Though our destination on this trip had been Pushkar, there was no way we could leave India without doing some major shopping.

Frenzied shopping

Again, as in Japan and Hong Kong, India was a shopper's paradise. In New Delhi I bought all kinds of decorative objects for my children's homes, only to find on our return that we could have done as well or even better buying the same items at Pier I Imports. I did, however, do well on purchasing fabrics. Surrounded by shelves of beautiful bedspreads, I sat on the floor as the shopkeeper unfurled one beautiful spread after another before me. Finally, I selected eight bedspreads at the ridiculous price of seven dollars apiece. For a pittance I had enough fabric for drapes and slipcovers for the "Indian room" in our McLean house.

John and me, with camels as far as the eye can see

The following year, in 1989, we made a trip was to Greece. We did not do the tour of the islands, but instead, headed for Crete where John was intent on hiking the Samaria Gorge, the longest gorge in Europe. This was a twelve-mile hike, very rocky, but manageable, even for me, a non-hiker. The descent into the gorge, however, was steep, going from a four thousand foot elevation to sea level within the first two miles. I made the mistake of always going down with my left foot first, the pressure on my big toe resulting in my eventually losing that toenail. Throughout our travels, John always managed to pick up some interesting souvenir from each place we visited. When we returned home, I mentioned that I had not seen him buy a souvenir from Crete. "Because I already had something," he said. He pointed to a little Chinese cloisonné pill box on his desk. "It's in there." On picking it up, I found, nestled on a bed of cotton, what appeared to be a shell of some kind, pink and curled. "But what is it?" I asked. He said, "You figure it out." And I did. It was my toenail. That souvenir was pure John, and it assuredly was a vivid reminder of Crete and our descent into the Samaria Gorge.

From Crete, we went on to Athens where John hosted his daughter's wedding in the Greek orthodox church. Ed, Annie's husband, her fifth, was an American of Greek origin. They had already been married for seven years, but his family was disappointed that they had not been married in the Greek church. Now, Ed was posted at the U.S. army base in Germany—he was in the military—and it seemed a perfect opportunity to carry out the Greek wedding. It was all very exciting, the church filled to overflowing with flowers. There was no procession walking down an aisle. The family, plus a dozen or more of Ed and Annie's friends from Germany simply followed them into the church and crowded around the altar. I remember little about the ceremony except for the priest placing a crown of flowers on each of their heads, and the bride and groom walking around the altar three times behind the priest at the end of the ceremony. For me, the party that followed was more memorable than the ceremony itself. On the dance floor the groom's mother was whirling around with a rose in her teeth. People were throwing money with abandon at the bride and groom. Two girls, their skirts flaring, were dancing on top of the tables. The music was blaring, the liquor flowing, and the sheer exuberance was something unmatched by any wedding I had ever experienced in America.

Our next trip of note was to Morocco in 1989. This time we joined a tour offered by a company called Cross Cultural Adventures. We were a small group of ten, three couples and two single women, plus our six-foot-seven Polish tour leader Piotr, and a local guide. Rather surprisingly, our group was distinctly geriatric, the youngest sixty, the oldest eighty-four, all of us well traveled. After a luxurious day in Marrakech, we boarded two Land Rovers for a harrowing drive to the magnificent mountains of the High Atlas. Piotre had informed us that two days of hard travel with no amenities whatsoever, would always be followed by a day in a first rate hotel to give us a chance to bathe, revive, and prepare for the next two days of roughing it. What Piotr had not told us was what to expect of the mountain roads. The higher we got, the worse they became. Several times the road had been partially washed away, and all of us would have to get out of the car and gather rocks to shore up the outside rut. Only then were the cars, precariously slanting toward the gorge, able to proceed over the makeshift road. Our longest and worst drive took sixteen hours over what could only be called non-roads, a few in high places after dark, but somehow we all survived. In this way we passed through many Berber villages, each with its own point of interest. In one, our whole group squeezed into a room that could barely hold our sleeping bags lined up side by side. Getting up in the dark to use the toilet was a tricky maneuver. In another, we were housed in the home of a villager who had ambitious intentions of converting his home to a hostelry. For this he had built a magnificent outhouse complete with large bathtub, washbasin, toilet, and even a bidet. It was lacking only running water. In another home, we slept on settees that lined the walls.

From one of the villages we had to abandon the Land Rovers to get to the next village six miles away. Some chose to walk. I opted for riding on one of the mules carrying our baggage, which was simply slung over the backs of the mules in heavy cotton bags. Unfortunately, while fording a stream, my muleteer, not wanting to wade through the water, jumped up behind me onto the mule, and in so doing pulled the bags off center. Inch by inch I could feel it slipping and kept leaning the other way to hold it in place, but by the time we reached the middle of the stream, everything, including me, slid into the water. The water barely came to my knees, but I was thoroughly soaked. But the sun was shining and a light breeze blowing, and soon it was as if the fall into the river had never happened. The others had gone on ahead, and atop the mule, singing at the top of my lungs with no one to hear except the bare mountains, I felt the most extraordinary sense of well being.

Among our group was a woman in her mid seventies named Bertha. She was a published author of some note whose book on home economics was still being used in junior high schools around the U.S. What made her so distinctive, however, was not her writing credentials, but her behavior. In our many days of hard driving there was no such thing as a rest stop as on U.S. highways. Instead, Piotr would call out periodically, "Pee stop!" at which point we would all dismount and look for a shrub or some rocks behind which we could relieve ourselves. But not Bertha. If a shrub was not immediately at hand, she would simply hike up her skirt, drop her pants, squat, and take care of her needs in full view of whoever was around. We labeled her Bare-bottom Bertha. When I think of Morocco, what always comes first to mind is Bertha, squatting, with her skirt hiked up, and the joy I felt, riding on a mule, singing with complete abandon in the bare mountains. Those are my warmest memories of that wonderful journey.

For the ten years after my retirement, from 1987 to 1997, it seemed we were in a constant traveling mode. We had a good trip to Norway where we visited the major sights of Oslo and Bergen, but our main purpose being to see the fjords, we went on a mail-packet steamer up the coast of Norway stopping at various cities to deliver mail. The first day on board I was awed by the stunningly spectacular scenery. Likewise, the second day. By the third, I was grateful I had my knitting.

Turkey was a fabulous trip we planned on our own. Though we spent several days in Istanbul, our destination was Cappadocia where the mushroom-like rock formations unique to the area were something I had never seen before. There, we chose to stay in what was called a cave hotel, our room literally inside a very primitive cave with walls and floor of bare earth. This was the

Our cave "room" at the cave hotel

type of accommodation frequented by young back packers, and sleeping in a cave rather than a hotel room was a unique experience. In Cappadocia we visited one of many underground cities, which at one time had been hiding places for Christians before Christianity was accepted in the region. This one was six stories deep and much like a warren of Swiss cheese. The ceilings were so low that John emerged with many bumps and scratches on his head, and also a sore back from having to walk long stretches in a stooped position.

While throughout our travels, John always brought home some unusual souvenir, I was always looking for new foods to add to our home menus. In Istanbul a vendor selling stuffed mussels from a portable cart drew our attention. The mussels were delicious. They were chopped, mixed with rice, pine nuts, currants, and flavored with dill and olive oil. But while we were still tasting, and before we had paid, the vendor, a look of pure panic on his face, suddenly folded up his cart and scurried off into the crowds. A uniformed policeman followed close behind. Those mussels, replicated when we returned home, drew rave reviews from friends.

Surprisingly, it was in Israel that I found more foods that I have copied and served to guests for many years since then. It was at Jerusalem's YMCA dining room (according to the travel guides, the best restaurant in the city) that we had, what for want of a better word I will call meat pies. No top crust, only a bottom crust pulled up at the edges to form a kind of pleated bowl. Inside, chunks of lamb, potatoes, onions, almonds and raisins. Having been exposed to the delicious *tagines* of Morocco, I detected a distinctly Moroccan flavor. I mentioned this to our waitress and within minutes the cook herself, Moroccan, was by our side, ready and willing to discuss the dish and to name the spices in it: turmeric, cumin, and coriander. Since our Israel trip, I have served this Moroccan pie again and again, often with chicken instead of lamb, to friends who have uniformly praised it. It was in the same YMCA dining room that we lunched on a sandwich of smoked salmon, grilled red peppers, and mozarella cheese on dark brown bread, unfortunately never found in America. Also, a delicious salad of Romaine lettuce, avocados, and anchovies, unique with the addition of fresh baby basil leaves. We have enjoyed these culinary discoveries through the years.

Israel was particularly noteworthy because in Jerusalem John managed to get us a room at the Mishkenot Sha'ananim, the highly privileged guesthouse for internationally acclaimed writers, artists, and musicians. I am not sure exactly how John got us accepted into this august institution, but assume he submitted the names of the various publications (some in Australia) in which his poetry had been published. As I signed the guest book I was awestruck by the signatures of many world-famous names that preceded ours: Heiffitz, Hemingway, Steinbeck, and others. I felt such a fraud. I couldn't help feeling somewhat embarrassed by the royal treatment we received from the staff who must have assumed we were among the internationally acclaimed.

Apart from the sights of Jerusalem itself, Israel was memorable to me for our visit with one of John's old college classmates. He was an orthodox Jew, and at dinner I was mesmerized by his beautiful chant before the meal was served. Dinner the following day at one of Israel's most successful Kibbutzes with another of John's Jewish friends was fascinating, but I couldn't help wondering how long the younger participants would tolerate its restrictive lifestyle.

By 1990, with John in his seventies, we started traveling with tour groups. Unfortunately, this mode of travel was disappointing, but we had reached the point where checking our baggage at airports, arranging transportation in foreign countries, and coping with hotel reservations had become more onerous than in our younger years. Often, though a tour would be billed as a group of no more than thirty persons, on arriving at each destination, we found our group combined with others and enlarged to up to one hundred people. Thus, as we boarded buses for the major sights, we felt much like cattle being herded on and off.

It was on a Grand Circle tour that we went to see the Oberammergau passion play performed only once every ten years by the residents of this small Bavarian town in Germany. I found the eight-hour-long show tedious and boring. The tour, however, also included a few of the major cities of Austria and Switzerland so we did get a taste of the beauties of those areas. We also did Portugal with Grand Circle Tours and again were disappointed. Driving along the coast in a bus, we saw cluster after cluster of condominium-type structures, all seemingly for foreign vacation seekers. Though individually the Portuguese architectural style would have been distinctive and beautiful, en masse they were monotonous in their uniformity. Also, if we had been making our own arrangements, we would surely have booked ourselves into one of the charming *pousadas* that had been converted from ancient castles or historic buildings, rather than the second rate hotels reserved by the tour group. However, we did take away from our Portugal trip a new food, or rather soup, to add to my collection. It was Calde Verde, a potato-based chicken broth, with lots of garlic and cabbage, its "verde" and distinctive flavor provided by chopped kale. It became another addition to our home menus.

Despite the limitations of group travel, we also joined a tour to the Copper Canyon in Northern Mexico. This was supposed to be comparable to the Grand Canyon in depth and scale, but to me, having seen the Grand Canyon in later years, Mexico's Copper Canyon did not compare to it in either beauty or grandeur. However, most of the trip was by train (going through eighty-eight tunnels), so going

The Richness of My Yesterdays 233

through the canyon did give us a totally different perspective than simply viewing it from above.

Then there were cruises. We did Alaska and the Panama Canal, both with the Holland America Lines. The part I enjoyed the best about the Alaska cruise was not Alaska or the cruise itself, but kayaking in the small inlets that were inaccessible to the big ship. I did this together with an old friend with whom we had often traveled in the past. She and I were both in our mid-seventies at the time, and it delighted us to see how much amazement, and even awe, we drew from fellow kayakers seeing two elderly ladies with the gumption to man a kayak.

The Panama Canal itself was impressive, but the cruise was memorable for another reason. I stepped into the bathroom in the middle of the second night aboard to find my feet in two inches of water. Our toilet had flooded the bathroom—luckily with clean water, and it took three days before the problem was repaired. In compensation, Holland American offered us a $100 credit on our "next" Holland America cruise. For us, there was no "next" on Holland America or any other cruise. We decided cruises were not for us.

Of all our travels, the most meaningful was our trip to China in 1995, fifty years after I had left. In the early seventies, after Nixon's visit to China and the re-opening of U.S./China relations, Americans had been flocking to the country that had been closed to tourists for over twenty years. One by one my friends, both Chinese and American, made the trip, some to rave about the country's wonders, others to deplore the changes. My own feelings were mixed. I had beautiful memories of a Peking I loved and was not sure I wanted to see those changes. But now I was thinking ahead to the memoir I had planned to write of my early years in China, and as I searched for memories, I found myself longing to see once more the home of my childhood. I was delighted that two of my children and their spouses wanted to join us.

We arranged a private tour for just our own family. The eighteen-day trip included all the "musts" for first-time visitors to China. It is covered in great detail in my since-published memoir *Adopted, the Chinese Way* so I will not repeat my account here, but instead refer any readers who are interested to the final chapter of that book. There is, however, one instance that bears repeating.

In China, at the time, there was a two-tier system for entry into tourist sites. Entry fees for tourists, *wai pin*, was more than double that for native-born Chinese, *nei pin*. Kathy, on one occasion, couldn't resist trying out her Chinese (learned when we were stationed in Taiwan), and was more than pleased with herself when she requested *nei pin* tickets and was charged the reduced price. To this, son Bean made the disparaging comment, "I don't see why you get such a kick out of pretending we're native. After all, we *are* tourists."

Looking back, I couldn't help being aware of what his words meant. We *were* tourists; we were American; *I* was American. I had left fifty years before, a Chinese, born and raised in China, but at the end of our tour I was ready to go home. I was American, and while China would always be a part of me, it was no longer home to me. For me, and for my children, *home* was America.

Chapter 26
The Downhill Road

In January 1997 we joined an expedition to the Antarctic. This is something John had wanted to do for a long time, but I had not shared his enthusiasm. He was now seventy-eight and was determined to go, with or without me. I could not let him go alone. Again, John made all the arrangements, for some reason choosing to go on a Russian ship.

Our Russian ship

We boarded the ship in Ushuaia, Argentina, and proceeded immediately through the treacherous waters of the Drake Passage. We had been told that we would be facing some of the roughest seas in the world, but on our first day on board the water could not have been more calm. The ship's crew, however, was clearly prepared for rough weather ahead. At our first meal in the ship's dining room we were surprised to see that the tablecloth was soaking wet. I thought that some water had been spilled inadvertently, but was told by our waiter that the wet cloth was to prevent the dishes and utensils from sliding. Still, the day proceeded peacefully, and we were on deck much of the time enjoying the sight of the albatross circling the ship and on the lookout for other signs of sea life. The next morning, however, as I was having my toast and coffee in the dining room, the ship took a mighty lurch and I was suddenly flung to the floor. I had not fallen off the chair; the chair, with me on it, had simply been hurled over onto its side. I was not hurt, only momentarily stunned, and picked myself up without any trouble. Others were not so fortunate. One man fell, broke his glasses, and had severe cuts on his face. Another suffered a dislocated shoulder. Worst was a woman who broke her hip.

The rest of the day was chaotic. The waves were huge; the ship bucked and rolled alarmingly. After a single venture onto the deck, John and I confined ourselves to the safety of the indoor lounge and to our cabin, content to view the massive waves and rolling sea through our porthole. The ship shook so violently that even lying in our bunks trying to read was difficult. Then, suddenly, as we neared the Antarctic peninsula, all was calm again.

During the next few days we took in much of what had been promised in our expedition brochures, everything meeting expectations and more. By now we were accustomed to being surrounded by ice and were very much aware that we were in the Antarctic, at the bottom of the world. From our ship we had seen countless icebergs and ice floes with groups of seals basking in the sun. Inflatable zodiacs had taken us to shore many times to see penguins, penguins, and more penguins. On our fourth day the loudspeaker blared forth that a zodiac would be leaving for a whale watch in an hour. We had had a busy day and John was sound asleep. I tried to waken him, only to have him dismiss me with a grunt. But I was not about to miss this opportunity. I quickly donned my rain gear and life jacket and joined the group departing for the whale watch.

The zodiac took us out into open water, and soon our leader killed the engine. The water was still, but suddenly, the whales, three of them. Three tails emerged, and swept above the water's surface, performing what seemed like a synchronized ballet. Totally in unison the three tails swooped in a graceful arch and then submerged. A few moments, and then a repeat performance, and then another, each time all three rising and then resubmerging together. It was almost as if the whales had been trained to perform for the visiting tourists. One sees pictures of this phenomenon, but to see it first hand and at such close quarters was a thrilling experience. The whales couldn't have been more than thirty feet from our zodiac. In fact, they had been so close that I was concerned that if they swam any nearer they might easily tip us over. Our guide assured us this could not happen. *But how could he be sure?*

When we returned to the ship John was already up and getting ready for a trip to view the penguin rookeries. I decided not to join him. Whale watching had been enough activity for me for one day, and I had frankly had enough of penguins. Instead, I lay down for a nap. I don't know how long I slept, but when I went back on deck there was an unaccustomed commotion. It seems there had been an accident of some kind. Before even inquiring what had happened, I

Rocky terrain, the site of John's fall

had this terrible foreboding. "It's John." All too soon my fears were confirmed. He had twisted his ankle on the very rocky terrain and had taken a bad fall. The crew had put him on a stretcher and brought him back to the ship in the zodiac, but there was no way they could hoist him up the gangplank. When I arrived on the scene one of the lifeboats was being lowered to bring him up. Then, to the ship's infirmary, where the ship's doctor, Russian, determined that John had fractured his hip in the fall. He took care of John's pain with generous doses of pain killer.

It was to be four more days on the ship before we would arrive again in Ushuaia. Those four days were a nightmare, not for John, who was heavily dosed with morphine, but for me. As a result of his fall, John had lost all bladder control, a situation not uncommon in older male patients who have undergone severe trauma. Under normal conditions a plastic urinal would have taken care of the problem, but we were once again traversing turbulent seas. The rolling and bucking of the ship prevented the urinal from staying in place, and even though I tied it up close to his body with a string around John's waist, the urine kept sloshing out. A catheter seemed to be the solution, but without a proper catheter with inflatable balloon to hold it in place, the ship's doctor had to make do with a rubber tube. As he attached this to John's penis with a roll of adhesive tape, I couldn't help thinking how painful this was going to be to remove. I need not have worried. It was soaked through in no time. With no catheter bag, the other end of the tube was placed in the plastic urinal, from which again, there was no way to prevent the urine from sloshing out. Since there was no such thing as rubber sheeting on board, I improvised by cutting open a plastic laundry bag and spreading it on the bed. The only way I could keep John in some semblance of dryness was to keep soaking up the urine with towels. In this way we passed the four days before reaching Ushuaia.

Meanwhile, despite the totally inadequate medical supplies on board ship, I could not fault the ship's staff in any way. The doctor made frequent visits to make sure John was not in pain; the kitchen staff brought food to our cabin. Most important, our expedition leader immediately contacted World Wide Assistance Services (WWA), the company from which we had had the good sense to buy private insurance. From this point on, WWA made all arrangements for John's care and for our repatriation to America. On our arrival in Ushuaia we were met by ambulance and taken to the local hospital. There, we were received by the hospital's director, whose first words were of apology. He explained, "We are a very poor country, but we do the best we can."

During the next few days we learned what a hospital is like in a very poor country. The hospital could not afford to provide sheets, towels, dishes, forks, knives or cups. The patients brought their own. John was assigned the luxury of a single room. His bed was bare. Since it was obvious that this newly arrived patient from America was without the necessary equipment, the family members visiting other patients immediately offered to lend us sheets and other items from their own supplies. Their generosity and desire to help was heartwarming.

On the second day after our arrival in Ushuaia a registered nurse arrived from America, courtesy of WWA. Our contract with the company promised medical assistance, referrals to local hospitals, and all transport and repatriation to our home country. We had not expected a private nurse. Her presence was invaluable. Not only did she immediately set about her nursing duties, but with the limited Spanish she had learned in high school she went shopping and bought all the things John needed for his hospital stay. Meanwhile, I was given permission to move into John's room at the hospital. And while the hospital's only two other non-Argentinean patients, both German, were complaining bitterly about being fed "entrails," John and I were enjoying the frequent servings of tripe, tendons, intestines, tongue, gizzards, and other innards. We found it all delicious. If I had not been so focused on John's condition I would have asked for the specific seasonings used, and added those foods to my home menus. We were well taken care of. Now we had only to wait for air reservations to take us home. It took five more days before stretcher space was available on the two heavily booked legs of the flight back to the U.S. This required ten seats, four rows of double seats for the stretcher, and two more for the nurse and me. The stretcher was positioned on top of the seats, and a makeshift curtain arrangement gave John the semblance of privacy, but I couldn't help noting that few passengers  boarding the plane could resist peering over the curtains en route to their own assigned seats. Changing planes in Rio Gallegos, John was transported from one plane to the other in a delivery truck. I recall cartons of Coke and some swimming pool equipment piled high beside the stretcher.

We arrived in Miami on January 29th, nine days after John's fall. At the Miami airport a Lear Jet, manned by a pilot and copilot,

John, ready for boarding the Lear jet

plus a flight attendant, was waiting for us. A quick flight and we were back in Washington and delivered by ambulance to Arlington Hospital where John underwent emergency surgery for a hip replacement. All arrangements, from the arrival of the nurse in Ushuaia to our safe return to Washington were made by WWA. In Ushuaia there had been few English speakers—at the hospital the only person who spoke

English was the hospital director—and I don't know how we could possibly have managed without their help. All expenses too were borne by WWA. The cost must have been enormous. The company even reimbursed us for John's hospital expenses in Ushuaia, all of $337 for his five-day stay, the charges unbelievable compared to what they would have been in the U.S. There was no charge for the days I spent in the hospital with John, or for my meals. All in all, we felt fortunate. John's fall had taken place toward the end of our trip, *after* he had accomplished his goal of seeing the Antarctic. This was not the case for the poor woman who had broken her hip *before* reaching our destination.

The aftermath of our Antarctic expedition, however, was not as auspicious. Following the surgery, John had weeks of rehab and physical therapy. He never regained full use of his leg and was never totally without pain. I insisted on his seeing another orthopedist for a reevaluation. The diagnosis was "a failed surgery." John refused a repeat operation, and for the rest of his life lived with this condition. He did not complain. But then, in June 1998, just a year and a half after the Antarctic expedition, the stroke.

We had finished dinner. John was working at his desk and I at mine. Suddenly, a loud crash. John had fallen off his chair. He was not hurt. He claimed to have simply swiveled around too fast on his swivel chair. Later, that same evening, another fall. And later, yet another. Each time, he picked himself up and assured me he was fine. But the next morning, getting out of bed, he was unable to stand. Each time he tried, his legs would not support him and he fell back onto the bed. I called 911.

The days, weeks, and months following John's stroke were again filled with rehab and therapy. A slight slurring in John's speech resolved itself in a week and he had no apparent cognitive impairment. Though there was no paralysis, it took months before he was able to walk unassisted. Visits to doctors,—the cardiologist, neurologist, internist, and urologist—became a routine part of our lives. A diagnosis of atrial fibrilation required frequent changes in his medical regimen, a constant monitoring of his heart, and a juggling of his prescriptions. He was plagued with recurring bladder infections. Other complications arose during the next two years, each requiring a procedure of some kind: a stubborn kidney stone, a prostate problem, a hernia, elevated blood pressure. All attempts to control his atrial fibrilation were unsuccessful. A pacemaker was installed in 2001.

And then there were the endless falls. Some were a mere crumbling of his legs with no injuries or only minor bruises. Others times, a broken rib, a cracked pelvis, some heavy bruising, and alarming swellings. There were several trips to the ER, and an occasional overnight hospital stay. But through it all, life went on. It did not stop; it simply changed. Though the stroke had not left any visible signs of cognitive impairment, John was definitely not as sharp with figures as he had once been. We had to make changes in the way we handled our finances. Throughout our marriage we had always had "his," "mine," and "ours." By mutual agreement, John had always been responsible for "ours." Now, I couldn't help noting that John was having difficulty balancing our checkbook and that the errors were in huge amounts. Now I took over management of our joint holdings. John was almost relieved to give up this responsibility.

Looking back, I am amazed at the change in my attitude toward money through the years. John and I had always been frugal. It never occurred to us to pay others to do what we could do for ourselves. And we had always traveled in the cheapest possible way. A friend asked me, "Why *did* you feel the need to be so frugal?" I did not have a ready answer. There had been no *real* need. John and I lived comfortably on our combined pensions, but for our travels we *did* have to draw on savings, he from his, and I from mine. And whatever we saved on one trip enabled us to afford the next. I supposed also we had been "saving for our old age." But now, "old age" had arrived. The years of panic when the three children's college tuitions were draining away my savings were long past. I was not a particularly astute investor, but the money I had invested in the stock market had appreciated. Also, I had invested Horace's life insurance money in two rental properties. These I had turned over several times, holding consecutively through the years eight rental properties, benefiting each time from their appreciation. I no longer needed to guard my savings.

I now had five grandchildren, two of Eric's, and three of Kathy's. I felt it was time they saw something of the world beyond their own backyards. As I didn't want these vacations to be a financial strain on any of my children, I decided to bear the full costs. For months we had been planning a trip to Italy. Unfortunately, John's stroke took place just two weeks before our scheduled departure. The children took off without us. It was an enormous disappointment for John and me to miss this, the first of our family vacations abroad.

Of the many places we rented in later years, Monte Vibiano, in Umbria was the grandest of all. It was not just a house. The property encompassed an entire mountain, the house, akin to a medieval castle, sitting on its crest. Its vineyards swept down the hill on all sides. The immediate surround included a gazebo-like teahouse, an evergreen maze, a swimming pool, replete with fountain at one end, and even its own

Monte Vibiano in Umbria

free-standing chapel. All this was described and photographed by my children in great detail.

After Italy, however, we enjoyed other family vacations. Some were within the U.S., and John was able to join us on vacations in the Adirondacks and another at Martha's Vineyard in Massachusetts.

Others were abroad. One vacation in Ireland was almost as grand as the one John and I had missed in Italy. There, we rented a castle in Tipperary. Silver candelabra and serving pieces adorned the buffet and the dining table, and we drank our wine from stemware of Waterford

Me and daughter-in-law Nora in front of our castle

crystal. Our sheets and pillow cases were of beautifully embroidered Irish linen. All of us were surprised at how trusting the owners were of their short-term renters, and I wondered if any had ever abused this trust by filching a goblet or two. Other years we rented a lovely villa in the Costa Brava in Spain, one in the South of France, and another in Quebec City in Canada. These family vacations brought our family closer in a way that Christmas or Thanksgiving get-togethers did not. The grandchildren got to know each other and their aunts and uncles, to know me, and me to know them. Bringing my family together during my lifetime was a far better use of my savings than leaving it to them after my death. My only regret was that John could not be a part of our family vacations abroad.

In 1985, when we bought our McLean townhouse, we had thought we would live out the rest of our lives in this house we loved. But by the year 2000, the stairs were getting harder for John to climb. We explored the possibility of an electric chair-lift for the staircase, but our stairs were u-shaped, making installation impractical. An elevator was a possibility, and though the configuration of our house *did* allow for it, it would be an ugly addition to an otherwise beautiful home, not to mention the cost. Both John and I were in agreement that it would be wiser to give up the house and to look at other options.

A "continuing care retirement community," was the logical course of action. We checked out eight of these CCRCs in the greater Washington area and put our money down to reserve a place at three. We were told the wait-time would be approximately three years. That was fine. We were not yet ready to move, but we were comfortable knowing we were prepared for whatever lay ahead.

Chapter 27
The Memoir

For years I had been planning to write a memoir about my family and my own early years in China, but there was always a reason to put it off. The trip to China, however, brought home to me how little knowledge, or even interest, my totally American children had in the Chinese part of their heritage. They knew I had been born and raised in China. They knew I was adopted, but knew little of the circumstances of my adoption. Except for our brief visits with my parents when we were on home leave, they knew almost nothing of their American grandmother or Chinese grandfather. They had no idea of the complicated relationships within a Chinese family, or the effect of a concubine's presence within a household. And they had no concept of how different my childhood had been from theirs. Our China trip did spark in them a glimmer of interest, but not much beyond that of any other American tourist. Yet, I felt there would come a day when, children grown and jobs long past, they might wish they knew more. It was time to put something down on paper.

I began my memoir with my birth and adoption in 1925, and ended when I left China in 1945 after the end of World War II. In writing of family relationships, I did include incidents that occurred in later years, but did not go further in writing about my own life in America. I had decided early on that the part of my life most meaningful for my children would be my years in China, the years of which they knew little.

The words came easily. The memoir was for my children and I was not particularly concerned with syntax or literary perfection. I was simply putting down all that I knew of my family and everything I could remember of my early years. From a somewhat battered file marked "Memoir," I retrieved scraps of paper I had been collecting for years, reminders of things I should include. "K rations for Xmas," "Mother's furs," "Sunrise in WH," a few newspaper clippings, and scribblings that were hardly legible. I was not a focused writer. I wrote only when the spirit moved me, which was only when I had nothing better to occupy my time. It must have been two years before I put it all together. For family and closest friends I had thirteen copies printed and assembled in ring binders at Kinkos. It was done. I was pleased that I had done what I had set out to do. But I knew too that it was not really done at all. I had told myself I was writing for my children, but at the back of my mind I had always known that I wanted to tell my story to a wider audience. With encouragement from friends, and particularly from my husband John, I started again, this time with hopes of publishing.

My first effort recorded all the facts, but looking objectively at the whole, I realized it was not even remotely in publishable condition. There was much work to be done. The following months were devoted to reading. I have never done so much reading in my life. I immersed myself in books on life in China. I read memoir after memoir, hoping that the qualities in the memorable ones would somehow, by osmosis, seep into my work. One, by Michael Ondaatje was so hilarious it made me laugh out loud. But *his* humor was no help to me. My family was not funny. *I* was not funny. Other memoirs were filled with the stuff of which tragedies are made. I had no tragedies in *my* family on which to draw. All the memoirs I read contained multiple anecdotes. I racked my brain, but could think of precious few. I would have to do with what I had. I noted that they all contained dialogue in varying amounts. My memoir was written entirely as a first-person narrative. I *could* make an attempt at adding dialogue. It was not a comfortable medium for me, but I would try.

I not only read memoirs, I also read book reviews, noting the features that were applauded, and particularly the qualities that were disparaged. Most disturbing was a withering critique by Jonathan Yardley, literary critic for the Washington Post. His scathing words about a newly published memoir surely doomed that author to literary obscurity. Yardley wrote that the author's descriptions of his boyhood were "self absorbed," and contained "far too much of himself in self-indulgent ways." This touched a nerve with me. Throughout my writing I had been very much aware, *and* concerned, that my memoir was too much about me, me, me. But was not a whole book entirely about oneself a monumental self-indulgence in itself? How did one avoid that?

Apart from that major problem, I realized too that my work needed major reorganization. I proceeded to dissect the ring-bound pages relentlessly. I moved whole chapters around. I cut lines and paragraphs from some pages and pasted them onto others. I expanded parts that I thought would resonate with readers. My stolen moments with *Lady Chatterley's Lover* at age twelve I expanded from three lines to two pages. Being jilted by my first love at age fourteen I stretched from six lines to six pages. *Were these not universal rites of passage?* I tried to bring situations to life by using dialogue rather than narrative. And I added many many details of Chinese things and places that I gleaned from the scores of books I read, things once familiar to me, but long since forgotten. It took me two more years to complete the revised version, but I felt the improvement had been worth the time and effort.

It was not until the end of 2000 that I was ready to start looking for a publisher. I knew this would not be easy. I spent hours at the library poring through the pages of *Writers' Market*, a hefty tome that was the single best resource for aspiring authors. I copied the names of countless publishers and their requirements for submissions. Some requested the first fifty pages; others, the first three chapters. I read all the books and articles I could find on how to get published. The cover letter, or "query," that accompanied a submission was all important.

It had to "sell" your book to prospective publishers. Following the instructions of all the "how to" books meticulously, I included the requisite introductory bio, a brief summary of content, the intended audience, and my reasons for why the book should sell. Whenever I could identify the particular interest of a publisher, I tailored the cover letter accordingly. I then assembled packages of my work and mailed them off to five publishers who had seemed most promising. Then I waited. And waited.

I had known this would be a long process, and was prepared for the wait. When one *did* come back, rejected, I repackaged it and sent it to the next publisher on my list. I learned quickly, however, that it was a mistake to wait for submissions to be returned before sending out more. More often than not it was two or more months before my pages were returned. Soon I was sending out copies every two weeks. Altogether, in an eight month period, I sent sample pages of my memoir with their accompanying documents to more than forty publishers with no success. I had, however, received many encouraging rejections, *if any rejection can be considered encouraging.* Knopf had said "the parts submitted have much charm." St. Martin's said my submission showed "terrific promise." Some editors had taken the time to write full-page letters with suggestions on how I could make my work more salable, and suggested alternate publishers. Others, in addition to the word "charm" added words like "interesting, fascinating, poignant, appealing, well told, and well written," but these words were always followed by the inevitable "but." The reasons given were varied: "Not strong enough to be competitive," "too particular to your own experience," "doesn't meet our needs," and most often, "not a good fit." Only one publisher, after receiving my sample pages, asked me to send my full manuscript. This gave me a glimmer of hope. I sent the full book, but heard not another word from them even after writing a follow-up letter. Then, of course, there were the many printed rejection forms. Three publishers, however, praised me and every facet of my submissions, only to explain how expensive the publishing process was, and to ask that I bear part of the cost of publishing. In each case the cost to me would be in the vicinity of ten to twelve thousand dollars. For that, I would receive five hundred books (the minimum cost-effective run) to sell or to store in my basement. Not an appealing prospect.

By midsummer of 2002, I gave up on finding a publisher, but I had worked too hard to give up. I looked for alternatives. By then, Print-on-demand (POD) publishing was beginning to make its presence felt in the publishing world. Relying entirely on digital printing technology, these computer-generated books could be printed in small quantities, even in single copies. For a given fee the POD publishers would not only print, design a cover, and handle royalties and mailings, but most important, they would obtain a copyright and take care of all the legal formalities of publishing a book. I checked out several POD publishers and elected to go with Infinity Publishing. com, primarily because they were the only ones who would permit me to do my own formatting. By so doing I would be able to have my pictures and sketches "accompany" the corresponding text, rather than be inserted in a block with other unrelated pictures. This was important to me. For me, a relative novice with computers, formatting was a challenging task, but when completed (with a great deal of help from my son Eric's wife Carolyn), I felt as pleased with this accomplishment as I had been with the actual writing of the memoir. The book was published in November 2002. Infinity had been a joy to work with. They delivered all

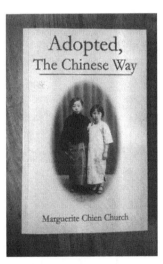

My published memoir

services as promised and within the stated time frame. From the delivery of my manuscript to the finished book, it had taken four months. Its selling price, determined by the publisher, would be $17.95, and was based on the number of pages. At a large discount on

my first order, I placed an order for one hundred books. Now I had to
sell them.

In addition to reading books on how to publish, I had also
been reading material on how to market my book. For self-published
authors the most frequent advice was to attend as many book fairs as
possible. For me this was not possible as my husband John's health
was such that I could neither take him with me nor leave him at home
alone. Other advice was to enlist the help of friends and family, to
have them host book-signing occasions on my behalf. This, I could
not bring myself to do. I did not want to put friends, or even family
members, in a position where *their* friends felt under pressure to buy
my book. For invitees it would be as bad as being pressed into the
obligatory purchase of plastic containers at a Tupperware party. No, I
would do the marketing on my own.

I began by hosting three book-signing events at our home in
Mclean. To the first I invited old and good friends, to most of whom
I gave the books as gifts. The second and third were for my tennis
group and for our housing community. These were not by invitation,
but only announced in the groups' monthly bulletins. Thus, there was
no pressure on anyone to come unless they were truly interested. Even
so, they drew a surprising number of people and resulted in numerous
sales. Apart from these three self-hosted book-signing events, I sent
copies of the book to the quarterly alumnae publications of my college
alma mater Smith College, and PAS, the high school I attended in
China. I also obtained interviews with writers from two small local
newspapers in the area, both of whom wrote enthusiastic articles
plugging the book. It was impossible to tell whether this advertising
produced any sales. I also sent copies of the book to the gift stores
of several museums specializing in Asian artifacts. Only two were
willing to carry the book, one of which was the Smithsonian's Sackler
Gallery in Washington, D.C. One of my grandsons, visiting the Sackler
with out-of-town friends, was surprised to see the book prominently
displayed on the store's shelves. He reported how impressed they
had been that his grandmother was a published author. The store

had placed an initial order of twelve books, but, disappointingly, the book did not sell well enough to warrant a second order. Still, the fact that the very prestigious Sackler had carried my book at all was an enormous source of pride to me.

Looking back at my marketing efforts, I believe that without the many marketing tools available via the Internet today, I did as much as one person could do at that time. Most sales were the result of meeting *with* and speaking *to* readers personally, mostly at book club events. The initial self-hosted book-signings at our home had led to invitations to speak to several book clubs. These in turn had led to more speaking engagements, some to book clubs, others to residential community associations, and to women's groups, each occasion adding to the book's sales numbers.

All in all, I was not unhappy with the way it had been received. I had accomplished my original goal of providing my children with a picture of the China of my early years. I had wanted the story to reach a wider audience, and it had (*though not as wide as I had once hoped*), not only through sales, but also through it's being carried in local libraries. I had done book-signings at both the Dolly Madison library in McLean and the Richard Byrd Library in Springfield. The attendance at both had been wretchedly poor—four people at each one—but despite the poor showing the Richard Byrd had nonetheless ordered nine copies for the Fairfax County's library system.

For a self-published book it had done far better than I expected, sales to date numbering over one thousand, and there had been an enormous bonus in the large number of friends, old and new, that it brought into my life. Letters came from friends who had known me at every stage—mostly from my years in China—and even from people I had forgotten I had ever known. Others came from perfect strangers who for one reason or another were interested in China. Many came from women who had themselves adopted a Chinese child. And some, from people without access to my address, were forwarded to me through Infinity Publishing. Today, thirteen years after the book's publication, sales are down to a mere trickle, but once or twice a year, I pick up my mail, and find an envelope from Infinity Publishing. In it is a small check, just enough to have dinner out. I can't help smiling.

Chapter 28
Downsizing

Toward the end of 2002, John announced, "It's time to move." I agreed. It was time. The stairs were becoming increasingly difficult for him, and our step-down living room, which had once been an attractive feature of the house, was now a distinct hazard not only for John, but for our friends of comparable age as well. For some time I had been noticing that when stepping down into the living room they frequently put their hands on the wall for support. To prevent any possible accidents, we had already installed vertical handrails. Also, there was the problem of coping with the snow in the winter months. Though our streets were plowed by the community, our long driveway was not. With John unable to help, and no teenagers in the vicinity to do the shoveling, I, close to eighty years old, was saddled with this chore. Yes, it was definitely time to move.

We contacted the three retirement communities where we had made deposits to check on availability. At one we were still far down on the waiting list. The second, which we had selected because it was in an urban area, near a shopping mall with restaurants and shops, and most important, a Metro station, was no longer feasible for us, as John was now unable to walk the long Metro platforms or the mall areas. But at the third, Greenspring Village, in Springfield, Virginia, a new building was under construction with several apartments available. We selected one with two bedrooms, two baths, *and* a balcony. It was one of the larger apartments with a square footage of fourteen hundred feet. Still, it was going to be hard to shrink from our thirty-four-hundred square-foot house to the smaller dimensions. We would have to do some serious downsizing.

At Greenspring we selected a move-in date in May 2003, giving us several months to sell our house and to dispose of what we would not need. We expected some cosmetic improvements would be necessary, but the friend and neighbor to whom we gave the listing assured us that the place looked great and would easily sell "as is." True to her word, on the first day the house was listed, as she was putting up the "for sale" sign on the front lawn, a prospective buyer appeared. He did a quick walk-through, returned with his wife, and by 4:00 that afternoon the sales contract was signed. I suspect that, in her eagerness to make the sale, our realtor had seriously underpriced the house. Our buyers, both realtors themselves, must have recognized instantly the value of their purchase. For our part, though we might have done better on the sales price, it was still more than twice what we had originally paid, and we were spared the grief of having to have the house constantly ready for viewing. Some of the neighbors, however, were irate because they felt our realtor had lowered the value of their property. Others were disgruntled at there not having been an "open house" at which they could have seen the inside of our house.

The house sold, we then had to take a hard look at our possessions. With five children between us, we knew we had ready takers for our excess Chinese furniture, rugs, and decorative items. However, they all had fully furnished homes of their own and would not be able to take everything. I had never been a collector of antiques, but still had many items of value from my family that had been kept in boxes for years and never displayed. Since none of my children were antique collectors either, we decided that now was the time to put up for auction those items of value. Sloanes and Kenyon auction house was happy to take the porcelains and paintings, but what really pleased me was that they were also willing to take an assortment of oddments that I had never known what to do with: embroidered headpieces, slippers for bound feet, antique Mandarin robes in poor condition, old Chinese costume jewelry, and yards of uncut "tribute silk." This silk had been made expressly as tribute for emperors, but it was not suitable for dresses, and was too sumptuous for any upholstery that I would be likely to use. In their catalogue sale, Sloanes and Kenyon offered these things in groups, and I suspect they were snapped up speedily by some interior decorator. We were pleased with the net amount we received from the auction.

The remainder of our belongings we would dispose of at a moving sale at the house *after* we had made the move to Greenspring. I was ruthless in limiting what we would bring. Books were a major problem. I told John we were taking two bookcases, and any books that would not fit in them would not come with us. I had taken careful measurements of our new apartment and knew exactly what pieces the apartment could hold and where they would be positioned. On May 3, 2003, the moving company had rugs and every piece of furniture in place, and boxes of kitchenware, books, linens, and clothing in their designated rooms. The following day, with the help of our cleaning girl's husband who owned a truck, we moved the more fragile items, lamps, pictures, and china, ourselves. Within the week pictures were hung, dishes were in their cabinets, books in the book cases, and clothes hung in the closets. Most important, John was settled comfortably in our new home. We had had the good sense to pick a settlement date on the sale of our McLean house a full month after our move-in date to Greenspring, leaving me with three more weeks to deal with what was left in the house.

The next step was to scout out local moving sales to see how they were run. Most of these were euphemistically called "estate sales" regardless of how small and insignificant the property, and most were operated by professional downsizers who took a hefty commission for their services. In addition, their contracts stipulated— in small print—that they be permitted to sell items not belonging to the house owners, "to enhance sales." They were in effect using the owners' home as a venue for their own sales. At a friend's moving sale we found the principal rooms filled with costume jewelry, and the closets jammed with used clothing, none of which belonged to our friends. We decided we would conduct our own sale.

For the month following our move I made daily trips from Springfield to McLean, each time sorting and organizing the remainder of our belongings. In this I had the help of daughter-in-law Carolyn and close friend and neighbor Marianne Potter. This was hard work and could have been an onerous chore, but we actually had a good time doing it. First we sorted, putting all like-kind things in one room: pictures and scrolls were hung in the master bedroom; linens for both bed and table, plus throw cushions, in a second bedroom; clothing in a third. Bric-a-brac and ornaments went in the living room. Antiques and Asian artifacts went in the dining room. Dishes and kitchen-ware were of course in the kitchen, tools and garden furniture and equipment in the garage. After the sorting we worked on pricing. I would hold up an item. Carolyn would say "Five dollars." Marianne would counter with "No, it's worth at least ten." I would declare, "Eight," and we'd slap a sticker on it. In this way, we went through everything item by item, feeling very pleased with ourselves when the job was done.

Our ad in the Washington Post described what our sale would include:

"Treasures from years in the Far East. Chinese antiques, ornaments, and accessories: standing cinnabar-colored screen, large wall screen, leather wedding boxes, rosewood Ming style altar table, porcelain umbrella stand, paintings (framed and unframed), many scrolls. Also, Mandarin robe, antique embroideries, beautiful hand-embroidered linens, Blue Danube china, glassware, garden furniture, rattan easy chairs, drop-leaf table, rugs. Steamer trunks, footlockers."

The wording may have been a mistake, for, though it drew hordes of buyers, it also brought numbers of dealers who were knocking at our door at 7:00 A.M. During the sale they were fighting with each other over who had seen an item first. I had to step in and physically separate them. On items on which I would not lower the price, the dealers returned the following day to try badgering me into a deal.

All in all, the sale was a smashing success. Many who came declared it the best organized moving sale they had ever attended. I'm sure we netted more for our efforts than any professionals could have, and the whole experience, though exhausting, had been exhilarating and fun. When the sale was over, our children came with their rented trucks and u-hauls and loaded up the things they were claiming. They had already taken the smaller objects, but we had needed the furniture pieces for display purposes at the sale. Son Bean, whose job with J.P. Morgan had him living in Japan, had already indicated what he wanted, and his items had to be taken to a mini-storage unit. There was very little left unsold, and most of this we carted off to Goodwill and the Salvation Army. There were no takers, however, for John's Hammond organ, which, apart from being a fine musical instrument, was also a beautiful piece of furniture. We then offered it to various churches and schools, but still there were no takers. We finally decided to advertise it in the paper. I called the classified ads section and explained, "I'm not sure where you would place this ad as I am not interested in selling, but want to *give away* an organ." To this, the woman in classified responded quite curtly, "I'm sorry we don't take that kind of ad." I found this hard to believe, and questioned her. "But surely there is some place in your column for give-away items." She repeated abruptly, "I've already told you. We don't accept ads like that." I persisted. "I don't see how you can run a classified column without a place for donations." At this, she became quite annoyed. "Ma'am, I've told you twice, we *cannot* accept your ad." On my pressing further, she gave me another number to call. But when I called that number and explained the situation, the woman answering my call was totally perplexed. "I can't imagine why you were given my number. We only handle medical reporting." With that, the light dawned; the problem was solved. Both she and I realized that there were "organs" and "organs," and ours had obviously been mistaken for a non-musical kind.

Following this misunderstanding, we did put the ad in the paper, specifying our preference that the organ go to a church or philanthropic organization. There was no response for two days. On the third we had several eager takers, but none could provide transport. When we had all but given up, we received a call from a man identifying himself as a church deacon. He and another came within the hour, and minutes after their arrival made off with the organ in their truck. They were two of the scruffiest looking black men I have ever seen. At the time, I had been skeptical, but they had produced a program from *their* church, and I thought that perhaps even church deacons are entitled to look slovenly on their days off. In retrospect, I was quite sure our beautiful organ, which had given us so many hours of pleasure, was not being played in any church. However, even if our scruffy church deacon made a few easy dollars from it, I only hope that some underprivileged child or family is enjoying it as much as we did.

The sale was done, and all of our unneeded belongings disposed of. I had lost six pounds in the process, but had a tremendous feeling of satisfaction over a job accomplished. Then came the settlement on the house. It was completed with no problems. It had been our home for eighteen years, longer than any other house we had ever occupied. It was now no longer ours. We would no longer see the view across the pond, beautiful in every season, or the swirls of goldfish that swarmed so often at the water's edge. We would miss the annual birthing of a brood of Canada geese who had made our pond their home, and we would no longer watch in fascination as the goslings made their first efforts at flight. I thought I would miss my garden too, as well as all the plantings I had put in on the far side of the pond, but surprisingly, once we moved, we both had no problem putting our old lives behind us.

We would now begin our resettlement at what we facetiously called our "old folks home," and in a way, that is what it was. At the first of the marketing events that we attended, it had been painfully obvious to us that all the other participants were "old." But no older than we. John was eighty-four; I was seventy-eight. It was unsettling.

I felt as if, in moving into Greenspring, we were resigning ourselves to *being* old. Still, if that was the case, Greenspring was a lovely environment in which to *be* old. It was beautifully landscaped, and totally surrounded by trees. The windows of our apartment were large, and all looked out onto the woods. Though our living space was little more than a third of that in our Mclean house, the living/dining area could comfortably hold six for the occasional get-together with old friends that we still expected to host. The second bedroom was large enough to use as our bedroom, and the master bedroom became the room in which we *lived*. It held everything our former family room had held, including a sofabed, an easy chair, both our desks, and the TV. I would miss having a guestroom, but how many days a year had it been in use? The sofa bed would serve the same purpose. Would we miss the basement recreation room? The only time it was ever used was when my five grandchildren visited and piled in with their sleeping bags. John *would* miss his jacuzzi. He had so enjoyed lying in that roiling water several times a day that we had actually redone our master bathroom, enlarging the windows to come down to the edge of the tub so that John could look out onto the pond as he soaked. The only thing *I* missed was having the space to keep my ironing board up and ready for use. Now, it had to be kept in the closet. But apart from that, rather surprisingly, the three rooms we now had met all our needs, and I wondered why we had ever needed all the rooms that had seemed so essential in our past lives.

The same feeling applied to many of the possessions we had cherished through the years. Most of them were now in our children's homes where we were still able to see and enjoy them, and also to wonder at why on earth we had ever owned so much. Admittedly, at our moving sale, I had felt a few twinges of regret as I watched eager buyers snapping up things I had haggled over relentlessly in some Asian bazaar years ago. They had meant so much to us then, but how much did they mean at this stage in our lives? They were material "things" we had enjoyed while we had them. It was hard to believe that their loss meant so little now. It was time to move on to the next stage in our lives.

Chapter 29
Another Life

Choosing Greenspring as our new home was a big move for us, and a happy one. Greenspring delivered well on all the glowing promises made in its advertising brochures. No longer was there a lawn to mow, leaves to rake, or snow to shovel. The single monthly fee was no more than our past expenses, and all the costs of maintaining a house were things of the past. Now, a simple call to our service department took care of all maintenance problems.

Settling in to our new home was no doubt easier for us than for the many who had lived in one home for fifty or more years. We had, after all, during our working years, been accustomed to moving to new locales and coping with new circumstances. The move to Greenspring was almost like being assigned to a new overseas station, with a few differences of course. The only major adjustment for us was at mealtimes. Accustomed to having dinner between seven and eight, we were horrified at first to find that dinner hours were between four and six (The wait staff was made up of mostly high school students who were required to be off duty by seven). However, surprisingly, we adapted to the new hours fairly easily. Instead of having an afternoon snack and a late dinner, we now had an early dinner and a late evening snack. What was a more difficult adjustment was having obligatory dinner companions every night. Both John and I were reasonably social beings, but exchanging our quiet candle-lit dinners at home for nightly social get-togethers in a large, noisy dining room was not always a welcome change. Mealtime was a lottery, never knowing what we would draw. Oftentimes our table-mates would be interesting, and the conversation lively and enlightening. Other times, an hour of making small talk with unresponsive partners was excruciatingly dull. However, all that said, we were glad that we were meeting and getting to know people from all walks of life. Mealtimes at Greenspring brought home to us how limited our past associations had been. Apart from our neighbors, our contacts had been confined to State Department or military personnel, members of academia, and the diplomatic world. Now, we were in real middle class America.

Greenspring was large, with two thousand residents, eighteen hundred of whom lived in "independent living" apartments. A separate facility on the same campus included "assisted living" units and full nursing care units. Its size was made somewhat less daunting by its encompassing three separate "neighborhoods," each with its own lobby, restaurant, and special facilities. All provisions and activities, however, were available to all residents across the board, regardless of which neighborhood was their home base. We had at first thought that Greenspring was far too large, but soon discovered that its very size was what made it such an active and vibrant community. The large number of residents brought with them a large number of talents. Writers led writers' groups, dancers organized dancing sessions, historians gave lectures, musicians not only gave performances, they brought in concert groups from their outside connections, and computer experts were there to rescue the computer illiterate when their children were unavailable. A brochure listed over two hundred activity groups, each one organized and run by residents. There was something for everyone, and if there was no activity that met your needs, you had the support of the community's staff in initiating one yourself.

For my part, though there was already a sing-along evening in another neighborhood, with my guitar I started a new one in ours. Since an acoustic guitar was not strong enough to carry a large group, our thrift shop, the Treasure Chest (also run by residents), without hesitation, provided the funds for two microphones (voice and instrument), the mike stands, and an amplifier. My singing had always been limited to soloing, but now I learned the chords for all the old favorites. Leading a sing-along was a new experience, and fun. I did this for four years, until I was rudely awakened by hearing a playback of my performance in one of our variety shows. Surely that weak, wobbly voice I heard was not me! The tremulous vibrato was very much that of an old lady. It was time to give up the sing-along and any other kind of singing in public.

John and I took advantage of much that the community offered, the lectures, the concerts, the movies, and were delighted to be charged only five dollars for performances for which we had once paid $30 or more at the Wolf Trap Center for Performing Arts. Years ago, when I first came to Washington as a young girl just out of college, I had gone only once to a movie by myself. Though the theatre was nearly empty, a man seated himself beside me, and barely into the movie, I felt his hand on my thigh. I had been too frightened to stay. After that experience I never again attended a movie alone, but now, for the first time in years, whenever John was unable to accompany me, I was comfortable going alone.

At the end of our first year we gave up our past primary care doctors for those at Greenspring whom we liked better than any doctors we had ever had. We also moved our bank accounts from our bank in McLean to the PNC bank's offices at Greenspring. We both joined the health club and used the many machines in the fitness center. I participated in some of the exercise classes, yoga, and aerobics, and I joined the small tennis group. Also, though I had thought gardening would be a thing of the past, I was able to continue in the 10' x 10' garden plots at our new home. I was kept busy filling mine with perennials. Our lives were more and more centered in Greenspring.

Surprisingly, it was at Greenspring, that I found a new calling that was as satisfying as any activity I had every pursued. We had been at Greenspring over a year when one day a ceramic sculpture appeared in my garden plot. It was of two figures under an umbrella.

I was quite sure someone had put it there by mistake and would soon reclaim it. However, a few days later, John and I were seated at dinner with the Woods, a congenial couple whom we had met the week before. Priscilla Wood's first words were "What did you think of my sculpture?" I was relieved to have found the owner. "Oh, it's yours," I said. "I'm so glad to know who it belongs to, but—." Before I could say more, she replied, "No, it *was* mine, but now it's yours. If you like it, that is, it's yours. I have absolutely no room in our apartment, and want you to have it." I was thrilled with this gift from a new-found friend.

When I learned that Priscilla was a professional potter, I persuaded her to show some of her work in Greenspring's upcoming art show. The end result? At the insistence of residents, she started a pottery class. I had always admired the beautiful pottery made in Japan, and that in Mexico too, but had never had any desire to own it, and certainly not to make it. I leaned more to finer, more formal china. But, to be supportive, I joined her class. It took only one session. I was hooked. Little did I know that after Priscilla's death five years later, I and one of the more experienced class members would become leaders of the group. Since that time we have consistently had twenty

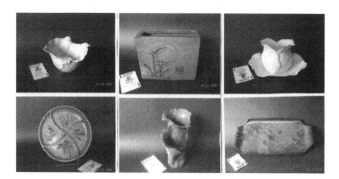

Some of my pots

or more participants in our twice-weekly sessions. We are fortunate that we are able to sell our pottery at Greenspring's annual bazaars and fairs, thus solving the problem that plagues every person engaged in a craft of any kind, that of disposing of one's work. Also, I was able to talk the manager of Greenspring's three convenience stores into allowing us to sell in the stores, this quite a concession as we occupied valuable display space that added nothing to the store's bottom line. The ever-present entrepreneur in me exulted in our actually making money from our work, and being able to donate our proceeds (from three to five thousand dollars annually) to Greenspring's charitable fund was a double bonus. But more important for me than dollars and cents was that, in my eighties, when I was daily more aware of my diminishing abilities in other spheres, I had found a new calling, one in which my abilities, rather than declining, could only improve.

Greenspring's charitable endeavors offered me yet another new and exciting experience. In one of its fund-raising efforts, the philanthropy department proposed printing a calendar. This was to be modeled after the British movie *Calendar Girls*, in which the members of a women's club are photographed, apparently in the nude, to raise needed funds. I was asked if I would be willing to be one of the calendar girls and was told they would understand if I preferred not to participate. I was thrilled to have been asked and could not

The Ladies of Greenspring calendar

imagine why anyone would even think of declining. After all, I would not have to *be* naked, only to *appear* so. I would wear my bathing suit, only dropping the straps, and my guitar would cover the crucial areas. I suspected that the reason I was asked was because I had this ready-made object to hide my supposed nakedness. The calendar was much publicized both on TV channels and in the local press. It was a great success, grossing over $40,000 in sales, and I was delighted to have been a part of it. It also gave me my few minutes of attention, if not fame. Walking into the post office, one of the postal clerks spotted me and shouted out, "That's Miss August," and immediately all eyes were on me. Another day, while on our shuttle bus, a fellow passenger said, "You looked so sexy." I had never in all my life *been*, or *looked* sexy. I took a perverse kind of pleasure in achieving a modicum of sexiness in my mid eighties.

Being a calendar girl also brought with it another kind of attention in the form of an unexpected phone call. The day before, I had met Priscilla's oldest son James and his family who were here for

the day, but still, I was surprised at his call. "Hi, this is James," he said. I immediately launched into a conversation, saying how glad I was to have met him and commenting on his many talents Priscilla had told me about. In the

Miss August

course of conversation he told me he had seen the calendar and thought the picture of me was great. He then added, "I do some modeling myself, you know." Since he looked very definitely middle-aged and not exactly modeling material, I asked, "You mean when you were young?" To which he responded, "No, now," and added, "Have you ever seen a picture of a well built man?" I thought of the pictures I had seen of body builders in muscular poses, and said, "Of course." To which he replied, "Then you might want to see some pictures of me. I'm very well hung." I was not sure I had heard right, and quite stupidly only one word came out of me. "What?" And he replied, "I'm very well hung, if you know what I mean." By then, I surely did know what he meant. I then made some excuse and hung up. I couldn't believe I had been taken in so easily, but up until the time he had brought his anatomy into the picture, we were having a fine conversation, with him picking up readily on whatever comments I made. The next day, still under the impression I had been talking to Priscilla's son, I asked some very probing questions of Priscilla and concluded, much to my relief that *her* James and my caller James were not one and the same.

Of all the calendar girls, only one other, my neighbor Virginia Scott, received a similar call. In her case the caller introduced himself by saying, "I'm a friend of Helen's." It so happened that Virginia *did* have a friend named Helen, and like me, she launched into a conversation about how Helen was doing. It wasn't until the subject of his anatomy came up that she realized things were not right and hung up. I don't know why we two were the objects of his calls, but it did make me aware that public visibility is not always desirable.

While I was totally energized by all these new activities, John was not doing as well. But despite his deteriorating health, he was happy. He loved our apartment. He loved looking out at the woods. He loved watching the beautiful sunsets through the trees. He liked it here, and an incident that occurred shortly after arrival gave him a feeling of security. During a heavy windstorm, John fell while boarding the shuttle bus. I was out at the time, but on my return learned that the security team had picked him up and taken him to the on-site medical center to be examined by the doctor. They also took him back to our apartment, and because he had some pain in his ankle, they later brought an X-ray machine to our apartment to ensure there was no breakage. All this without my being present. John felt secure.

Knowing that help was always at hand even during my absence, and knowing that John *felt* secure, I was less concerned about leaving him for short periods. Before our move to Greenspring, I had been unable to join my children on several excursions, and had been especially disappointed in not being able to make a visit to London during the two years my son Bean was working there. Now, he was living in Tokyo, and I felt comfortable accepting his invitation to visit him there and to join him and his wife Nora on a trip to Laos and Cambodia. Bean had planned the whole vacation with consideration for my limitations: each day filled with a morning of strenuous sightseeing, an afternoon of total relaxation, and a luxurious dinner at the end of the day. Looking back, I'll always remember that vacation as the most wonderful gift I have ever received. After years of low-end travel, it was a joy staying in elegant hotels where breakfast buffets were more sumptuous than any I had every known. All this would not have been possible if I had not felt secure knowing John was well cared for at Greenspring.

There was no question that John was getting weaker. The cane he used his first two years at Greenspring was supplanted by a walker, then by a rollator, and then by a motorized power chair. His continued falls were a constant worry, and with each fall, it was becoming harder for him to get up. The time it took to move himself nearer to a chair, the bed, or anything he could grab onto to hoist himself up was interminable, and even with my doing my best to lift him, we often had to call security for help.

Two consecutive falls early in 2009 left him unable to stand at all. From the ER he was taken to Fairfax Hospital, and from there to Greenspring's nursing home where he had to endure the thinly disguised irritation of his daytime caregiver each time he needed help or had an accident. There, he underwent intensive therapy for almost a month. His stay was not covered by Medicare. Our long-term-care insurance policy for nursing-home-care did not kick in for ninety days, but we were fortunate in that we had also bought a home-care policy that was effective immediately. We brought John home. We replaced our queen-sized bed with a hospital bed and a twin. We acquired a wheelchair, and a bench for the bathtub. We had railing installed by the toilet to help him in "transferring." I hired a caregiver for an eight-hour day. This, however, I soon cut down to four, preferring to care for John myself those extra hours rather than putting up with the oppressive presence of George, our six-foot Haitian caregiver, for the entire day. John had not had a stroke, but his condition was much as if he had. George bathed him, dressed him, helped him brush his teeth, put in his hearing aids, and tried to walk him a few more steps each day. John slept most of the time. But added to his increased inability to function on his own, was a problem that none of his doctors had ever been able to account for. John always felt cold. In the past, during the day, he would warm himself by soaking in the jacuzzi, usually several times a day. Now, the shallow bathtub replaced the jacuzzi. It was the nights that were the problem. He slept in long johns, and on top of those, fleece tops and pants that I made for him. He also wore socks, a hat, scarf, and often, gloves, and still, claimed to be cold. I was convinced this was a neurological problem, for in fact his body was always hot, and his doctors said his circulation was so good they could feel his heartbeat in his feet. Also, his hearing, even with top-of-the-line hearing aids, was almost non-existent. Sitting across from him at our small dining table, it was impossible to have any kind of conversation. And worst of all was the continuing and steadily worsening problem of incontinence. I was getting up with him three or four times a night, each time having to remove his layers of clothing to change his diaper. Many times, not wanting to disturb me, he would go to the bathroom himself using his wheelchair. He could remove the diaper, but was unable to replace it. There were frequent changes of bed linen, and many loads of laundry. Life was difficult, and I was constantly amazed that John was able to remain as cheerful as he did.

On October 23rd we celebrated John's ninetieth birthday. I was stunned that his son Jocko would not be present at this milestone in his father's life. He had made other plans. But the rest of the family, his daughter Annie, and my three children and their spouses, most coming from afar, gathered for a wonderful lobster dinner with all John's favorite side dishes. A wealth of presents followed, and John, surrounded by love and attention, was simply beaming throughout the evening. Three months later, almost to the day, on January 22nd, he was gone.

The night before, quite surprisingly, he had suggested himself that he would try to do some walking. This was unprecedented for him. It had always been, "I'll do it after dinner," or "After my bath." Always it was "later." I pushed him to the hall in his wheelchair, positioned his walker before him, and helped him stand up. As usual, I followed close behind with the wheelchair. He took four steps and fell back onto the wheelchair with the words, "I can't do it."

I told myself he was tired. At least he had tried. Later in the evening, as I was getting him ready for the night, he had summoned enough strength to roll over one way and then the other as I put on his diaper, but he had not been able to raise his hips enough for me to pull up his long johns or his fleece pants. He tried again, and again, and again, but could not do it. I covered him as best as I could, and exhausted, he fell asleep. I slept fitfully that night, agonizing over how we would cope.

The next morning, as on most other days, even before opening my eyes, I reached across the bed for John's hand. It was cold, so cold. I felt the tears rising, and just as quickly, receding. I was glad. I was glad John was gone. Glad he would no longer be facing the indignity of being incontinent, of wearing a diaper, glad he would no longer be cleaned by a stranger's hands, and mostly, glad that he would not be ending his days in the nursing home without me by his side. I lay there, still holding his hand, for several minutes, replaying the events of the night before. I knew even then that I would no longer be able to care for him at home. He must have known it too. Perhaps it was the knowing that made him give up.

Finally, almost reluctantly, I released John's hand and pulled the pull cord. In minutes, security appeared. Soon after, the room was full of people, among them, I supposed, a police officer. I was asked a few questions about the circumstances of John's death. I knew only that he must have died peacefully for I had not been aware of any tossing or turning in the night. They asked about the disposition of the body and I told them it was to go to Howard University's Anatomy

Department. They made a call and within the hour he was taken away. I was left alone. I sat down on the edge of the empty bed. The tears came. This time they did not recede.

Chapter 30
The Aftermath

Once again I was a widow. It was so different from the first time forty-one years ago. Then I had my children. Even without Horace, I had had a family, and I had friends. Now, after being at Greenspring for almost seven years the new friends I thought I had made suddenly felt like no more than congenial acquaintances. In a community of two thousand people, I was alone. I *felt* alone. Except for two truly old friends of more than fifty years, David and Mary Dean, I had not needed the others. I had had John.

I immersed myself in all the tasks that death brings in its wake. First, a memorial reception, not a church service, for John was not religious. I wished I could have given him the sendoff he really wanted, a real Irish wake. We had once attended the wake of an Irish friend. The body in an open casket was laid out in the family's bay window, and most of the guests got royally smashed drinking toasts to the dear departed. It had been a glorious bash, and John had said then, "That's the way I want to go." Of course, he himself made this impossible by later deciding to donate his body to Howard University. He was enamored of the idea that some young black medical student would be thrilled to have a white body to work on. Still, though we couldn't give him his Irish wake, we did our best to give him a good sendoff. The reception was held on January 30, 2010. Unfortunately a major blizzard swept through America's eastern seaboard on that day, dumping ten inches of snow on the D.C. area. This prevented our *old* friends, our non-Greenspring friends, from being present. At the reception, John's son Jocko, daughter Annie, and grandson Mikey, each recalled their memories of John, after which, I too spoke. I was aware that it was unusual for a widow to be speaking in memory of her husband, but I wanted those at Greenspring to know the person John had once been rather than the reduced person he was when we came to Greenspring. Any concern I had about this break with precedent was dispelled by several letters received after the reception thanking me for "bringing John to life."

The reception over, other tasks lay ahead. I tackled them with a vengeance. George, John's caregiver, was the same size as John, and was happy to take much of his clothing. All the medical equipment, the walker, rollator, power chair, wheelchair, bath transfer bench, and other miscellaneous medical aids I was relieved to turn over to Greenspring's thrift shop. But then there was the inevitable paperwork that follows a death. Death notifications had to be sent, certificates to be filed, insurance claims to be made, and most important, distribution of John's assets according to the terms of his trust. None of it was complicated, but everything took time. Finally, all the necessary things were done, and all that was left was for me to go through John's papers. I put that aside for later.

The year following John's death was filled with medical problems that put my life temporarily on hold. First, the discovery of a lump in my breast. It was malignant, but luckily, the cancer was caught in its early stages. A lumpectomy was followed by six weeks of daily radiation treatments. Next came artheroscopic knee surgery. According to my son-in-law and friends who had had this procedure, this was supposed to be a piece of cake, but for me it was almost six months before my knee felt normal enough for me to return to my usual physical activities. After knee surgery the dermatologist found a malignant melanoma on my arm. Again, as with the breast cancer, it was in the early stages and taken care of by a simple excision. So simple, in fact, that as I watched, I thought, "If I had an extra pair of hands, I could do it myself."

I couldn't help being aware of how lucky I had been that both the cancer and the melanoma had been discovered early. But I was going through what all widows and widowers must go through when losing someone who has been a major part of one's self. Without John to care for, I felt my life was devoid of purpose and totally aimless. I felt lost. I had no real concerns about my health. Yet, possibly somewhere in my subconscious I *was* disturbed, for from the day I first discovered the lump in my breast, almost to the day, I was unable to sleep at night without the help of sleeping pills. I enrolled in a VIVA program, which, through a series of tests, evaluates one's physical, mental, and emotional state of health. Though I proved physically and mentally to be in well above average condition, the tests indicated that emotionally I was depressed. The same conclusion was borne out by my doctor at Greenspring. More than a doctor, she was a caring person, and in recent visits I had found myself tearing up again and again when I met with her. She, and also the VIVA counselor encouraged me to talk to Greenspring's social worker. I did not follow through. I told myself I could pull myself out of this hole I was in. I did not join the grief support group. I was already doing all the things one is supposed to do. I was keeping busy, engaged in a full schedule of activities. I was making myself go down to dinner even when socializing was the last thing I wanted. I didn't see that a social worker could do much more for me.

Toward the end of 2011 I learned of the formation of a new class in creative writing. Though I had already published a book, I had never thought of myself as a writer. I wrote that first book only because I had a story to tell and things I wanted to say to my children. However, I knew that I needed to do something to take my mind off myself, and with some persuasion from the group's leader Marcia Boyles, I joined the class.

At the first few sessions it was apparent that there were divergent interests among the group's members. Some wanted to focus on writing fiction. Some, more specifically wanted to work on play-writing. I did not feel myself capable of creating scripts or stories, and felt I could write only about what I knew. I could continue with memoir, with a goal of recording my life *after* leaving China. Only one other person, Betsy Renner, was also interested in memoir-writing. Soon, the original group broke off and we were left with just Marcia, Betsy, and me. For me, the smaller number was a boon. I had never taken a writing course of any kind, either in college of after. Other than my husband John presenting me with a copy of Strunk and White's *Elements of Style* immediately on reading the first chapter of my first memoir, I had not had any writing instruction at all. Now, I had what amounted to a private tutorial in writing.

For the past three years, I have submitted a chapter each month for Marcia and Betsy to critique. The experience has been invaluable. I learned a great deal, both about my writing and about the content of my work It also gave me something to focus on, to occupy my time, and to lift me out of the depression I had been in. And as I near completion of this memoir I realize too how the very writing of it has enriched my life. It has enabled me to relive my past with all its highs and lows, its happy moments and its sad. Once again I relived the wonder of owning our first home. Again I returned to my glory days of a hushed audience waiting for the first strum of the guitar and me, singing. Those and other happy times returned. But I relived too the sad moments. I wept again when writing of my first husband Horace's death, and yet again, recounting the devastation of being cast off by his family. But those sorrowful events were far outweighed by the other joyous memories that bubbled to the surface, memories of friends, of family, and of my children, all too numerous to record here.

Now, the individual chapters are written, and I am assembling the pieces, looking at the whole. As I review the sum of my written words I realize how full and varied my life has been. Having a Chinese father and American mother, I had the benefit from the start of two cultures, living my early years in one, the rest in the other. In my adult years, again, I lived in both a Chinese world and an American one. In my personal life, I had not only the rewarding years as a wife and mother, but also the later years of a challenging career. And though I would never wish on anyone the death of a spouse, especially at the early age at which I lost Horace, his death allowed me to have not one, but two good marriages, and within those marriages two different lives, the first, sophisticated and cosmopolitan, mixing freely with the rich, the prominent, and the powerful; the second, one of simple middle class anonymity filled with adventurous travel and a foray into the entrepreneurial business world. In the process I also raised three children, all of whom are leading meaningful and productive lives. Looking back, I feel I had more than any one woman could ask for. I had it all.

Well, I have written my memoir, and in so doing have lived my past twice over, once in real time, and once in memory. But the past is past, and I must return to the present. I am approaching my ninetieth birthday and am in better health, both physically and mentally, than any other ninety-year-old I know. My only problem, and a big one: I CAN'T HEAR!!!

I have been wearing hearing aids in both ears for the past twenty years, upgrading them regularly to keep up with state-of-the-art improvements. My comprehension of speech has deteriorated markedly in the past three years, and is rated by my audiologist as severe to profound. I no longer attend lectures and discussion groups. In large gatherings I catch little of ongoing conversations. I hesitate to ask questions because I don't grasp the answers. Large groups are now more a chore than a pleasure. I hear the words but don't know what has been said. Worse, I can no longer enjoy music and have stopped attending musical programs, which for me have become no more than a cacophony of sounds. I cannot identify tunes, even ones as simple as "When Irish Eyes Are Smiling." I have attended presentations on hearing loss. I have read books on the subject. I am told to choose my environments, and to "create" environments in which I can hear. I am doing that. In Greenspring's dining rooms, I sit only at small tables for two or four. I invite people to my apartment singly or in twos and threes where there is no peripheral noise. I am trying, really trying, to accept, or rather, "to adapt" to my present circumstances, but more and more I find myself chafing at my limitations. I nod appreciatively when others speak. I laugh when others laugh. But it is hard to nod and to laugh at words that have no meaning.

However, all that said, I am well aware of how blessed I am. My three children and their spouses are attentive and caring. My five grandchildren are responsible, independent adults. My health, other than my hearing loss, remains good. I wake up each morning with no aches or pains. I square dance, go to zumba classes and yoga. I lead a pottery class. I make pots. With the aid of subtitles, I watch TV. I go to movies at Greenspring's theatre where again I am assured of subtitles. I read. I write. I use the computer. I surf the internet. I love the apartment, which for the past twelve years has been my home. I never cease to delight in the view from my windows, beautiful in every season. I see the tender green of new growth in the spring, the lush green foliage of summer, and the riot of golds

View from my Window

and reds of fall. But it is the winter view that I like best, when the trees are bare, and every branch, large and small, is outlined clearly against the sky. And it is only in winter that the glorious colors of the sunsets glow through the naked branches. It is winter now and the tree tops look feathery, forming a lacy band across the skyline. All this I have.

As for the future, when the weather warms I will check my small garden plot for the first signs of green, the promise of spring. As summer approaches, I will plant a tomato plant in the large pot on my balcony and delight in each bud that one day will become a tomato. In the first days of autumn I will be joined by my entire loud, exuberant brood, children *and* grandchildren, for a family gathering in a beautiful lakeside house. That is as far into the future as I care to look. As for the present, my days are full. My life is full. I am grateful for the richness of my yesterdays. I am grateful for all I have in my life today. And tomorrow? Whatever tomorrow brings, I cannot ask for more.

Made in the
USA
Middletown, DE

76509303R00163